A FIELD GUIDE TO HUMANS

The Natural History of a Singular Species

Ronald M. Smith

Lava Fields Publishing

DEDICATIONS

To Edward O. Wilson for opening the door,
Steven Pinker for leaving bread crumbs, and
Robert Trivers for helping me understand who
was looking back at me in the mirror.

And to René for unceasing encouragement
and mastery of The Chicago Manual of Style®.

A FIELD GUIDE TO HUMANS

For information, contact Lava Fields Publishing at
lavafieldspub@icloud.com.

ISBN: 978-0-9990006-0-1

Published by
Lava Fields Publishing

Cover Design by Tim Green

Table of Contents

Introduction

THE IDEA OF a field guide to humans might seem odd at first. Of course, like the author, all readers of this book are members of the same species, have years of contact with other humans, and possess self-awareness. We all recognize ourselves and others as individuals. We have consciousness.

But knowledge of human nature is not inherent. We have to learn what it means to be human and personal experience typically yields only limited insight. The ancient Greek admonition "know thyself" reflects the reality that self-knowledge is elusive and that achieving it on a personal basis is a long and challenging project, and perhaps—until recent discoveries—not even possible.

This field guide is designed to tell the story of human nature from a naturalistic perspective, a perspective developed through the careful study of the natural world. Just as human naturalists carefully observe and then describe the characteristics and behaviors of other species, this guide aims to do the same—only with humans, themselves, as the object of study. And like other field guides, this one attempts to maintain a certain distance from its subject to promote as much objectivity as possible.

The narrative of this field guide is intended to tell a rather complete story of humans as it might be told by a naturalist from another planet making first contact with us and intent on understanding our species. This story has only been made possible by relatively recent scientific studies, most published within just the last twenty years. What has emerged is a view of humans as a complex animal with a deep and influential evolutionary history—just one of the millions of species of organisms on Earth—but one with some unique characteristics that has positioned us to become the dominant life form on the planet.

Why read this book? Two reasons come to mind. First, from a personal point of view, understanding a naturalistic view of human nature can help you anticipate and influence what other humans are likely to do individually and collectively in given situations. Solving problems of all kinds depends on being able to predict behaviors and act appropriately to channel a course of events.

Second, as a member of an exceptionally social species completely reliant on cooperation, a naturalistic understanding of human nature shared by a critical mass of other humans is necessary to secure a sustainable future. Many problems confront humans as a species. Successfully addressing these problems requires a broad common understanding of what it is to be human and how to engage together to achieve positive outcomes.

As you read this guide, think like a naturalist and contemplate all of the diversity within our single species. Then do some field work of your own and admire some of the variety firsthand.

FORMAT AND CONTENT

This field guide to humans is based on a format similar to guides commonly used to identify and describe other species such as wolves, seabirds, wildflowers, or snails. The goal is to describe the natural history of humans so that when you see one you will have a more coherent understanding of the species, from physical characteristics to behavior. Like other field guides, this one can be used as a reference, meaning you need not read it from cover to cover. Each chapter is relatively self-contained (though you will occasionally find cross-references to other chapters so you can pursue a topic in more depth if you wish). Feel free to read the chapters in any order that appeals to you.

The field guide begins by introducing the environment for life on Earth. A considerable amount of time is spent describing the physical characteristics of the planet, creating context for the humans that inhabit it. Further context is established by placing humans in the greater web of life currently found on Earth, and the process of organic evolution that has unfolded over hundreds of millions of years.

With the stage set, in the next chapter, the specific evolutionary origins of the human species are shared with a recounting of the major historical milestones of the most recent fifty thousand years leading up to the present. This is followed by a discussion of the current human range, population size, and habitat.

Next comes a multi-faceted description of physical characteristics that distinguish humans from other species. This includes a range of topics from body mass to coloration to vocalizations. The categories used are the same as the ones human naturalists would typically use to describe other animal species in field guides. The discussion of physical characteristics also includes information about the range of variation seen among individuals.

Diet and health are then considered followed by a discussion of mating habits and the characteristics and development of human offspring. The next chapter on behavior is long and detailed, reflecting the fact that human behavior is varied and distinctive among the species on Earth. Special attention is devoted to the role of genetic and environmental factors in the development and ultimate expression of behavior. The importance of collective knowledge and individual learning are highlighted.

The last section of the guide discusses the current conservation status of humans and their future prospects as a species. A forecast of near-term challenges is provided, along with thoughts about how humans might adapt to improve their viability as a species.

ORIENTATION

A number of conventions are followed in the guide to support readability. Even though the International System of Units (SI, or "metric system") is more commonly used and preferred on a worldwide basis, units of measure in this book are generally presented in the U.S. English System. This reflects the fact that the book is being initially published in the United States where fluency with the metric system is not common.

The one major exception to the U.S. English system is the use of the micron (micrometer) to describe very small objects. This unit of measure will be discussed in detail momentarily.

Among the conventions used in this book, of special importance is the convention for characterizing time. Units of time for historical events are all presented as "years before present" or simply as BP. Determining a date using this system involves counting backward from the "present" to the year in which an event occurred. Recent events are generally known with reasonable precision while those in the more distant past may be broader estimates. Using the common calendar system, the base year for events in the last five hundred years is 2015. For earlier events, the base year is generally 2000. Since earlier events are generally estimates, a more general base year causes no real perspective problems.

The following table (Figure I-1) provides some sample conversions from the commonly used Gregorian calendar system, which is divided into two calendar eras, the common era (CE or AD) with numbering beginning about 2000 years ago, and all earlier events before the common era (BCE or BC) counted backward from that base year.

Date Conversions	
1,500 AD/CE	500 BP
1 AD/CE	2000 BP
1,500 BC/BCE	3,500 BP
10,000 BC/BCE	12,000 BP

Figure I-1. Date Conversions

Once you become accustomed to the "before present" dating convention, tracking historical events becomes much simpler and the temporal relationships among events become clearer.

To prepare to read this field guide, also spend a little time recalibrating your sense of scale, ranging from very small to very large values. Being able to shift among these frames of reference comfortably will enhance your ability to fully appreciate the sweep of human history.

The guide contains many references to time that span many orders of magnitude, some of which will be far outside the scope of normal human experience. For instance, the guide points out that the Earth is about 4.8 billion years old. Yet, how do we relate to a billion years when our own lifespans are measured in a few decades? At another extreme, the diameter of a carbon atom is about .0003 microns. That's certainly very small, but how small is it really compared with the objects we handle regularly?

We humans don't relate well to very large or very small values because they are not part of the direct experience of daily life. But to better understand the human story we need to be able to relate to long spans of time, great distances, large population numbers, and small dimensions characteristic of molecules like deoxyribonucleic acid (DNA) that can't be seen with the naked eye.

Through some simple exercises, it's possible to gain a sense of scale linking large and small quantities with those that we do understand concretely. First, let's start with an exercise to gain perspective on large quantities. Use a timepiece that can measure seconds. Prepare to count out loud for a full minute. Start counting to sixty, naming one number every second. This is your base rate for contemplating a range of larger numbers. A minute is a time interval we all understand concretely.

Suppose we were able to continue counting numbers, one per second, until we reached specific larger quantities. Assuming you could say a number name every second (which quickly becomes impossible once you reach about one thousand) how long would you have to count? Determine the time required to count continuously to reach each of the values in Figure I-2 and record your answers in the table. (Check the answers provided at the end of this chapter.)

Quantity Comparisons	
A. Seventy-Five	
B. One Thousand	
C. Fifty Thousand	
D. One Million	
E. One Billion	

Figure I-2. Scale Model of Quantities

Compare your results with the answers, beginning with the realization that seventy-five is about the number of years in the average human life span. Try, especially, to comprehend the idea of a billion. When you encounter large numbers in the field guide, periodically return to this page and recalibrate yourself with this scale model.

Now let's turn attention to small numbers. Our unit of choice, the micron, equals one millionth of a meter (.00004"). The micron is useful because it gives a better sense of relative size among small things. The key to understanding this unit of measure is to connect it to a tangible object.

Take a human hair, cut it in half, and hold it so you are looking at the cut end in a bright light. You should just be able to see that it has a very small width. A typical human hair has a diameter of about 75 microns. This is about the smallest dimension that can be seen by an unaided human eye with 20/20 vision.

Now draw a circle one meter (39.4") across on a large sheet of paper or other convenient surface (Figure I-3). The circle represents the cut end of the human hair you just inspected. Anything inside this

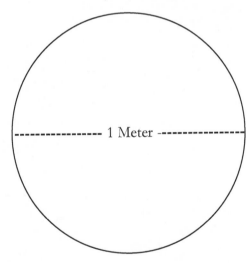

Figure I-3. Scale Model of Small Objects

circle is microscopic in real life—it can't be seen with the unaided human eye. Find the center of the large circle and draw a new circle around it, this time with a diameter of only about 4 centimeters (1.5"). In our scale model, this new circle represents an actual diameter of 3 microns. This is about the size of a typical single-cell organism like a bacterium.

Now draw one more very small circle around the center point with a diameter of just about .25 centimeter (.1"). This represents a diameter of about .13 microns. This is about the size of an influenza virus. Place the smallest point you can right in the center of the circle. If you have a very sharp pencil, the diameter of this point might be equivalent to around .0065 microns, the size of a molecule of hemoglobin, the oxygen carrying protein in red blood cells. (Figure I-4)

Object	Model Size	Actual Size
Human Hair	100.00 centimeters	75.0000 microns
Bacteria	4.00 centimeters	3.0000 microns
Virus	.25 centimeters	.1300 microns
Hemoglobin	pinpoint	.0065 microns
Carbon Atom	NA	.0003 microns

Figure I-4 Comparison of Small Objects

Using our current scale model, nothing smaller can be shown. A molecule of water, for instance, is about thirty times smaller than the central dot. These are sizes that are mostly incomprehensible to us even with the exercise of substantial imagination. Step back and look at your scale model. We started with a large circle representing the diameter of a human hair and scaled ever smaller objects without reaching the atomic level of matter. This exercise is worth revisiting when you come across references in the field guide to small objects or phenomena that pertain to humans, such as those associated with the molecular mechanisms of genetics. A solid command of differences in scales is essential to truly appreciating the human story.

Prepare yourself for an exciting adventure through space and time in pursuit of insights into your own humanity.

Answers for Figure I-2
A: just over a minute
B: about seventeen minutes
C: about fourteen hours
D: about eleven and half days
E: a little under thirty-two years.

A Field Guide to Humans

1 Environmental Context

THE EARTH ORBITS a G-type main-sequence star of moderate mass and above-average luminosity called the sun. It emits a white light that, at the top of Earth's atmosphere, is received as fifty percent infrared, forty percent visible, and about ten percent ultraviolet light. The atmosphere blocks about seventy percent of the harmful incoming ultraviolet light, and the planet's strong geomagnetic field deflects most of the charged particles of the solar wind, thus making the surface habitable for carbon-based life forms. The sun is the source of nearly all of the energy needed to drive surface processes on Earth, ranging from weather to life itself.

The sun and its solar system are part of a much larger celestial structure called the Milky Way Galaxy, which is about one hundred lights years across and contains more than two hundred billion stars (along with vast quantities of gas and dust). It is a barred spiral galaxy with two major arms, two minor arms, and two minor spurs. The sun is located just on the inside of one of the spurs, the Orion Arm, and is about twenty-seven thousand light years from the galactic center and about twenty light years above the galactic plane. The entire Milky Way Galaxy is rotating around its center, which is the home of a very massive black hole. Based on the sun's location in the Galaxy, it has a rotational velocity of over five hundred thousand miles per hour.

Planetary Characteristics

The Earth (Figure 1-1) is the third planet from the sun in a solar system with a total of eight planets and several dwarf planetoids (Pluto and Ceres, for example). It has a mean distance from the sun of 92.96 million miles. It both rotates on its own axis and orbits the sun. A complete rotation occurs every twenty-four hours with a surface velocity of about 1,040 miles per hour. When seen from above the north pole, it appears to rotate counter-clockwise. Rotation causes the surface to be exposed to daily periods of direct sunlight and periods of

Figure 1-1. The Earth Viewed from Space

darkness. The duration of these periods vary over the course of an orbit except near the equator.

Every 365.27 days the earth completes an orbit around the sun. Its orbital speed is about sixty-seven thousand miles per hour. When viewed from above the solar system plane, the earth orbits the sun in a counter-clockwise direction. Because the planet's axis is inclined about twenty-three degrees relative to the plane of the sun, energy distribution varies over the course of an orbit, resulting in rather strong seasonal variations at higher latitudes. The axis also wobbles slightly over long periods of time (for instance, one such cycle is twenty-six thousand years long) due to various solar system gravitational effects. Wobbling effects drive climate variations to varying degrees, which in turn impacts life forms living on the surface.

Earth has one moon that orbits it at an average distance of 238,900 miles. It completes an orbit every twenty-seven days. An important gravitational interaction between the Earth and its moon is the creation of tidal bulges in the Earth's ocean which result in regular variations in sea level at coastal locations.

The Earth has a mean diameter of about 7,918 miles and a circumference at the equator of about 24,902 miles. It has a solid iron inner core, surrounded by a liquid iron outer core. Above this is the rocky mantle with convection currents that transfer heat toward the surface. This heat is partially the residue left over from planet formation about 4.5 billion years ago (twenty percent) and from the ongoing decay of imbedded radioactive elements (eighty percent). Riding on top of the mantle is a relatively thin layer of crust made up of lower density silicate-rich rocks. The whole system is dynamic with plates of crust moving slowly in response to the mantle convection currents. Volcanic and earthquake activity is still prevalent, particularly along plate boundaries.

The Earth's mass exerts a gravitational pull at the surface of about 32.2 ft/s^2. This means that a dropped object will fall about thirty-two feet in the first second, an additional sixty-four feet in the next second, ninety-six feet in the second after that, and continue to accelerate in the same fashion until it impacts the surface or reaches terminal velocity (around one hundred twenty-two miles per hour near the Earth's surface), where friction and buoyancy in the air limits the maximum downward speed.

Surrounding the solid Earth is an atmosphere composed primarily of nitrogen (seventy-eight percent) and oxygen (twenty-one percent). About one percent is composed of a variety of trace gases, including water vapor, which is particularly important for maintaining life on the surface. The density of the atmosphere decreases with height, with most of the gases concentrated in the first forty thousand feet from the surface. The average pressure of the atmosphere at sea level is about 14.7 pounds per square inch. Compared with the mass of the Earth, the atmosphere is very thin. A twelve inch diameter ball covered with an oil film .001 inch thick would approximate the relationship between the dimensions of Earth and its atmosphere. From the surface, on a clear day, the atmosphere appears blue due to the strong scattering of the blue frequencies of sunlight passing through it.

The atmosphere is very dynamic, driven by the Earth's rotation and differences in solar heating from the equator to the poles. Weather happens as energy is redistributed within the atmosphere. Common weather phenomena include clouds, rain, snow, and wind. These are associated with areas of high and low pressure and with the fronts separating air masses that sweep across the surface. In addition, more severe weather events are fairly common including, thunderstorms with lighting, tornadoes, and hurricanes/typhoons. Most air temperatures range from -40°F to 100°F. The average global temperature of the atmosphere at sea level is currently about 59°F. Long-term patterns of weather define regional climates, which vary over the planet and over time.

The Earth is essentially a water planet. Over seventy percent of its surface is covered by that fluid, with the vast majority (96.5 percent) found in a single, large planetary ocean that averages ten thousand one hundred feet deep. All of this ocean water is saline, containing on average about 3.5 percent dissolved salt. Fresh water is found on land surfaces in lakes, rivers, ice caps, glaciers, permanent snowfields and in groundwater aquifers. Most of the freshwater (about seventy percent) is in frozen form stored in ice sheets and glaciers in the higher latitudes and at higher elevations. Like the atmosphere, water forms a relatively thin film on the surface of the Earth compared with the mass of the planet itself.

The portion of the Earth's surface not covered by water consist of a few large landmasses and thousands of islands of various sizes. The dry land surface includes a variety of landforms such as mountains, plateaus, deserts, plains, valley and coastlines, among others. The dry surface ranges in elevation from fourteen hundred feet below sea level to an elevation of almost thirty thousand feet. The northern and southern pole regions are covered with permanent ice caps, though this is in the process of changing, particularly in the northern hemisphere, as the mean surface temperature is rising due to recent global warming.

The landmasses have been classified into latitude zones based broadly on climatic conditions. There are two polar regions that comprise a little over eight percent of the Earth's surface, two temperate zones that comprise fifty-two percent of the Earth's surface, and the tropical zone straddling the equator that comprises forty percent of the Earth's surface. Within these zones there are many different climatic variations influenced by geography that have a significant effect on the distribution of life forms.

BIOSPHERE

Humans are part of the biosphere, which is the very thin veneer of the earth's surface that can support life. It is comprised of all the life forms on the planet and the non-living components of the environment, including the lithosphere (dry land), hydrosphere (the oceans and terrestrial bodies of water), and the atmosphere with which they interact. The biosphere is characterized by a complex, interdependent network of living things and their environments. Some interactions have planetwide consequences and some have more local impact. Planetwide, there is a continuous cycling of matter and flow of energy, which is driven almost entirely by solar radiation.

From the various environments on Earth, called ecosystems, organisms extract the resources needed to maintain their life processes. Of these resources, water is particularly important, as it is a primary constituent of living things. A variety of other nutrients, particularly various forms of carbon, are also needed for living things to assemble the complex molecules that make up their forms. These forms range from single-cell organisms to very complex, multicellular organisms like humans, that are composed of billions of differentiated cells.

There are three broad categories of life on Earth. First are the *primary producers*, mostly green plants, that have the capacity to convert sunlight into food. Two particularly important categories are phytoplankton—microscopic organisms that float near the surface in the oceans—and flowering terrestrial plants that concentrate energy to produce foodstuffs, like fruits and seeds, that were particularly important to the evolution of humans. Photosynthetic organisms form the base of the food chain on which all other organisms depend, both for food and the atmospheric supply of oxygen needed for respiration. Surprisingly, about half of all the ongoing photosynthesis on Earth arises from microscopic phytoplankton (though they comprise only about one percent of global biomass). Their role in supporting life on Earth is pivotal.

The second broad category of life is made up of *consumers*. These are organisms, the animals, that eat producers to extract the energy they need for life. They form the second level of the food chain. In turn, there are consumers of consumers, forming third and even fourth levels of energy transfer. But all of the consumers, including those at the top of the food chain like humans, are ultimately dependent on producers and their conversion of sunlight into food.

The third category of life forms is made up of *decomposers*. All living things have finite life spans and eventually cease the functions of life. The decomposers are the organisms that break down dead remains into simpler components for recycling into the biosphere. These organisms, including many kinds of single-cell microbes, produce some of the key raw materials to support the next generation of living things.

BIOLOGICAL DIVERSITY

Carbon-based life is abundant on Earth. At present, over 1.7 million living species have been described and named. A species is a population of similar individuals who can reproduce sexually with each other, thus comprising a shared gene pool representing the total range of genetic options available within a population.[1] The exact number of species on Earth is unknown at this time, though it is estimated to be minimally several million more than the number already identified. A great many of the unidentified species are insects, though there are still many unknown species in other families as well. For instance, there are likely many forms of bacteria yet to be discovered. On the other hand, almost all large plant and animal species have been identified and described.

Living things are found all over the Earth, but not in equal numbers or in the same ranges. Numbers vary greatly, with individual, single-celled organisms by far the most abundant. On the other extreme, some species of animals on the edge of extinction may be reduced to just a very few breeding pairs. Distribution generally depends on environmental conditions that vary greatly around the planet. Organisms have preferred environments. Some organisms tolerate more diverse environmental conditions and thus can have a wider distribution. Others require very specific conditions that occur only in very limited areas. These specific areas of distribution are called habitats or niches.

Organisms live together in ecosystems where they share complex interdependencies with each other. For instance, flowering plants rely on insects for reproductive support through pollination. There are

---

[1] Defining a species for organisms, like bacteria, that reproduce asexually is more complicated and generally is based on genome analysis.

many such ecological relationships needed to keep ecosystems healthy. When one or more of these relationships is disturbed, adverse consequences ripple through the system. The sum total of all the organisms and their ecological relationships with each other constitute the planet's web of life.

Environmental conditions on Earth are subject to change through a range of processes. Such changes can have a significant impact on living things.

EVOLUTION

The collection of organisms on Earth today, both in kind and number, is just a snapshot in time of a constantly changing biosphere. The collection of organisms has been much different in the past and will be much different in the future. This is a consequence of the process of organic evolution that is continuously modifying the expression of life.

Members of a species that are well-adapted to their environment tend to produce more offspring than other organisms who are less reproductively successful. Therefore, the characteristics (genes) of more successful organisms become more widely spread in a breeding population. In addition, random DNA mutations also occasionally introduce new characteristics that are more adaptive to a population, and are passed along more frequently to future generations. As a consequence, over many generations, a population gene pool slowly changes, eventually yielding offspring with characteristics significantly different from earlier generations. At some point, members of a new generation can no longer mate successfully with others in their population and a new species arises.

A changing environment favors different biological adaptations. Organisms all have varying degrees of sensitivity to changes in environmental conditions. For instance, most corals living in oceans are sensitive to relatively small changes in the alkalinity of ocean water. If the water becomes less alkaline (more acidic), coral colonies suffer and may even experience wide scale die offs. However, some corals may be more tolerant of changes and, if they survive the harsher conditions, will experience more reproductive success. Their genes will become more common in future generations.

Changes in the environment thus drive natural selection, in turn modifying gene pools over time. As long as the environmental changes are gradual, adaptations better suited to new environmental conditions will spread in a population, eventually leading to the rise of a new species. However, relatively rapid changes can lead to the deaths of all the members of a population, resulting in the extinction of a species.

Environmental changes have been the norm throughout Earth's history and will continue to drive evolutionary changes for millions of years to come.

Geologic Time Milestones

The Earth coalesced out of the local solar nebula about 4.8 billion years before the present (BP) as part of the larger process that formed all of the planets in the solar system. At first, the entire planet was a seething ball of molten material. As it cooled, the surface solidified and a primordial atmosphere formed. Ongoing precipitation of water vapor from this atmosphere formed a single planetwide ocean by around 4.4 billion years BP.

The first simple, self-replicating life form appeared in this ocean sometime before about 3.5 billion years BP. After life appeared, the mechanisms of organic evolution began differentiating forms.

Marine single-celled organisms evolved and thrived for more than a billion years. During this time the component mutations leading to photosynthesis began to spread in populations. By about 2.4 billion years BP, photosynthesis was well-established and free oxygen released by single-celled photosynthetic organisms increased significantly in the atmosphere to around .2 percent (compared with twenty-one percent today). This was enough oxygen to put new biological and geochemical processes in motion, of which surface oxidation was one. All dry land turned from dark gray to red as it oxidized (rusted).

Single-celled organisms continued to diversify for the next billion years, with evolution laying the foundations for multi-celled organisms yet to come. One of the important innovations during this period was the development of cells with a nucleus, the basic template for multi-cellular organisms. Life was still confined to the oceans but increasingly concentrated in coastal and near shore environments where nutrients were widely available. Crustal plates were in motion, driven by heat convection currents in the mantle, so the geography of dry land changed on a scale of millions of years.

Climate remained relatively stable during this billion-year period, until around seven hundred seventy-five million years BP when the

Earth entered a period of dramatic climate oscillations brought on by massive atmospheric feedback loops largely involving changes in the concentration of carbon dioxide. At times, the surface was frozen solid, at others, surface temperatures were well above those of modern times. These extreme climate changes accelerated organic evolution.

The first multi-cellular organisms—the first animals—appeared by at least six hundred and thirty-five million years BP. By five hundred seventy million years BP, the first living things—probably algae—began to colonize the edges of dry land. Multi-cellular life exploded when, around five hundred and thirty million years BP, animals evolved the capacity to surround themselves with hard, protective shells. These shelled organisms were incredibly successful with wide distribution and huge populations.

Around four hundred fifty million years BP, oxygen levels in the atmosphere reached near modern levels, which helped stabilize climate cycles. It also led to the formation of the ozone layer of the atmosphere that protects life forms from ultraviolet radiation. This made it possible for organisms to inhabit the land surfaces for the first time. The first of these were green plants which were widely distributed by four hundred million years BP. Insects soon followed.

Animals with backbones—the fish—had appeared and were evolving in the oceans. These became abundant and varied by four hundred million years BP. By around three hundred and fifty million years BP, amphibians evolved from the lineage of fish and became well-established on dry land. Next, reptiles evolved and became common by about three hundred twenty million years BP. They became the dominant land animals and remained so for millions of years.

Around sixty-five million years BP, mammals—the biological lineage of which humans are members—appeared. They rapidly diversified and filled niches all over the planet. Flowering plants also evolved and became abundant in this same time frame. From this point forward, flora and fauna, though continuing to evolve, began to more closely resemble those found in modern ecosystems.

Environmental conditions on the Earth's surface varied greatly over these long spans of time, with periods of intense cold and extensive glaciation to long periods of quite warm conditions planetwide. At times the concentration of atmospheric oxygen increased to as high as thirty-five percent, to be followed by periods with levels below current conditions. The ongoing movement of continental plates, periods of massive volcanism, and the occasional impact of large meteors ensured that the surface environment was very dynamic—and challenging for life. Terrestrial life forms, in particular, were sensitive to these environmental changes.

Over the last five hundred million years, there have been several major extinction periods that dramatically reduced the number of species and the populations of those that survived. In the most

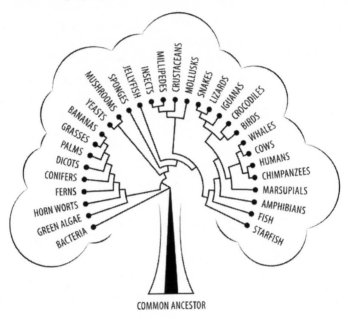

Figure 1-2. Very Simplified Tree of Life

extreme case, which occurred about two hundred fifty million years BP, more than ninety percent of marine species and seventy percent of land species became extinct. Yet life was resilient and, in time, refilled all of the niches that had been vacated.

TREE OF LIFE

All of the organisms on Earth today share a common original ancestor. They are related genetically to each other to varying degrees. When these relationships are shown visually, the diagram is reminiscent of a branching tree, the tree of life on Earth (Figure 1-2). The trunk represents the common ancestral life form and the branches show the various species produced through the processes of evolution. All of the branches that reach the outside of the canopy represent life forms on Earth today. However, there are many branches within the canopy that are truncated, representing species that have gone extinct. A full tree, representing all of the species that are currently found on Earth and all those species that have previously gone extinct, would have millions and millions of branches.[2] But despite the fantastic diversity, they all share the same root.

The figure portrays a small sample on the outside surface of the evolutionary tree. The branching structure shows how just a few of the types of organisms on Earth today have arisen from a common ancestor over millions and millions of years of biological divergence. Whole groups of once successful organisms—such as dozens of species of dinosaurs—are no longer part of the current community of life. The only remnant of their lineage is found in the existing, heavily diversified, community of birds.

A scale model of the tree of life would have somewhat unique dimensions. If it's height was based on the passage of time, with an inch equaling a million years, the tree would be about two hundred ninety-one feet tall based on when life first appeared. The trunk, the distance from the first single-cell life form to the first multi-cellular organism, would be about two hundred and thirty-eight feet high. The entire crown of the tree would occupy the next fifty-three feet. The start of the mammalian lineage would arise just five and half feet from the top and the human twig would be less than an inch long at the top of one tree branch.

The Earth's environment continues to change in response to many forces, now including the actions of humans. Adaptations will be required by many species and many will meet the same fate as the dinosaurs. The biosphere is inherently subject to modification driven by environmental change over time. Such is the nature of organic evolution, which constantly drives change in life forms through natural selection in a constantly changing world.

■ ■ ■

Now, after more than three billion years of evolution and countless episodes of environmental change, the biosphere hosts abundant and varied life forms, including humans. In the great span of geologic time,

---

[2] About ninety-nine percent of the species that have ever lived are now extinct.

they are all just temporary members of the ongoing stream of life forms to inhabit the Earth.

Humans are one species of animal in the mammalian lineage of the current tree of life. At present, they are the dominant life form on Earth and have extensively modified ecosystems across the planet through a huge population presence and the use of powerful technologies. This ability to modify the environment even includes changing global climate. As a species they have an enormous and growing impact on the planet and the other organisms they share it with. However, they are still subject to the forces of natural selection. They will continue to evolve along with all other life forms, though their manipulation of the environment will most certainly change the trajectory of the selection process.

2 Origins and History

HUMANS, LIKE OTHER life forms on Earth, arose through a process of organic evolution—changes in physical form and function fueled by randomly occurring genetic mutations and shaped by natural selection over long periods of time. Their evolution and history can be usefully divided into seven periods that are organized into two stages (Figure 2-1). All timeframes are shown in years before the present (BP).

Stage	Period	Timeframe	Theme
1	1	220 million – 7 million BP	Evolution of Mammals
	2	7 million – 100,000 BP	Human Species Emerges
	3	100,000 – 50,000 BP	Modern Behaviors Appear
2	4	50,000 – 11,000 BP	Migration & Colonization
	5	11,000 – 5,000 BP	Settlement & Agriculture
	6	5,000 – 500 BP	Dense Settlement & Cities
	7	500 BP - Present	Scientific Revolution

Figure 2-1. Stages and Periods

Stage 1 includes periods 1-3, which focus on the evolutionary history of mammals, of which humans are a member, and the emergence of the human species. Stage 2 includes periods 4-7 and presents the history of humans over about the last fifty thousand years, a very brief period of time from an evolutionary perspective.

Key milestones are presented within each period. A milestone is an event that is particularly important to subsequent developments in the human story. The focus is placed on just a few of the most important milestones that have led to the modern humans that inhabit Earth today. They will help make sense of the unusual human story.

Now for a reminder. The chronology that follows includes extended periods of time. Please refer back to the strategy provided in the Introduction, if necessary, to again calibrate your sense of large numbers. To fully appreciate the various intervals involved, it's important to put them in perspective with each other. Though this is not easily accomplished, understanding the human story depends on comprehending the time scales associated with it.

ORIGINS—PERIOD 1: EARLY EVOLUTION

Though life on Earth got its start about 3.5 billion years ago and all life forms evolved from this single source, the line of animals—the mammals, which led to humans—emerged only about two hundred twenty million years ago.

Figure 2-2. Early Mammal

The first mammals were small (a few inches long) insect eaters who were active primarily at night to avoid predators (Figure 2-2). They had several new-to-the-animal-kingdom characteristics, including being warm blooded, covered with hair (usually in the form of dense fur), birthing their offspring live, nourishing them with milk produced by mammary glands, and having relatively large brains compared with the size of their bodies.

For millions of years mammals continued to evolve and differentiate into new forms in difficult ecosystems dominated by reptiles (including dinosaurs). They were not star players in the animal kingdom. Instead they formed a minor group of animals living in a small, somewhat specialized ecological niche. Around one hundred thirty million years ago, another important evolutionary milestone was reached: flowering plants appeared on Earth for the first time. These plants, which produced seeds, nuts and fruits, became dominant, providing a critical new food supply for animals. Mammals coevolved with the flowering plant kingdom and were very dependent on it.

About eighty-five million years ago, a new line of mammals, the primates, first appeared. They were the next branch in the tree of life leading to humans (and monkeys and apes). These mammals were well adapted to living in a particular habitat, the canopies of trees in tropical forests. They were small and furry with important new adaptations, including three-dimensional color vision, flexible joints, and grasping hands and feet. They were vegetarians exploiting the fruits and nuts of the recently evolved flowering trees. The primates survived a massive asteroid strike sixty-five million years ago that led to the extinction of the dominant dinosaurs, and like other mammals, they took advantage of the newly vacated niches and rapidly expanded.

By about ten million years ago, the population of primates leading eventually to humans was made up of monkey-sized, furry, small-brained, fruit-eating, tree dwellers living in rain forests in equatorial Africa (Figure 2-3). They were not particularly important players in their ecosystem and were fairly low on the local food chain. They were just one of many animal species sharing the forest together.

ORIGINS—PERIOD 2: HUMAN EMERGENCE

Then, about seven million years ago, a group of primates acquired an important new adaptation, walking upright on two legs. This was most likely in response to a long period of climate change, which reduced the area of tropical forests and converted large areas to more open savannahs. To adapt, some primates had moved out of the trees, at least part of the time, and started to exploit the more open terrain for new food sources. Their stereoscopic vision, combined with a new

Figure 2-3. Early Primate

upright posture, gave these animals the ability to see over tall grasses to find food and avoid predators, a formidable advantage.

Over the next several million years, the evolution of the pre-human physical form continued. During this time, another important adaptation arose, a thumb that was flexible enough to touch all the other fingers of the same hand, which made precision grasping and manipulation of objects possible. This eventually led to the invention and use of wood, bone and stone tools, which increased success in obtaining and processing food.

Relatively late in this time period, fire was first used in campsites to provide warmth, extend the length of the day during which humans could be active, ward off predators, and cook food. The campfire, which humans still admire today, is an ancient innovation.

Cooking became a standard part of food preparation and had several important effects. It allowed humans to predigest their foodstuffs, making it easier to obtain the nutrients in them. As a result, over many generations, cooking allowed for the natural selection of a smaller digestive system. The human gut became smaller because cooking made it easier to extract energy from the food that was eaten.

Cooking also led to additions to the human diet. For instance, vegetable material like tubers, which could not be eaten raw, became edible when cooked. And a whole new food source, meat, was exploited. Meat became a regular part of the food supply, probably scavenged at first from the kills of other animals and then later obtained proactively through individual and group hunting. Meat provided an important new source of concentrated energy and was made more digestible by roasting over an open fire.

But cooking brought about one more incredibly important change. Due to the fact that humans could now extract more energy from their food and that cooking facilitated the addition of more concentrated foodstuffs, there were now sufficient calories available to support the higher energy needs of a larger brain. With adequate fuel, natural selection favored genes for more brain power.

By the end of this stage, one hundred thousand years ago, humans ranged through most of eastern Africa from the southern tip of the continent up to the start of what is now the Sahara desert, somewhat north of present day Ethiopia. Africa was in the midst of a long drying and cooling period. The human habitat was primarily savannahs. The total population was perhaps around ten thousand divided among many hunter-gatherer-scavenger bands marking and defending foraging territories.

The modern physical form of humans had pretty much fully evolved. These animals were now significantly larger, mostly hairless, larger-brained omnivores who lived on the ground and walked upright on two legs. Because the modern physical form was in place, these animals could now be considered to be members of the modern species. From this point in time and going forward, these animals and all their descendants are properly considered humans.

But though they now looked like modern humans, they did not yet possess some key behavioral adaptations. More important evolutionary changes were to come.

ORIGINS—PERIOD 3: MODERN BEHAVIORS AND CULTURE

This was a critical period for the humans, when changes in the environment led to a population crisis and a rapid reshaping of the gene pool, which concentrated new adaptive genes.

The drying and cooling period in Africa continued into this period and reached its maximum at about sixty-five thousand years ago. Tropical forests had retreated and deserts had expanded. The primary human habitat, the savannahs, were drier and food was less abundant. The sea level was around two hundred twenty-five feet below the current level as a result of ocean water being locked up in glaciers in the higher latitudes.

The human population dropped to around five thousand and was concentrated in a relatively small area of perhaps one thousand square miles in what is now Ethiopia (Figure 2-4). Of the five thousand or so remaining individuals, perhaps only half were in breeding pairs. These were difficult times. There was a possibility that the species was headed for extinction, just like so many others before them in the Earth's history.

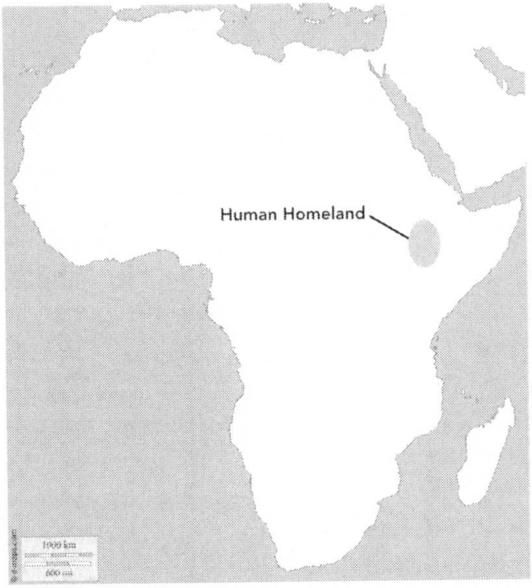

Figure 2-4. African Range

But humans narrowly survived this population bottleneck, though with some significant biological changes. Perhaps the most important of these were modifications to the throat that permitted humans to make new sounds and control them with precision. These modifications, along with processing changes in the brain, eventually made spoken language possible. And natural selection quickly spread these adaptations through the small human population.

Once humans started talking to each other using a shared language, a whole new universe of behavioral options became available. Language made possible new levels of cooperation, planning, and resource exploitation never before seen in the animal kingdom. With language, humans became more adaptable, innovative, and successful. They were definitely beginning to out think other animals.

And with the creation of a shared language, culture became increasingly important. In fact it exploded in importance, launching humans onto a new lifestyle trajectory, the results of which are seen in the complex modern societies that dominate the world today.

Culture is learned behavior that is shared by the members of a human group. It is transmitted, largely through language, from generation to generation. Culture conveys the rules and expectations for individual behavior and membership in the local group. It also provides explanations for why an individual should behave in certain ways or why things happen as they do (or at least why the members of the group imagine that things happen as they do). Culture is the glue that helps humans understand the world and work together effectively.

Here are some examples. Through culture, individuals learn who is likely to be a friend and who is likely to be a foe, and how to interact with each. Culture establishes the norms for how to behave toward kin and other members of the tribe, the expectations for sex roles, and the appropriate interactions with members of the opposite sex. Culture provides the skills needed by a hunter-gatherer, such as which plants to collect and which to avoid, which game animals are preferred and how to hunt them, and which predators are to be avoided. The methods for making tools and preparing food are passed along via culture, along with any specific community preferences. The expectations associated with camp life and rank in the local social hierarchy is part of culture. Culture also provides explanations for how the world works, and how to attempt to gain the favor of supernatural forces. The rules for mating, avoiding contaminations, treating illness, and caring for the dead are all prescribed and shared within the culture. Culture is essential for group cohesion and success.

Since culture is learned and new individual and collective experiences continuously add to the existing knowledge base, culture is constantly expanding and changing. In fact, culture can be thought of as evolving, like organisms evolve, as new human experiences modify or replace older practices. The culture adapts to new circumstances and the needs and wants of its participants. It is always a work in progress.

Language plays a pivotal role in this process. Language provides the means to share culture, not only in the here and now, but also across the generations. Since during this time period there was no writing or any other communication method (other than some sign language perhaps); talking was the only means of communicating the details of the local culture. Humans memorized stories, myths, and descriptions of procedures, and shared them with each other and their children. Skillful storytellers were highly regarded. But stories are easily, quickly and sometimes arbitrarily changed. This turns out to be very important for the evolution of culture.

Unlike the very slow rate of change characteristic of organic evolution that unfolds over many generations, cultural evolution can occur very rapidly with noticeable changes possible within a single human generation. With culture, know how, know when, and know why can be stored in a shared knowledge base and modified as needed, often on the fly. For humans, during this period, the power of instinct was reduced compared with other animals, replaced by flexible social learning.

By the end of this period, humans were equipped with skills, tools, and social organization to be at the top of the food chain in their African homeland. They were on the rise and showing signs of their potential. They were on the brink of a fateful choice.

■ ■ ■

Evolution, working over long periods of time in Africa, produced a line of animals that, by fifty thousand years ago, had some unique characteristics. They had an upright posture, walked on two legs, had hands capable of a precision grip, had stereoscopic vision, and possessed large, language-processing brains. And with language, they started accumulating knowledge that could be passed from generation to generation. The behaviors of these animals were increasingly influenced by culture generated from within their social groups.

So while the members of this new species were not especially big, fast, or strong, they were well-equipped to cooperate with each other, to learn from experience, and to think ahead to an extent never before seen among organisms on Earth. The species was showing some signs of unusual intelligence.

History—Period 4: Migration and Colonization

The page now turns in the story of the humans, transitioning from Stage 1, a review of evolutionary origins, to Stage 2, an accounting of historical milestones. At this point, it's worth noting that from an evolutionary perspective, humans are a relatively recent addition to the animal kingdom compared with other species, and they now have some adaptations unlike any previously seen. From this point forward, events will unfold that flow continuously to the present. To acknowledge this continuity, it seems appropriate to declare the start of human history, which will be presented as a sequence of four successive time periods. See *Timeline A* (p. 55) for a scale model overview of these time periods and how they relate to each other.

History began with what seems like a small, even routine, activity. About fifty thousand years ago, a small group of humans left their ancestral homeland in Africa, never to return.[3] Recall that the human population in Africa had dwindled to a few thousand individuals, spread among three or four different, but related, family trees. From one of these lineages, a small tribe of around one hundred fifty decided to migrate from their home territory in what is now Ethiopia and venture northward, possibly driven by population pressures in their home range. Remember that foraging territories had to be quite large and could only support a limited number of hunter-gatherers. When a population in a territory reached a certain size, some members would need to leave the tribe and seek out new territory.

While the migration of a few humans may have seemed like a minor event at the time, it was to have momentous consequences. Once the migration commenced, it continued on for tens of thousands of years until humans had colonized all of the landmasses on Earth. One small tribe became the root of a family tree that includes all humans on Earth today.[4] Refer to *Timeline B* (p. 56) for information on the key milestones of this period and their relationships to each other.

The Migrants

As we have seen, the members of the human population at the time of the migration had developed physical and behavioral characteristics that made them more adaptable and resilient. Those that decided to migrate were curious, adventurous and pretty self-confident. They believed that they could survive the challenges and reap the benefits

---

[3] The actual start date is unknown. It is likely that the migration started sometime between 55,000 and 50,000 years ago, based on the evidence obtained from various sites along the migration route. For the purposes of this chronology, I have somewhat arbitrarily set the start of the migration at exactly 50 thousand years ago, subject to revision as more evidence becomes available.

[4] It is possible that there was more than one migration event or even a small, steady stream of migrants over a sustained period of time. But any subsequent migrators came from the same gene pool as the original migrating tribe. All migrants were members of the same genetic lineage.

associated with moving forward into previously unknown territories. What were these founding ancestors like?

The migrants were relatively tall and lean, mostly hairless, with dark skin and quite possibly almond shaped eyes, similar to humans living in Asia today. They had good stereoscopic vision, sensitive hearing, substantial lung capacity, strong hearts, and a robust cooling system based on perspiration. They had strong hands with precision grips. They had brains as large as modern humans and they had very fine-grained control of speech sounds.

These characteristics were well adapted to the conditions they had faced at home in Africa. The melanin in their skin was a natural sunscreen. Their cardiovascular systems helped them cope with sustained and strenuous exercise. Their height allowed them to better see over the savannah grasses, helpful in avoiding predators and spotting game. They were distance runners, chasing prey across large, open savannahs under a hot equatorial sun. And, as it turns out, these physical characteristics were also very well suited to a range of environments they were to face as the migration unfolded.

As has already been noted, the migrants shared a spoken language that allowed them to work together very effectively. They had a tribal form of social organization composed of individuals with differing degrees of status and headed by a chieftain. They were patriarchal. Males and females formed relatively durable pair bonds for mating and child rearing. They had stone, bone and wood tools and weapons that effectively supported their hunter-gatherer lifestyle. They had established campgrounds. They defended territory and caches. They also had some basic navigation skills that they used to set courses and track their locations.

They had control of fire. They cooked and preserved foods for future consumption. They also knew how to find and carry fresh water in dry landscapes, and how to fish and harvest shellfish. They knew how to build dugout canoes. They constructed and wore sewn clothing and ornaments. They told stories to pass along knowledge and folklore. They were religious, believing that the world was inhabited by all kinds of spirits that could help or harm humans. They had ceremonies and rituals. They sang and danced. They looked after the sick or injured and buried their dead.

But though there were similarities within the group, there were also differences. The members of the migrating tribe were not clones of each other. Just like in modern groups, there were differences in physical form such as height, weight, build, coordination, stamina, and fertility. They also varied in intelligence, temperament, social skills, language proficiency, and practical competence. All this variation comprised the gene pool that would be contributed to descendants of the founding tribe and on which natural selection would act over the next few thousand generations.

Migratory Process

During the migratory period, almost forty thousand years long, all humans lived in the wild and had only one lifestyle, that of the hunter-gatherer. The migration process was grounded in this reality.

The idea of a migration may conjure up images of a punishing journey of many miles a day through inhospitable lands with countless hardships. However, the migration out of Africa was, for the most part, quite different from this scenario. The departure from Africa wasn't a rapid forced march. Rather, it was more like a slow, intermittent expansion along a frontier.

Of course the migrants had to carry everything, just like any other day of traversing the foraging route in their home territories. There were no wheeled carts or domesticated animals for riding or hauling goods. So all their possessions, including the complete tool kit with fire starter (or the embers from the last fire) were carried along by the members of the tribe as they moved from one camp to another, but this time into unknown territory.

Imagine a group of one hundred fifty traveling together out of their familiar home range. Some members undoubtedly scouted ahead while the main party, including women with children, followed. Others were out foraging for food. Progress was likely about the same as on a regular day making the circuit back in the ancestral foraging grounds. After a few miles, camps would be established, probably near a water source. If the foraging went well, a good campsite might become the center for a new foraging territory that could be occupied for some time. If the foraging conditions were poor, the group might push ahead in search of better conditions.

From the migrants' point-of-view, there was no particular destination in mind. The goal was simply to find and inhabit an unoccupied territory with a good supply of food and water. For a group of one hundred fifty hunter-gatherers, this might require an area of around fifty square miles based on an average availability of foodstuffs. Once a new territory was established, it might be home for decades or until the most preferred food supplies were exhausted.

Partly because the humans used hunting tools to become the top predators in their local environments, they were reproducing very successfully and the birth rate in a tribal group consistently exceeded the death rate. Local populations increased. Once it became too large to be comfortably supported within the current foraging territory, conflicts over resources typically increased.

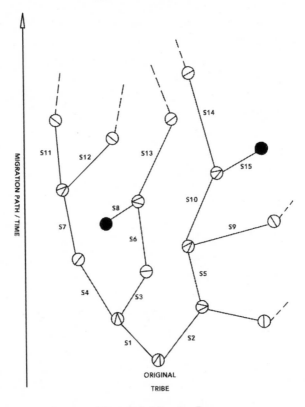

Figure 2-5. Migration Process

As a result, the migrant group would then split, some would stay behind and others would push forward on the frontier to establish a new territory. Such splitting would occur over and over again, and was the typical process driving expansion and colonization (Figure 2-5 showing splits and a couple of unsuccessful relocations).

Imagine this same process at work for the better part of forty thousand years: successfully colonizing a new territory, successfully reproducing and increasing the local population size, and eventually dividing the tribe and continuing the migration. Though the migration was intermittent and though some of the migratory groups were probably unsuccessful, the overall effort was a huge success. Humans went on to colonize all of the continents and their total population increased substantially.

Dispersal Timeline

Remembering that the initial migration started fifty thousand years ago, here's a sketch of the migration and colonization timeline (Figure 2-6). The dates of initial contact in various regions are approximate. The leading edge of the human wave of migration reached different landmasses at different times, strongly influenced by climate conditions prevailing in those areas. For instance, Europe could not be colonized until periodic glacial conditions eased. In another example, Australia could not be colonized until sea levels dropped due to extensive glaciers at higher latitudes. And even then, there were still daunting ocean channel crossings that had to be undertaken.

Region	Initial Contact
Middle East	49,000 BP
India	48,000 BP
Australia	45,000 BP
China	40,000 BP
Europe	38,000 BP
North America	16,000 BP
South America	14,000 BP
Pacific Islands	4,000 BP
New Zealand	800 BP
Antarctica	60 BP

Figure 2-6. Colonization Timeline

Many islands in the Pacific were colonized much later, including New Zealand, which was reached by humans only about eight hundred years BP. In the southern polar zone, the continent of Antarctica saw its first permanent human settlement only about sixty years BP, after technological innovations made it possible to construct and supply buildings that could withstand the harsh climatic conditions.

To put the general rate of migration in perspective, assume that a migrant typically walked a leisurely five miles in a day (perhaps a total of three hours-worth of walking). If this activity was repeated every day for a year, a walker could cover a total of one thousand eight hundred twenty-five miles. If this pace continued for ten years, a walker could cover eighteen thousand two hundred fifty miles. With this in mind, note that the migrants who left what is now Ethiopia colonized the Middle East, about fifteen hundred miles away, in around a thousand years. This is an average migration rate of 1.5 miles *per year*. The migrants had plenty of time available to explore and exploit a new territory for years before a new sub-group moved beyond the current frontier. The migration process was generally slow and intermittent, but persistent.

The migration route branched somewhat like a tree with groups moving in different directions at different times, colonizing different areas, and sometimes even temporarily retreating from a territory if the climate conditions grew difficult—during an ice age, for instance.

Population Growth and Physical Changes

During the migration period, the human population grew substantially. Remember that the founding population was small, around one hundred fifty individuals (or at most a few hundred). Between the start of the migration and around twenty-two thousand years ago, the total world population increased to about one million over twenty-eight thousand years. While not an explosive growth, significant increases were occurring. Humans were now much more numerous than they had ever been in Africa.

Though there may have been some setbacks from climate changes and large scale natural disasters like volcanic eruptions that made some territories largely uninhabitable, humans were greatly expanding their range and experiencing reproductive success.

By the end of the period, eleven thousand years ago, the total population had risen to something above ten million. Keep in mind that this growth was all due to a dramatic increase in the amount of land that had been colonized and the ever-increasing number of foraging territories established. Because hunter-gatherers can only support a limited number of offspring, birth rates worldwide remained largely stable.

Throughout this period, humans were becoming dispersed over very large areas with minimal contact. While there were most certainly some interactions along the boundaries of adjoining territories, most tribes were isolated from all but their closest neighbors.

As tribal groups split repeatedly and moved away from their kin, reproductive groups remained rather small and increasingly remote from each other. In these small groups, genetic traits could change relatively quickly. New environments favored some traits over others and just plain luck influenced what traits got passed on to children born in the group. For instance, one person with a unique trait like a particular eye color might die from an accident before having any offspring, so that eye color would disappear from the local tribe.

As an example of this process of change, when humans colonized an area like northern Europe, that environment with its less intense sunlight favored individuals with lighter skin that could absorb more Vitamin D with a minimum risk from the lack of the melanin pigment in the skin. As a result, over many generations, the original dark skin of the migrants was replaced in the local population with light skin coloration. Evolution was at work modifying the physical characteristics of all the migratory groups in all their different environments.

Small hunter-gatherer tribal populations, unique environments, strictly local intermarriage, and isolation rather quickly reworked the thousands of human gene pools. Changes in physical traits from the rather homogeneous founding population were substantial.

Cultural Evolution

Cultural evolution was also at work, bringing changes of its own, but even more rapidly. Recall that the founding tribe spoke a common language. But language is very subject to modification in word meanings, grammar, and speech sounds (accents). As groups split and occupied territories remote from each other, their spoken languages rapidly diverged. In just a few generations, spoken languages had become so different that had previous kin met, they would no longer have been able to understand each other. Without the ability to communicate, cooperation is difficult or impossible.

Every part of every culture changed in detail and kept changing as human experience in various environments drove new adaptations. Languages changed, food preparation methods changed, mating practices changed, social roles changed, dances changed, religious practices changed, garment styles changed, artistic preferences changed. Isolation would be caused not only by sheer distance (a ten mile walk might be enough to separate kin permanently from each other) but also by geography where a mountain or river might completely isolate one group from another.

Cultural evolution promoted deeper genetic changes as well, especially of the behavioral sort. For instance, cultural practices that favored close cooperation between members of a tribe could have favored less aggressive, more communicative individuals. Again, over many generations, this might have reshaped the local population to include more genes for cooperative behavior. In a different environment with hostile neighbors, strength and aggression might be more adaptive and the genes that supported them proliferated.

The process of selecting mates could also change local populations. For instance, a legend might have become part of a local shared culture that caused women to prefer taller men. As a result, taller men might have had priority as mates and ended up more successful in producing offspring. As a consequence, the average height of males in the local population would increase, quite apart from there being any other natural selection advantage associated with height.

During this period, hunter-gatherer tribes spread throughout the world, each establishing and defending a foraging territory. There were literally thousands of independent evolutionary pockets diverging from each other all over the world. The net result of all these evolutionary forces is the diversity of the physical and cultural differences we see among modern humans. Humans not only dispersed, they also, as a consequence, became much more varied in physical details and cultural forms.

Environmental Impacts

From a broad ecological perspective, the migration of humans was not benign. When they entered a new territory, they entered as the top predator. This had some consequences, mostly negative, for the species already living in new foraging territories.

Initially, the migrating humans shared the planet with at least four and probably more types of archaic human-like animals (hominids), including a very close relative, the Neanderthals. These species, which had all evolved in Africa like the humans, had migrated out of Africa much earlier and lived in small populations spread throughout Eurasia.

Humans surely encountered and interacted with members of these species as they established new territories. In any case, by about thirty thousand years ago, all of these other human cousins had become extinct. Humans probably played a role in this as they and their cousins were competing for the same resources. Perhaps humans simply out-competed their rivals using their better tools and superior social skills. Or humans may have taken a more direct approach through confrontation and warfare. Given the aggressive and territorial inclinations of humans, this is certainly plausible. Most likely, it was a combination of these forces that led to humans occupying the hunter-gatherer ecological niche all by themselves.

As has already been noted, the migrating humans were at the top of the food chain in every territory they established. They were accomplished pack hunters with a versatile tool kit. They could take down the largest prey. Their population was growing and they were hungry.

The numbers of large mammals living in any area in the human migratory path were significantly reduced once humans arrived. Throughout the world, many large species of all kinds went extinct during this period. While it's possible that climate changes also played a role, human hunting certainly reduced populations of animals quite rapidly and changed every ecosystem that was encountered.

It is worth mentioning one species that did benefit from the human migration. About fifteen thousand years ago, humans in central Asia domesticated the least aggressive of wolves, and enlisted them to assist in hunting and guarding their camps. Dogs became formidable allies and their use spread quickly among hunter-gatherer tribes.

Talking about ecosystem impacts associated with the period of human migration leads to an interesting observation. In the modern world, some humans are concerned about what they call invasive species of plants and animals. These are species that are intentionally or accidentally introduced into environments in which they are not native. Such introductions, even when intended to accomplish a worthwhile objective, often have unintended effects on native plants and animals, sometimes even catastrophic consequences. With hindsight, this seems somewhat ironic, as humans are perhaps the most invasive of all species on the Earth. This still continues to be the case in the modern world where humans are continuing to modify environments to the detriment of other life forms, some of which are essential for the maintenance of the healthy ecosystems on which humans rely.

The migration process, which created many new tribal groups, created the conditions for social conflict. It would be a mistake to think that the migration was a long period of peace and prosperity (though there may have been moments like this). The fact is that humans are territorial, aggressive, and deeply suspicious of other humans who are not members of their own tribe. They are also opportunistic when it comes to resources. Camp raids, theft of caches, and open warfare between tribes were not uncommon events and were probably the norm, especially when adjacent populations became too large to be supported by the local foraging territory.

Cultural evolution also undoubtedly amplified these tendencies. Stories celebrating the exploits of the tribe along with stories outlining the evil character of outsiders were perpetuated and transmitted to the young. Religious practices were also adjusted to justify the actions of the tribe and seek (in vain) the support of supernatural forces to defend the community.

While there were aspects of cooperation between adjacent tribes, such as trade and mate exchanges, there was a deep undercurrent of defensiveness and rivalry between tribes that persists among human groups even today. Some dark elements of human nature were clearly expressed during this long era of humans living in the wild.

Meanwhile, Back in Africa

Thus far the focus has been on the human migration out of Africa. Most of the kin of the original migrators stayed home while their restless relatives went on to populate the rest of world. Those that remained were also successful hunter-gatherers at home and their populations increased. Old territories in all of southern Africa were re-entered and re-colonized, along with the coastal fringe of northern Africa. Any archaic hominids in Africa also became extinct, just as they did in Eurasia.

While the migration was unfolding elsewhere, physical and cultural evolution continued within African populations, with substantial long-term interbreeding among tribal groups. Just as there was divergence among the groups of migrators, divergence arose within Africa as well. By the end of this period, there were around two million humans in Africa, the vast majority of whom had originated there.

■ ■ ■

Fifty thousand years ago, a small tribe of humans started a migration out of Africa that would result in the colonization of all the landmasses on Earth. These humans had the language skills, tools, and social skills needed to establish and succeed in new, never-before colonized territories. The migration was a slow, intermittent expansion along a broad frontier that lasted more than forty thousand years.

The process of expansion produced thousands of relatively isolated hunter-gatherer territories where physical and cultural evolution proceeded independently. Consequently, populations began to diverge from each other in both physical traits and cultural practices, so that by the end of this period there was much greater diversity among humans than when the migration had begun.

During this period, the human population worldwide grew from a few thousand to around ten million. Colonization resulted in significant ecological changes in areas occupied by humans, including the extinction of other hominids and many species of large mammals.

HISTORY—PERIOD 5: SETTLEMENT AND AGRICULTURE

Around eleven thousand years ago, even though the migration was still in progress, a new human lifestyle emerged for the first time. A tribe of hunter-gatherers occupied a territory in what is now Iraq. In it they had several campsites, but one that was especially attractive. It provided access to good water and game animals. It was also close to some of their favorite wild plant foods. It offered a rich supply of resources to meet their needs. Settlement beckoned. Refer to *Timeline B* for key milestones of this period and their temporal relationships to each other.

Agriculture, Part 1 – Domestications

Rather than follow their regular foraging circuits, the members of this tribe began spending more and more time at their main campsite. After a while they stayed in the same camp most of the time and only foraged for food during the day. This offered several benefits: the campfire could be maintained all day long, children could be looked after more easily, food caches could be continuously guarded, it was less taxing for the elderly, and its relatively permanent stone-working sites made it easier to produce high-quality tools. The tribe was becoming more settled by working from a home base rather than circulating constantly through their foraging grounds.

As time passed, some tribal members noticed that some of the wild cereal grains (wheat, barley, lentils) they especially valued grew close to camp. One day, an enterprising individual dug up some seedlings and brought them back to camp and replanted them. They seemed to do fine, and even better when a little water from the nearby stream was applied. And thus, agriculture and one new occupation, farming, were born. Other nearby tribes learned of the new practice and liked the idea of growing their own foods nearby. In this way, the tending and propagation of wild grains spread quickly through the Middle East.

Now move forward a thousand years. In the same region, a hunting party collected a couple of young wild sheep and brought them back to camp rather than killing them in the field. This turned out to be a good idea. A makeshift pen of wood and stone kept them nearby. The lambs ate the grass (inedible by humans) near camp and grew fat. The first living food cache, made possible by settled camp life, had been created. And so started the domestication of animals intended as a food source, living in close association with humans.

Settlement, followed by the adoption of agriculture was a momentous milestone for the humans. Though most humans would maintain the hunter-gatherer lifestyle for several thousand more years, the new lifestyle caught on quickly. Human settlement seems to have stimulated the development of agriculture. When settled life became established in any new area during the migration, some form of agriculture was soon to follow.[5] As a result, pockets of agriculture arose independently all over the planet.

The practice of agriculture created two new conditions for humans. First, territories could be smaller, much smaller. Compared with foraging territories, farms required much less land. As a result, human groups of farmers could live in closer proximity. Human population densities increased. And second, in connection with these

---

[5] The plants and animals that were domesticated varied based on the wild varieties that were available locally.

trends, more offspring could be supported. Populations in farming communities increased substantially.

Farming also brought cultural changes. Higher population densities created the opportunity for new types of cooperation. Trade possibilities also increased. And more frequent social interactions stimulated changes in religious practice, the content of stories, and the nature of collective rituals. Cultural evolution went back into high gear in the new farming communities.

But agriculture was a mixed blessing, particularly as it became a more established way of life. Humans had to work longer and harder to keep the food flowing. Ironically, nutrition may have gotten worse because of reliance on a more restricted diet. And new diseases became a problem as a result of sharing living spaces with farm animals. All of these factors may have combined to actually reduce life spans in farming communities.

Villages

As settlements grew larger, humans started producing more permanent structures (the use of mud brick was common) and to cluster these together, giving rise to the first villages. The larger local populations soon outstripped the capacity of the traditional tribal form of governance to maintain order, fostering substantial social experimentation. The balance between cooperation and aggression was regularly tested. New forms of social control evolved to help resolve disputes and strengthen cooperation. Religion was often enlisted to help improve group cohesion.

Toward the end of this period, domesticated animals (oxen) were first used to supplement human labor on farms. They added energy that improved farm productivity and output. This innovation, combined with further selective breeding of domestic plants and animals, set the stage for the production of food surpluses which would transform human communities in the next historical period.

Despite the negative side effects already described, farming was a huge success for humans. More and more hunter-gatherers settled and started farming where the climatic conditions supported it. Throughout this period, the new lifestyle was increasingly adopted, eventually changing the course of history.

History—Period 6: Dense Settlement and City Formation

This period marks the beginning of the most recent ten percent of human history and the start of a revolutionary and broad-based set of changes to the human lifestyle. Refer again to *Timeline B* for information on the key milestones of this period and their temporal relationships to each other.

Agriculture, Part 2—Innovations

The farming lifestyle continued to spread and replace the hunter-gatherer tradition. Two new innovations, large-scale irrigation and the use of dung from domesticated animals for fertilizer, greatly improved farm productivity and led, for the first time, to significant food surpluses in some localities. In addition, farmers discovered that their domesticated animals were more than just food caches for later consumption. Cows and goats produced milk and sheep produced wool, which were useful and attainable without harming the animals themselves. In addition, surpluses of these items could be traded for other goods and services.

Plant and animal domestication continued, increasing the number of species controlled, and improving crop yields. As an example, wild emmer wheat was transformed into a more productive variety through selective breeding: the repeated collection of the best seeds from a harvest were used for the next planting season. Over many generations of wheat production, a plant with larger seed heads emerged, yielding more food per plant.

Around five thousand years ago, the wheel and axle were invented, making it possible to more efficiently move materials around in carts. Five hundred years later, horses were added to the list of useful draft animals, providing yet another new source of energy to support farming activities. All of these changes to farming methods improved yields and opened up new possibilities for local trade and commerce.

Cities

Agricultural surpluses, combined with continuing population increases promoted the growth of villages, a group of dwellings and other structures where humans lived in close proximity. Eventually one of these villages in Iraq grew to exceed ten thousand inhabitants at the beginning of this period, five thousand two hundred years ago. It was the first settlement of such size and complexity worthy of being called a city. The era of urbanization, the concentration of humans in close relative proximity, had begun.

Specialization

The formation of cities drove new social innovations. The availability of local food surpluses made it possible for some city dwellers to pursue activities other than farming. Craft specialists such as potters, clothing makers, mud brick builders, tool manufacturers, leather workers, and food preservers proliferated. Religious specialists also appeared to organize and guide the rituals and special events that at one time had been maintained only within the tribal unit. Other city dwellers specialized in the arts of war to defend the city when required. All of these specialists eventually formed cooperative work groups (the precursor of guilds) to foster cooperation among members, promote commerce and train new recruits.

And one more type of specialist also appeared. Since cities far exceeded the size that could be managed using the traditional tribal forms of governance, new social arrangements for maintaining order and facilitating cooperation were needed. So new forms of relatively large-scale governance arose, supported by bureaucrats responsible for the administration of rules and regulations, resolving disputes, and collecting tributes (taxes). Sometimes these arrangements were merged with the local religious authority. But, regardless, these bureaucracies were prepared to support the social order through force, if necessary, and a male from a hereditary power base almost always headed them.

Of course city life also had some downsides. Since humans are hierarchical, class differences appeared that adversely affected some community members while benefitting others. Though it's not clear when and how slavery first started, captives from wars during this period most likely were brought back to cities. The use of slave labor was a widespread practice.

Sanitation in cities was undoubtedly a problem, and when combined with the widespread tending of domestic animals, caused disease to become more prevalent. Without the tight social control and personal accountability of tribal life, dishonesty, petty crime, and freeloading became more common. Periodic shortages of food and water were also likely in larger towns and cities, due to underdeveloped distribution systems.

The advantages of the cities lay in their access to specialized skills, cooperative commerce, shared rituals, and provisions for common defense. They also provided a platform for regional trade with other villages, towns, and cities. A few of these regional networks grew very large, forming agriculture-based civilizations. Such civilizations arose in Egypt, Mesopotamia (Iraq), the Indus Valley (Pakistan) and somewhat later along the Yellow River in China. Eventually agrarian civilizations also formed in the Americas in Mesoamerica (Mexico) and the Andes (Peru). They were characterized by large urban populations; monumental building projects; many, and often elaborate, cultural artifacts; large-scale religious practices; and strong social cohesion. None survived into modern times, most likely due to their large, concentrated populations and a range of practices that were ecologically unsustainable.

Writing

At the beginning of this period, associated with the rise of cities, another important innovation appeared. To account for various trade activities and to track crop yields in and around cities, some form of recording system was needed. Writing was invented to meet this need (Figure 2-7). Though it started modestly, writing was to become an innovation with a huge impact on humans. Writing appeared

Figure 2-7. Clay Tablet with Cuneiform Writing, circa 2,000 BP

independently in just a few places and was reserved for the elite. By the end of this period, almost all humans on Earth were still illiterate— unable to read or write. Spoken language was still dominant.

Collective Learning

Near the end of this stage—about one thousand years ago—the first universities were formed, initially in the Arab world, and then in Europe. This was a very important development for expanding the collective human knowledge base. These new institutions brought together many of the most intellectually able humans in their regions of influence. The work undertaken in the universities accelerated the creation of new knowledge at an unprecedented rate. Scholarly work began to flourish.

After the invention of the scientific method at the very end of this period, universities would become particularly important for the development of the various scientific disciplines, which rely on a community of similarly trained scholars to review and critique hypotheses, experimental designs, data sets, and the conclusions reached by individual researchers. Universities would provide this kind of environment and, as they matured, became increasingly important in generating new theoretical knowledge and then applying it to the invention of new technologies. Many of these would come to have important commercial value.

By the end of this period, farming had become widespread and was still the lifestyle practiced by a majority of humans. And with it came its characteristic higher birth rates. During this period, the human population grew rapidly. By three thousand years ago, the total world population reached about one hundred million. By the end of the period, five hundred years ago, it had topped four hundred million and was accelerating (Figure 2-8).

During this period, conflicts between human groups continued, became more organized, and were practiced on a larger scale than ever before, especially in the major zones of settlement around the world. Full-time soldiers and armies appeared. Bronze tools and weapons were replaced by iron ones a bit over three thousand years ago. Horses and chariots came into use for battle. Warfare was becoming more lethal. Regional military alliances were formed and dissolved with great regularity. The chances of being touched by human violence during this period were reasonably good.

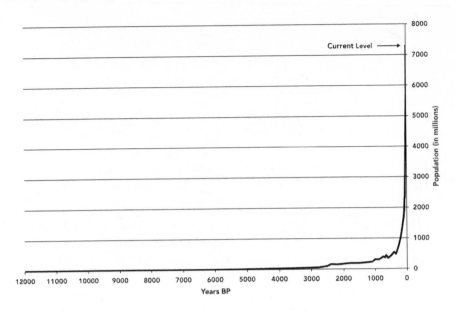

Figure 2-8. Population Growth

History—Period 7: Scientific Revolution

It's now time to consider the most recent period in human history covering just the last five hundred years or so—one percent of the total fifty thousand years of history. It has been a period of rapid and unprecedented changes for human lifestyles. The collective human knowledge base has expanded at an incredible rate and continues to accelerate. Humans occupy all habitable corners of the planet. Increasingly, countries have emerged, consolidating earlier forms of social organization around the world. (See Chapter 3 for more information) Culture and language diversity, which were at a peak early in the period, diminished somewhat as groups became less isolated from each other. Secular institutions arose to regulate human activities and to standardize cooperation. Institutions are sets of rules and customs that regulate a particular sphere of human life in a given society. Examples include laws and associated methods of enforcement, medical practices, educational practices, political organization, military forces, economic systems, marriage and family norms, and forms of mass media. Institutions are stabilizing forces and yet, somewhat ironically, are subject to continuous modification.

The human population exploded, reaching seven billion, and continues to climb. Urbanization continues and is accelerating. Trade and communication networks are now worldwide. By the end of this period, humans had caused large-scale habitat changes and even, somewhat unintentionally, started to modify the Earth's climate. By the present day, their impact had become immense. See *Timeline C* (p. 61) for some of the key milestones in this period and their relationships to each other.

What accounts for these transformations in such a short time? While it is difficult to identify the key drivers of all the changes, four stand out: the discovery and use of the scientific method, the exploitation of fossil fuels, the wide-scale transmission of the human knowledge base through compulsory education, and the invention of computer software.

Scientific Method

Throughout history, humans have been curious observers of the natural world and have developed a range of ideas about forms and processes, with varying degrees of accuracy. At the start of this period, some new ideas developed about how to gain a better understanding of natural phenomena. The core principles of the scientific method were articulated.

The scientific method is a particular way of studying the natural world. It includes several recurring steps (Figure 2-9). Science is always a work in progress, where new insights are viewed as tentative and subject to revision. Its practice relies heavily on the expectation that any experiment can be repeated to produce the same result as earlier work. It is also a public process that requires scientists (often anonymously) to critique and challenge each other's work. Each new insight is rigorously tested before finding acceptance. Mathematics was adopted as a particularly effective way of precisely expressing the relationships that science was revealing. This proved to be a particularly powerful innovation.

The use of this method spread quickly across many different fields of study, feeding more specialization. As noted in the last section, the university became an important incubator for scientific thought. It provided the community of scholars and other resources needed to promote new discoveries and it accelerated the production of new knowledge.

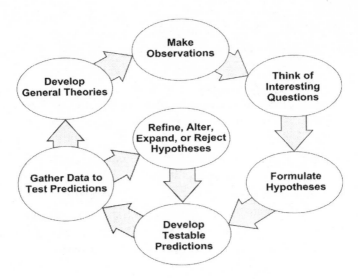

Figure 2-9. Scientific Method

Not simply satisfied with greater understanding of the natural world, scientists also asked how the new knowledge might be applied. Science therefore also fueled technological innovation. And technological innovation fueled a vast array of new products and services that flowed into the ever expanding commerce networks. This synergy has rapidly transformed the standard of living for many (but not yet all) humans.

Fossil Fuels

Another major milestone during this period was the harnessing of fossil fuels to generate useful forms of energy. Coal, petroleum, and natural gas (methane) are all products of geological processes that led to their formation millions of years ago, and subsequently made them accessible close to the Earth's surface. Coal was mined first, and first used to power the industrial revolution that started in Europe with the invention of the steam engine, about two hundred fifty-five years BP. Natural gas was harnessed next for commercial uses, about two hundred ten years BP, and then the relatively large-scale extraction of petroleum followed, about one hundred sixty years BP. With the invention of the internal combustion engine, about one hundred fifty years BP, petroleum production dramatically increased, as it could be refined into gasoline that powered newly-developed engines. Fossil fuel energy was converted to electrical power, and distributed commercially for the first time one hundred thirty-six years BP.

Throughout the last half of this period, and on an increasingly large scale, fossil fuels and their refined products supplemented and then replaced human and animal labor. These new sources provided humans with vast supplies of energy to support their activities. Once plentiful and controllable sources of energy became available, thousands of new uses were invented and shared through ever expanding networks of trade and commerce. These new innovations spread rapidly worldwide. The modern world is now almost completely dependent on the fossil fuel economy.[6]

Though the exploitation of fossil fuels has substantially raised living standards worldwide, their use poses some challenging problems for humans. First, the supply of fossil fuels is limited. Once they're gone, they're gone for good. At the projected rate of use, all reserves will be used in less, quite possibly much less, than five hundred years.

A second problem for humans is that burning fossil fuels creates a variety of toxic by-products that are harmful to life forms, including humans themselves. In addition, burning fossil fuels causes the formation of large volumes of carbon dioxide that, in high concentrations, cause the average temperature of the atmosphere to increase. This warming causes a range of ecological problems which have yet to be dealt with.

Finally, the global distribution of fossil fuel energy is substantially unequal for a variety of social and economic reasons. Not all humans have benefitted from the deployment of fossil fuel energy systems and the higher living standards that they provide. Though some efforts are underway to address this issue, there is no clear path to its resolution.

Compulsory Education

Writing made it possible to organize and transmit the expanding human knowledge base much more efficiently. The limits of human memory were largely offset by the ability to supplement it with external objects—books. Humans who could read and write enjoyed a tremendous cognitive advantage compared with the illiterate.

---

[6] While there is substantial dependence on fossil fuels, dependence is not complete. Solar, wind, hydro, biofuel and nuclear power systems make up about eighteen percent of the current total global energy supply. In some sectors of the world economy, efforts are underway to reduce the use of fossil fuels.

During the early part of this period, formal education first gained some traction, though it continued to be reserved for members of the upper classes. By about four hundred years ago, the first system of universal education was introduced in Europe, where the expectation was established that most children should learn to read and write. But literacy spread slowly. One hundred fifty years ago, only about ten percent of the world population could read and write in their native languages.[7]

Systems of universal, compulsory education spread rapidly, so that currently the literacy rate worldwide is now around ninety percent. Of course, reading and writing are now seen as just the basic skills needed to master an increasingly vast curriculum of useful knowledge and skills that demand disciplined study. And the addition of new knowledge has become so rapid and extensive, that disciplined study is now pretty much required throughout the human lifetime to support informed decision making.

Through the deployment of formal education, humans are promoting the further expansion of knowledge, particularly scientific knowledge, which will likely lead to new waves of cultural and technological change.

Computer Software

One outstanding characteristic of humans has been their ability to invent and use tools. A recent invention, the computer, is proving to be the most important tool yet devised. Though the first commercial computer was introduced just sixty-five years BP, the technology has evolved and spread worldwide in the intervening years.

A computer is an electronic device that can store, retrieve and process information in a digital form. It is a programmable machine that can follow a defined set of instructions with great fidelity to produce a pre-defined result. Different sets of instructions (programs or software) produce different outcomes, making the machine very flexible for performing many different kinds of tasks. Modern computers can perform very complex instructions rapidly and reliably. Many humans now use these devices regularly for work and recreation.

---

[7] Even today there are more than three thousand languages spoken by small numbers of people around the world that have no known written versions.

Because the technology is so new, humans have not yet fully grasped its impact. But already it's clear that computers have dramatically improved human performance and productivity. For any given individual, a computer and the network of resources to which it is connected provide almost immediate access to almost all of the content in the human knowledge base, which has grown to enormous proportions. It also allows them to solve difficult mathematical problems, model complex systems, evaluate multi-faceted alternatives, create intricate designs, and produce rich multi-media representations of abstract ideas.

Software, in particular, has been transformational, as it is a means to share intelligence with others. Specialized software programs are typically developed by humans with deep knowledge and expertise in a narrow domain of knowledge and skills. Through their efforts, they make it possible for those with less specialized training to solve problems normally reserved for a small pool of experts. In this way the experts share their expertise. Really good software improves the performance capability of many other humans. It raises the level of intelligence in the whole population of humans who use it.

Computers and the software systems they support are in an early stage of development, and though the results have already been enormous, they just hint at the possibilities ahead.

■ ■ ■

Many historical forces are currently at work as human societies continue to evolve. For the first time in history, more humans live in cities than in the countryside. Non-agricultural specialists outnumber farmers. And the hunter-gatherer lifestyle has almost disappeared altogether, except for a few isolated tribes in remote areas.

Nearly all humans now live in societies organized as countries. There are currently about one hundred ninety-five such political units in place, varying greatly in size and population. Perhaps around a dozen are completely dysfunctional, having been unable to establish and maintain even basic institutions. Another dozen or so are very fragile.

Technological changes made possible through the application of the scientific method and the exploitation of new energy sources have transformed the standard of living for some, but far from all, humans. Worldwide, about half of the humans live on the equivalent of US $2.50 or less per day (less than $1,000 per year). Many humans capable of productive work are unemployed or are underemployed (wanting to work more or are in positions that don't make full use of their skills), without the means to maintain even a basic level of subsistence. In addition, nearly a billion people suffer from some degree of chronic malnutrition, even though there are sufficient foodstuffs produced to meet everyone's basic needs.

Literacy has become widespread, though the majority of humans are still undereducated in terms of the knowledge and skills needed to fully participate in modern societies. Access to quality education is uneven across societies, due largely to a variety of local and regional forms of discrimination. On the positive side, the average intelligence of humans seems to be rising, keeping pace as the cognitive demands of life are increasing.

Human conflicts continue, though the incidence of violence has declined somewhat overall.[8] Warfare reached new levels of scale, technological complexity, and lethality, achieving a dubious milestone with the use of the first atomic weapons only seventy years BP. Presently, substantial conflicts are still underway in the Middle East and Africa. Tensions are clearly evident among many of the most powerful countries. Substantial resources, approaching 2.5 percent of the world gross domestic product (about US $1.7 trillion) continue to be devoted annually to military operations.

Overall, ecological sustainability is an issue. Already, the human population has exceeded the carrying capacity of the planet, based on the lifestyles practiced by the humans living in the wealthiest localities. So, although many outward features of human life have changed, the handprints of the past are still evident and are still shaping events in the modern world. Even though hunter-gatherers are mostly gone, their inherited impulses shaped by eons of evolution remain, despite the fact that these impulses are not particularly well-adapted to the typical conditions in the modern world. The human presence on Earth is still a work in progress.

---

[8] Two atomic bombs were dropped on Japanese cities at the end of a widespread period of conflict that started about seventy-five years BP. During the conflict dubbed World War II, around sixty million soldiers and civilians were killed through the direct actions of other humans, about three percent of the world population at the time.

Timeline A

Overview of Human History

Scale: 1 dot equals 100 years

50,000 **1** . . . .
. . . .
. . . .
45,000 . . . .
. . . .
. . . .
40,000 . . . .
. . . .
. . . .
35,000 . . . .
. . . .
. . . .
30,000 . . . .
. . . .
. . . .
25,000 . . . .
. . . .
. . . .
20,000 . . . .
. . . .
. . . .
15,000 . . . .
. . . .
. . . . **2** . . . .
10,000 . . . .
. . . .
. . . .
5,000 **3** . . . .
. . . .
. . . . **4**
. . . . *Present*

Periods

1 Start of migration out of Africa (about 50,000 BP)
2 First permanent settlement and start of agriculture (about 11,000 BP)
3 Beginning of dense settlement and formation of cities (about 5,000 BP)
4 Beginning of the scientific revolution (about 500 BP)

Timeline B

Major Human History Milestones: 50,000 BP to Present
Scale: Each dot equals 10 years, each row equals 500 years

References periods:
- Typical modern human life span (80 years)
- Typical years per reproductive generation (30 years)

50,000 **1** . . . .

49,500 . . . .

49,000 . . . .

48,500 . . . .

48,000 **2** . . . .

47,500 . . . .

47,000 . . . .

46,500 . . . .

46,000 . . . .

45,500 . . . .

45,000 **3** . . . .

44,500 . . . .

44,000 . . . .

43,500 . . . .

43,000 . . . .

42,500 . . . .

42,000 . . . .

41,500 . . . .

41,000 . . . .

40,500 . . . .

40,000 **4** . . . .

39,500 . . . .

39,000 . . . .

38,500 . . . .

38,000 **5** . . . .

37,500 . . . .

37,000 . . . .

36,500 . . . .

36,000 . . . .

35,500 . . . .

35,000 . . . .

34,500 . . . .

34,000 . . . .

33,500 . . . .

33,000 . . . .

32,500 . . . .

32,000 . . . .

31,500 . . . .

31,000 . . . .

30,500 . . . .

30,000 . . . .

29,500 . . . .

29,000 . . . .

28,500 . . . .

28,000 . . . .

27,500 . . . .

27,000 . . . .

26,500 . . . .

26,000 . . . .

25,500 . . . .

25,000 . . . .

24,500 . . . .

24,000 . . . .

23,500 . . . .

23,000 . . . .

22,500 . . . .

22,000 6 . . . .

21,500 . . . .

21,000 . . . .

20,500 . . . .

20,000 . . . .

19,500 . . . .

19,000 . . . .

18,500 . . . .

18,000 . . . .

17,500 . . . .

17,000 . . . .

16,500 . . . .

16,000 7 . . . .

15,500 . . . .

15,000 8 . . . .

14,500 . . . .

14,000 9 . . . .

13,500 . . . .

13,000 . . . .

12,500 10 . . . .

12,000 . . . .

11,500 . . . .

11,000 11 . . . .

10,500 . . . .

10,000 12 . . . .

9,500 . . . .

9,000 13 . . . .

8,500 . . . .

8,000 14 . . . .

```
7,500  . . . . . . . . . . . . . . . . . . . . . . . . . . . . . . . . . . . . . . . . . . . . . . . . . . .
7,000  . . . . . . . . . . . . . . . . . . . . . . . . . . . . . . . . . . . . . . . . . . . . . . . . . . .
6,500  . . . . . . . . . . . . . . . . . . . . . . . . . . . . . . . . . . . . . . . . . . . . . . . . . . .
6,000  15 . . . . . . . . . . . . . . . . . . . . . . . . . . . . . . . . . . . . . . . . . . . . . . . . .
5,500  . . . . . . . . . . . . . . . . . . . . . . . . . . . . . . . . 16 . . . . . . . .17 . . . . . . .
5,000  18 . . . . . . . . . . . . . . . . . . . . . . . . . . . . . . . . . . . . . . . . . . . . . . . .
4,500  19 . . . . . 20 . . . . . . . . . . . . . . . . . . . . . . . . . . . . . . . . . . . . . . . . .
4,000  . . . . . . . . . . . . . . . . . . . . . . . . . . . . . . . . . . . . . . . . . . . . . . . . .
3,500  . . . . . . . . . . . . . . . . . . . . . . . . . . . . . . . . 21 . . . . . . . . . . . . . .
3,000  22 . . . . . . . . . . . . . . . . . . . . . . . . . . . . . . . . . 23 . . . . . . . .
2,500  . . . . . . . . . . . . . . . . . . . . . . . . . . . . . . . . . . . . . . . . . . . . . . . . .
2,000  . . . . . . . . . . . . . . . . . . . . . . . . . . . . . . . . . . . . . . . . . . . . . . . . .
1,500  . . . . . . . . . . . . . . . . . . . . . . . . . . . . . . . . . . . . . . . . . . . . . . . . .
1,000  24 . . . . . . . . . . . . . . . . . . . . . . . . . . . . . . . . . . . . . . . 25 . . 26 .
  500  27 .            See Timeline C for Details              .Present
```

Milestones

1. Migration begins (about 50,000 BP).
2. Migrants reach India (about 48,000 BP).
3. Migrants reach Australia (about 45,000 BP).
4. Migrants reach China (about 40,000 BP).
5. Migrants reach Europe (about 38,000 BP). This general territory is initially shared with another human-like group, the Neanderthals. By the end of this period, the Neanderthals have become extinct.
6. Worldwide glacial maximum occurs. Earth's climate significantly colder and dryer than today. Large amounts of seawater locked up in glaciers in northern and southern latitudes substantially reducing sea level. Total human population reaches one million (about 22,000 BP).
7. Humans cross a land bridge from Siberia (and/or travel in boats) into the Americas and begin colonizing the continent (about 16,000 BP).
8. Migrants reach South America (about 15,000 BP). In Eurasia, the first animals (wolves) are domesticated. The keeping of dogs spreads quickly through human populations.
9. Total human population reaches ten million (about 14,000 BP).
10. Ice age ends. Overall world climate becomes warmer and wetter (about 12,500 BP).

11. First permanent camps and first domesticated plants (barley and wheat) are cultivated (about 11,000 BP).
12. First farm animals (sheep and goats) are domesticated (about 10,000 BP).
13. First cows and pigs are domesticated (about 9,000 BP).
14. Permanent dwellings of mud brick begin to be built (about 8,000 BP).
15. First draft animals (oxen) are used to provide farm labor (about 6,000 BP).
16. Bronze invented and used for tools and weapons (about 5,300 BP).
17. First city settlement (more than ten thousand people) established. Written language is invented (about 5,200 BP).
18. Wheel and axle is invented (about 5,000 BP)
19. Horses first used as draft animals (about 4,500 BP).
20. First book written using papyrus (about 4,400 BP).
21. Iron ore first mined and smelted to produce tools and weapons (about 3,200 BP).
22. Worldwide population reaches one hundred million (about 3,000 BP).
23. Money is invented to promote local commerce (about 2,600 BP).
24. First universities established (about 1,000 BP).
25. Printing press invented. Mass production of written material begins (about 575 BP).
26. European migration to the Americas begins (about 525 BP).
27. Scientific revolution begins (about 500 BP).

Timeline C

Detail of Most Recent Historical Period: 500 BP to Present

Scale: one dot equals one year; one row equals 25 years.

```
500    . . . . . . . . . . . . . . . . . . . . . . . . .
475    . . . . . . . . . . . . . . 28 . . . . . . . . .
450    . . . . . . . . . . . . . . . . . . . . . . . . .
425    29 30 . . . . . . . . . . . . . . . . 31 . . . . .
400    . . . . . . . . . . . . . . . . . . . . . . . . .
375    . . . . . . . . . . . . . . . . . . . . . . . . .
350    . . . . . . . . . . . . . . . . . . . . . . . . .
325    . . . . . . . 32 . . . . . . . . . . . . . . . . .
300    . . . . . . . . . . . . . . . . . . . . . . . . .
275    . . . . . . . . . . . . . . . . . . . . . 33 . . . .
250    . . . . . . . . . 34 35 . . . . . . . . . . . . .
225    . . . . . . . . . . . 36 37 . . . . . . . . . .
200    . . . . . . . . . . . . . . . . . . . . . . . . .
175    . . . . . . . . . . . . . . . . . . . . . . . 38
150    39 . . . . . . . . . . . . . . 40 . . . . . . 41 .
125    . . . . . . 42 . . . . . . . . . 43 . . . . . 44
100    . . . . . . . . . . . . . . . . . . . 45 . . .
75     . . . . . 46 . . . 47 . 48 . . . . . . . . . .
50     . . 49 50 . . . . . . . . . . 51 . . 52 . 53 . .
25     . . . . . . . . . . . . . . . . . . . . 54 . . Present
```

Milestones

28. Foundations of scientific method first articulated, (about 460 BP).
29. Microscope invented (425 BP).
30. First universal (compulsory) education introduced in a German Duchy (423 BP).
31. Telescope invented (407 BP).
32. Steam engine invented (317 BP).

33. Industrialization begins (factory production using machines); extensive use of coal begins (255 BP).
34. Invention of the modern flush toilet (240 BP).
35. European Americans declare independence from Britain (239 BP).
36. Human population worldwide reaches one billion (211 BP).
37. First commercial use of natural gas (210 BP).
38. Discovery that germs can cause disease; development of scientific medicine begins (151 BP).
39. Literacy rate of world population reaches ten percent (150 BP).
40. Invention of commercial electric light bulb; widespread use of electricity begins (136 BP).
41. First automobile sold (127 BP).
42. First commercial motion picture (118 BP).
43. First radio broadcast (109 BP).
44. First commercial airplane flight (101 BP).
45. First commercial television broadcast (79 BP).
46. First nuclear weapon used in warfare (70 BP).
47. First commercial computer sold (65 BP).
48. Structure of DNA discovered (62 BP).
49. Human population worldwide reaches two and a half billion (47 BP).
50. Humans land on the moon for the first (46 BP).
51. First personal computer sold (34 BP).
52. First cell phone sold (31 BP).
53. Human population worldwide reaches five billion (BP 28).
54. Human population worldwide reaches seven billion (BP 4).

3 Range and Population

ONE OF THE clearest indicators of human dominance on Earth is their range, which extends to all habitable parts of dry land, and even into some areas that are only marginally or seasonally habitable. They even have a presence on and under water, and in low earth orbit above the planet. This chapter describes the full extent of the human range, the size and composition of their population, and the scope of their worldwide distribution.

As already noted in Chapter 2, fifty thousand years ago there were no humans outside of Africa, and even within Africa, their range was small. Over the last fifty thousand years humans undertook a spectacular migration and experienced a significant population expansion. Chapter 2 also included an overview of the routes and general timing of this migration and outlined the population growth that accompanied it. By ten thousand years ago, humans had entered and begun colonizing every landmass except for Antarctica and some remote islands.

As humans transitioned from the hunter-gatherer lifestyle to a more settled lifestyle based on agriculture, they began to use land more intensively, and created food surpluses that made higher levels of reproduction possible. Populations grew rapidly, and around five hundred years ago the rate of growth accelerated greatly. In the last few hundred years, humans have become the most common large mammal on Earth by a significant margin.

CURRENT RANGE

Humans currently inhabit every ecological zone on Earth, though their distribution is uneven. With their technologies, they can inhabit climatic zones that would normally be too harsh for long-term human survival. For instance, they have permanent settlements on the Antarctic ice cap; they temporarily host thousands of humans at a time on the surface of oceans in large ships; and they even maintain a small colony of humans in orbit around the earth in a space station. Though these may be extreme examples, it's indicative of the human capacity to adapt to unusual environments.

Most humans live in the temperate climate zones in the northern and southern hemispheres and in other areas that, due to local conditions, share a similar moderate climate. These are also the zones most suitable for agriculture.

Since agriculture is an essential component of the human lifestyle, they predictably occupy areas where farming can be successfully practiced. About eleven percent of the Earth's dry land is arable, that is, suitable for growing domesticated crops. About another thirty percent, though not suitable for crops, is being used by humans for livestock pasture. In total, about forty percent of all dry land is currently being used by humans for agricultural purposes.

But land use changes. In some areas of the world, humans are converting native forests, wetlands, and arid environments to agricultural purposes using a variety of technologies. However, the expanded use of land for agriculture is offset somewhat by the conversion of existing farmland, especially adjacent to cities, for other commercial and residential uses. At present, a total of about nineteen million square miles of the Earth's land surface (more than fifty-seven million square miles) is in some degree of agricultural production.

Roaming Habits

Humans do not participate in genetically-determined seasonal migrations like some other animals, such as species of birds. However, humans do travel extensively within their home territories and beyond for business or pleasure. While some prefer to remain close to home, others travel extensively, logging thousands of miles of travel around the world in a lifetime. This kind of travel is a recent development, as the normal foraging circuit for a hunter-gatherer tribe may only have been a few miles in length. Though modern travel may involve a quest for food or resources, as it was for ancestors living in the wild, modern purposes are more varied, and almost always include the pursuit of interactions with others.

Humans have invented transportation technologies and built specialized infrastructure to support and coordinate travel. Machines such as automobiles, trucks, buses, trains, ships, and airplanes have come to be the dominate forms of transport having replaced animals (such as horses) in just the last couple of centuries, as a primary means of personal transport or moving freight. Vast resources have recently been invested to create extensive transportation grids.

There are currently more than a billion motor vehicles in use around the planet, supported by more than thirty-nine million miles of roadways (of varying quality). Railroads have been constructed to move freight and passengers between key population centers. There are more than eight hundred thousand miles of train tracks dispersed around the planet. More than thirty-five thousand commercial ships transport cargo across large and small bodies of water. Aircraft fly around one hundred thousand flights a day, connecting more than forty thousand airports around the planet.

Many modern humans are not sedentary by nature. They are almost constantly on the move, undertaking a broad range of activities. Some even mimic migratory animals by living seasonally in different localities, sometimes thousands of miles apart. Though this is relatively rare, it illustrates again the flexibility of human behavior in situations where the necessary resources are available.

POPULATION

At present, the world human population is more than 7.3 billion. Remember that only fifty thousand years ago, the lineage of all humans on Earth today was founded by a tribe numbering perhaps 150 people. And also recall that most of the population growth has been in only the last five hundred years. It is estimated that the total number of humans will reach eight billion by about 2025 and eleven billion by about 2100, a bit more than eighty years from now.

If the lifestyle typical of humans living in wealthy countries, such as the United States, was available to everyone, the current population size would most certainly exceed the carrying capacity of the Earth. With the current infrastructure and technologies, a world population size of ten billion will ensure that large numbers of humans will suffer hunger, malnutrition and premature death, and that the worldwide standard of living will be reduced substantially for nearly everyone.

Population Characteristics

The founding tribe was composed of just a few extended families and the members of these families provided the genetic variety available to subsequent generations.[9] All humans alive today are members of the same species and can potentially reproduce with each other. Each individual is a member of a lineage going back to the founding tribe. But not all humans are the same genetically.

During the migration period, thousands of hunter-gatherer tribes established territories in different ecosystems at different times and were quite isolated from each other. Reproductive isolation is the key point. Each tribe had its own gene pool with limited opportunities to add new genetic variety. Consequently, thousands of small populations began to diverge from each other genetically.

In small populations these changes can be quite rapid. As children with new combinations of particularly adaptive genes are born, beneficial mutations are added to the local gene pool. Genes are lost when a carrier of a rare trait dies without reproducing. When particular traits become prized by potential mates, or when changing environmental conditions favor specific new traits, genes are passed on.

These were the dynamics shaping the genetic composition of small populations for more than the first forty thousand years of human history. Only after settlement took hold and humans started living in closer proximity did gene pools begin to comingle on a larger scale through migrations and military occupations. The more extensive flow of genetic material among populations has really only been significant for the last five hundred years or so.

Genetic Variation

Despite the genetic comingling that has occurred, ancient population lineages are still discernable in human DNA. As a result, the physical and behavioral characteristics of modern populations differ, on

---

[9] While the founders provided the entire initial DNA, other sources were added through some limited interbreeding with Neanderthals, and probably other archaic hominid species encountered during the migration. Also, natural DNA mutations continued to occur and bring changes to the human gene pool.

average, from one another. However, within a population lineage there is typically more variability in individual characteristics than there is *between* the averages of any two population lineages. Even though there is substantial variability within a population, differences in population averages are real and not trivial

For physical characteristics such as skin color, eye color and shape, hair color and texture, and stature and body shape are examples of easily observed differences across populations. For instance, the

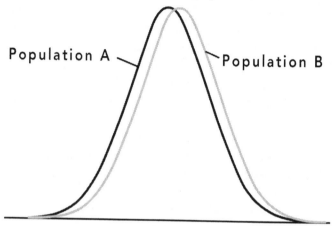

Figure 3-1. Population Differences

average height of northern European males is about five feet eleven inches, while the average height of males living in China is about five feet six inches. But the distribution of individual heights in each population overlaps significantly (Figure 3-1).

There are many examples of how evolutionary forces have shaped the genetic characteristics of populations. Typically among mammals, breast milk is not digestible by the young after weaning, but in some European populations who kept dairy cows, a trait for the long-term toleration of milk became widely distributed. In some African populations, a trait that conferred resistance to malaria became widespread, though in one form it caused a deadly disease: sickle cell anemia. For a population living on the high plateau in Tibet, a trait that produced more oxygen-carrying blood cells became widespread. And for populations living in Japan, a trait that produces thick, black hair follicles on the head became very common.

In addition, just as with physical characteristics, cognitive characteristics also continued to evolve in isolated populations, giving different groups somewhat different average characteristics compared with others. Intelligence is one such characteristic that has been studied by humans in some depth. Here again, just as with physical characteristics, the range of variation within a population lineage is significant so that any two populations substantially overlap with each other, though average values may be somewhat different.

Using genome-wide association studies, humans are beginning to understand these population level differences. Such studies, which compare genomes for many individuals, seek to find specific DNA sequences that are common to a trait in a population. Based on the current rate of analysis, it will take about another decade before population lineages will be fully mapped. Thousands of full genome sequences from representative individuals will be needed, which presents a formidable challenge, though the technology now exists to achieve the goal.

Understanding all of this human variation is important because it can help identify performance or health risk factors, for which positive interventions can be designed.

Each of the 7.3 billion humans on Earth has a unique DNA configuration.[10] Each configuration is the product of a lineage stretching back tens of thousands of years. Many related genetic configurations arose in isolated populations typical of hunter-gatherers, driven by known evolutionary factors. Though much comingling of gene pools has occurred, particularly over the last several hundred years, the effects of ancient lineages can still be seen. Genetic variations in modern humans are spread over a wide continuum of physical and behavioral characteristics. Understanding this variability is important to provide the best life outcomes possible for every individual.

GEOGRAPHIC DISTRIBUTION

The distribution of humans is not uniform over the Earth's land masses (Figure 3-2). Humans prefer the temperate climate zone, and this is where the major population concentrations are found. While

---

[10] Except for identical twins that have (very nearly) identical genomes. Worldwide there are about three twin sets born per one thousand births (.3 percent). Within the current world population of more than 7.3 billion, there are more than twenty million sets of identical (monozygotic) twins.

humans were hunter-gatherers, they were sparsely distributed in fairly large foraging territories. Densities only started to increase with the transition to settlement and agriculture.

Persons/sq km
<2
2-10
11-40
41-100
101-500
>500

Figure 3-2. Human Population Density

Though villages, towns, and cities first arose more than five thousand years ago, most humans continued to live on subsistence farms or on livestock grazing ranges until quite recently. About two hundred years BP, only about three percent of humans lived in urban areas.[11] One hundred years BP, this had increased to about fourteen percent. By fifty years BP this number had increased to thirty percent. Today more than half (fifty-four percent) of the world population lives in urban areas and this trend is accelerating.

As the proportion of people living in urban areas has increased, the actual population size has exploded. Currently there are over one thousand urban areas on Earth, each with a population greater than five hundred thousand. The largest urban area, Tokyo, Japan, alone has a population of around thirty-eight million. It is estimated that by 2050,

---

[11] An urban area is defined as the region around a city, town, or village where the population is dense and supported by human-made infrastructure such as roads, rail lines, electricity distribution grids, water distribution systems, and sewage disposal systems.

in just about thirty-five years, two-thirds of all humans will live in urban areas. And remember, the human population in 2050 is expected to be over nine billion.

This poses huge challenges for humans. Vast resources will have to be invested to upgrade infrastructure all over the world to accommodate all of these people in safe, healthy, and ecologically sustainable urban environments.

POLITICAL DISTRIBUTION

Another important dimension of the distribution of humans is their division of the landmasses into (currently) one hundred ninety-five geo-political territories called states or countries, and their assigning of citizenship status to most of those who live within their boundaries (Figure 3-3). Countries are a fairly recent development in human social organization. Only about twenty of the currently recognized countries

Figure 3-3. Geo-political Boundaries in Europe

existed before two hundred years ago. All the rest have been formed since then. Countries range in size from Russia, with a land area of 6.3 million square miles (eleven percent of the Earth's land surface), to Vatican City, a religious enclave, with an area of .17 square mile.

The borders of the existing countries have historical roots and have generally been established as a result of political negotiations and/or conflicts, including warfare and colonization. Many boundaries are still contested, with the most recent new country formed in Africa only five years BP. It looks likely that the boundaries, social organizations, and total numbers of countries will continue to change for the foreseeable future.

The creation of social groupings like countries is a direct expression of the territorial impulses of humans. In addition, they are sustained largely by human impulses to form tribal allegiances and create social hierarchies. At their best, countries promote higher levels of productive cooperation among their citizens by establishing and supporting many kinds of social institutions like financial systems, commerce standards, communication networks, legal systems, schools, and various types of security forces. In addition, they can pool resources and undertake useful large-scale public works. At their worst, some current countries are completely corrupt and dysfunctional, or they use their tribal motives to promote conflicts with others externally or even internally. Humans have a long, dark history in this regard. Ultimately, all of the territorial boundaries are arbitrary human constructions subject to change. Further changes appear inevitable.

4 Habitat

HABITAT GENERALLY REFERS to the physical environment in which an animal lives. But humans are an unusual case. As was noted in the last chapter, humans live everywhere, not because they can tolerate severe weather and climate extremes, but because they build and inhabit artificial environments that shield them from the elements. Of course, other mammals build burrows, dens and sleeping nests for shelter, but the human versions are fantastically varied and elaborate in comparison.

There is also another type of habitat that is unique to humans. This is a kind of psychological rather than physical habitat, which comes from the human needs for social learning and connections. Humans live in a variety of societies that have distinctive cultural characteristics. These include languages, social customs, education methods, judicial systems, financial norms, architectural styles, music and art traditions, and religious preferences. There are thousands of these cultures found in different locations around the planet with varying degrees of similarity and difference. A human that lives in a culture is very much affected by its influence. This is why culture is an important aspect of the human habitat.

This chapter will describe some of the physical and social aspects of the human habitat. These descriptions will again highlight the adaptability and creativity of humans.

PHYSICAL HABITAT

Humans still prefer their ancestral African landscapes, but can and will live just about anywhere. More specifically, humans prefer verdant, savanna-like environments, which are open grasslands with clusters of bushes and trees spaced so their canopies don't overlap. They prefer undulating terrain with vantage points and some views to the horizon, along with views of water or evidence of its nearby presence.

Ancestral hunter-gatherers depended on landscapes where there were ample game animals and a variety of plant life, including flowering and fruit-bearing shrubs and trees. Humans today still prize these kinds of landscapes, but have used technologies to adapt to a much wider range of landforms ranging from deserts to arctic tundra.

The savanna landscape is also the environment that was most responsible for shaping the physical and psychological characteristics of humans over at least two hundred thousand years. It was here where natural selection reshaped the human gene pool and produced the lineage leading to all humans on Earth today. No wonder humans find the savanna landform so attractive.

Historical Perspective

Humans have had for thousands of years a preference for seeking out or creating shelters, especially at night. Before the start of the migration out of Africa fifty thousand years ago, humans had already developed skill creating temporary shelters. So instead of just enduring whatever the natural conditions were at a campsite, humans had learned to create simple structures that provided some shelter from the elements and from predators as tribes foraged their territories.

Hunter-gatherer camps were established at regular locations. Some of these were intended for short-term visits of one or two nights. They would have been in the open-air, probably near a source of fresh water, with no more amenities than a ring of rocks for containing a campfire. But a few campsites were probably designed for longer stays. Just like the more temporary campsites, they were likely near a good water source. But these might have also been selected for better security from predators and uninvited human guests, and might have included a more elaborate hearth, a food cache, a tool-making anvil, and sleeping shelters.

Sleeping structures were likely constructed of locally available boughs, long grass straw, and mud, perhaps supplemented with animal

Figure 4-1. Hunter-Gatherer Shelter

skin coverings (Figure 4-1). They were most likely made to be easily disassembled between uses and reassembled on the occasion of the next visit to the same campground. They offered some protection from the elements, but were very rudimentary and small, just accommodating a family. The basic design of these shelters remained mostly unchanged for thousands of years and served hunter-gatherers well.

Once the migration began, humans moved into new, and often more challenging environments. As this occurred, shelters were adapted to meet the new environmental conditions. For instance, as an adaptation to a colder climate, shelters may have been enlarged and the hearth been brought inside. New locally available materials such as animal bones were used to create the framework for a shelter. The migrants were creative and opportunistic in exploiting their environments, which made their survival possible. Temporary shelters in foraging territories were the norm for most of human history.

The next major habitat innovation occurred when humans began to adopt a settled lifestyle starting about ten thousand years ago. Permanent settlement meant that shelters could be designed for relatively long-term use, and the idea of a permanent home became the norm. With the sense of permanence came the concept of ownership. Though territoriality had long been part of the human mindset, the idea of a home and its grounds firmly established the expectation of private property. The natural next step was the adoption of inheritance practices, with properties normally transferred from one generation to the next, with few exceptions, through the male line of decent.

Settlement resulted in the use of new materials and construction methods to improve weather tightness, durability and security. Mud bricks—blocks of sundried clay—became the material of choice and were used initially to form round dwellings with tree branches or fronds for roofing materials. Later, the same mud bricks were used to form straight walls, and roofs were constructed of more substantial wooden materials, often covered with straw and mud (Figure 4-2). As construction methods continued to evolve, mud brick walls and dirt floors were sometimes plastered with mud and sand. Thatched roofs, which were relatively watertight, came into common use. Homes of mud brick are still being constructed today in less economically developed parts of the planet.

As villages with higher population densities appeared about five thousand years ago, mud brick structures with shared walls became common. Some dwellings had more than one room, reflecting

Figure 4-2. Mud Brick Home

emerging class and wealth differences among individuals and families. Clay ovens came into use to supplement open fire hearths for cooking.

When humans migrated into areas with wetter, cooler climates with extensive forests, they relied more on wood and stones as primary construction materials. Tools and techniques for constructing shelters slowly improved over many generations as humans sought to make better use of locally available raw materials. As humans fanned out around the planet, new construction innovations appeared in various regions. In some arid regions, mud brick dwellings were plastered with mud, straw or animal dung. Walls of interlaced branches were constructed and plastered (called wattle and daub).

Where available, stones were stacked and mortared with mud to create walls and, after the development of the appropriate tools, blocks of stone were fabricated and used for home building. Windows and doors, which were just holes in walls, became widely used for the first time. Regional differences in materials, methods, and tastes gave rise to distinctive home styles in different locales, particularly for more wealthy families. The vast majority of people continued to live in simple one-room huts.

About two thousand years ago, a significant new construction innovation appeared in Greece: the first use of cement. Cement, a combination of powdered lime, sand, and clay, created an exceptionally strong mortar when mixed with water, and was used when constructing walls of bricks, stones, or stone blocks. Its use greatly improved the stability and durability of structures. The Romans next mixed cement with small bits of volcanic rock, thus producing a new and very important construction material: concrete. This new material, which had the consistency of rock after it dried, made it possible to construct new, large architectural forms, including multi-story homes. Unfortunately, these innovations were lost for several hundred years after the decline of the Roman Empire.

The function and style of homes continued to evolve over the next several hundred years. Humans tending animals in the countryside, and even in villages, shared their homes with their animals, both to protect them and to use them as a source of heat. The use of brick, stone or rubble stone foundations for new homes became more common. Fired clay tiles began to be used for roofing in instances where walls were substantial enough to support the weight. Entrances were fitted with wooden doors; windows gained shutters; and, by about five hundred years ago, framed glass for windows was used for the first time. Chimneys were incorporated in homes only about four hundred years ago.

As class and wealth differences in societies grew ever greater, property ownership became concentrated. As a result, fewer people owned their own homes or the land on which they were situated. Until recently, most humans were peasants, and though some owned their own small subsistence farming plots, the great majority only rented their small farms from large landholders. Their homes continued to be small and simple. Cities continued to grow with a range of homes from large and opulent to poorly constructed, unsanitary shanties.

With the start of the industrial revolution, only about two hundred years ago, came many new innovations in construction techniques and materials—all supported by mass production methods. Wood was milled in standard sizes, metal nails became widely available, and kiln-fired bricks were common. The advent of Portland cement (cement that will harden underwater) and the use of reinforcing steel made it possible to construct enormous apartment buildings in cities. Running water, indoor toilets, central heating, and eventually the widespread distribution of electricity revolutionized home life. And vast networks of asphalted or concrete streets and roadways connected humans with each other.

Contemporary Variations

Today on Earth there are great variations in human physical habitats generally reflecting differences in wealth. At one extreme, perhaps two percent (fifteen million) of the human population has no dwelling at all and simply lives on the streets of cities or in the open countryside. Just slightly better off than the homeless, are humans that live in ramshackle, often interconnected shelters that make up the expansive slums of most large cities. Perhaps fifteen percent (about one billion) of the world population lives in these conditions with no safe water supply, inadequate sanitation facilities, or insecure living conditions. Another fifteen percent live in primitive circumstances in the countryside. The availability of drinkable water and the proper disposal of human waste are only marginally better.

Currently, the average human household, composed of four or five related individuals, lives in a simple home or apartment of around five hundred square feet. This provides enough space for two or three small rooms. Some space is set aside for food preparation and, if located in a city, there may be a simple indoor toilet. If the dwelling is in the countryside, an outdoor privy is more likely used for sanitation. There will typically be a piped water supply (or a shared well), though the quality of the water may be poor. Wood or a wood byproduct like charcoal will be used for cooking and space heating during cool periods. Electricity will be available, at least intermittently. There will be an entry/exit door and a few windows, normally fitted with glass. Furnishings will be few, simple, and hand-built. Most dwellings like this are in Africa and Asia, where most of the world's population lives (Figure 4-3).

The average annual household income is somewhat less than the equivalent of US $10,000. The relative purchasing power of this level of income varies substantially from locale to locale. However, at best, it provides the means for only a basic subsistence lifestyle. Remember, this is a description of the average physical habitat and household environment, which means that about 3.4 billion humans live at or below this level.

Figure 4-3. Typical Contemporary Home

Because the quality of habitats is related to wealth, most people (two-thirds) on Earth inhabit dwellings very similar to the average one. There are fewer amenities below the average and a few more above the average, but the commonalities are greater than the differences.

Wealthier humans, those in the top one percent of the world population (seventy-three million people) are widely distributed around the planet but are most commonly found in Europe and the Americas. The entry level to this group is an annual income of only about US $35,000. About half of the wealthiest humans in the world live in the United States. There, the typical home size is around twenty-two hundred square feet. Such a home has two or three bedrooms, a kitchen, at least two bathrooms with indoor toilets, a dining room, a living room, piped clean water with several faucets and drains, a central heating and air conditioning system in climates where they are needed, weather-tight and insulated construction, reliable electricity with multiple wall outlets, broadband coaxial cabling delivering television and internet services, and a garage for one or two automobiles.

Kitchens typically include electric refrigerators, gas or electric cooking ranges, an electric dishwasher, and a microwave oven. There are generally two or three televisions of various sizes used in different rooms to access audiovisual entertainment, and one or two general-purpose computers. The average home will generally have a room dedicated to an electricity-powered clothes washer and drier. Every room is furnished with amenities appropriate to its function: tables, chairs, desks, couches, beds, cabinets, light fixtures, and art works used for decoration.

Those considered very wealthy have annual household incomes of US $380,000 and above. Roughly half of these households are in the United States and the rest are found primarily in various cities around the planet. They represent about 0.1 percent of the total population, or around just seven million humans.

Their homes are often large (sometimes with footprints larger than ten thousand square feet) and lavish, with many rooms and

Figure 4-4. Mansion

amenities, and with formally landscaped grounds. Many have more than one residence. Wealthy families typically have several automobiles, a boat or yacht used for pleasure activities, and maybe even an airplane for personal use. They often are able to employ other humans to perform a variety of helpful support activities such as cooking, cleaning, childcare, gardening, running errands, and driving vehicles. Though they are a relatively small portion of the total population, these families control perhaps a third of all wealth available to humans on the planet (Figure 4-4).

Though the total range of habitats is great, the vast majority of humans live in rather modest circumstances. In absolute terms, the quality of the average physical habitat has improved substantially since hunter-gatherer days. Still, millions of humans live (and die) in squalid conditions more harsh than were encountered by their foraging forbearers.

Monumental Structures

Humans started building structures not intended solely for habitation about ten thousand years ago. Sophisticated techniques for constructing structures with sun-dried bricks and blocks of stone were developed, especially in zones with large-scale civilization centers, such

Figure 4-5. Egyptian Pyramids

as in Egypt and Mesopotamia (Figure 4-5). Early on, these monuments were typically constructed for religious reasons. Especially common were large burial tombs and temples. In addition to their ceremonial functions, monumental buildings were often constructed as part of an effort to consolidate political control within a region. They were visible reminders of the local power structure.

With the advent of cities, about five thousand years ago, buildings were also constructed for more practical commercial purposes. For example, markets, workshops, and stables provided services in neighborhoods. Increasingly, walls were built around towns and cities to make them more secure. Fortresses and castles were built to provide protection from other hostile human groups.

By two thousand years ago, Greeks and then Romans became very sophisticated in their architectural designs and mastery of building materials. In addition to temples and other religion-inspired monuments, these civilizations produced many civic projects such as amphitheaters, sports stadiums, aqueducts, bridges, and paved roads, remnants of which still survive today. Other civilizations in this time frame also independently produced monumental buildings in civic centers on every continent except for Antarctica.

Through the next fifteen hundred years, architectural design and materials continued to evolve with significant regional differences in esthetics. Fortification, religion, arts, and scholarship were major themes in the creation of public buildings. Castles, cathedrals, museums, and universities sprang up all over Europe, with similar developments in Asia. Some structures, like cathedrals, were massive projects taking two or three generations to complete.

Since the industrial revolution, humans have built many kinds of structures to support a wide array of specialized activities.[12] Using steel-reinforced concrete, much larger and more sophisticated buildings became possible. The skylines of cities have been remade through the introduction of high-rise buildings—structures with twelve or more stories. In cities, these are common and are divided into apartments, offices, retail spaces, or some combination of all three (Figure 4-6). Currently, the tallest occupied building in the world is a tower in Dubai that is about twenty-seven hundred feet tall and incorporates one

---

[12] Examples include factories, office buildings, museums, libraries, schools, houses of worship, athletic performance venues, barns, warehouses, and courthouses.

hundred sixty-three floors of retail, office, and residential spaces. With new materials and methods, architects, engineers, and contractors have been able to build imaginative forms merging art with functional spaces.

Because most current humans live in cities or their surrounding suburbs, they rarely interact with the natural world except for planned recreational activities, like camping in an intentionally preserved green space like a national park—and even then, the experience is buffered by technology like tents, camp stoves, and coolers filled with beverages and prepared foods. Few humans experience sustained, direct

Figure 4-6. High Density Cityscape

interaction with wild nature like their hunting and gathering forebears. Human-modified environments now dominate the human physical habitat.

Social Habitat

For humans, social habitat is just as important as their physical one because they all rely on social learning to develop the behaviors they need to survive and prosper. Social learning is passed from generation to generation, primarily through language and other means of socialization—the process of adapting behavior to the norms of the local community. You have to learn a great deal to be a human. But the details of what is learned will determine what kind of human you will become and with which social group or groups you will affiliate most strongly.

Historical Perspective

When history started about fifty thousand years ago as a human tribe migrated out of Africa, social life was simpler. The tribe was an intact society with its own culture. A culture is the sum total of all the knowledge and norms commonly expressed by the members of the society. It includes conventions like spoken language, social customs, preferred foods, education methods, gender expectations, moral codes, means of exchange, art forms, music traditions, and religious practices, among other social features.

The founding tribe's culture was quite homogeneous. But given the method through which the migration unfolded, local tribal cultures soon diverged from each other. Part of this was due to the fact that humans had to adapt to different environments using different strategies, and part was due to the general human capacity for innovation and change. Even a culture that remained rooted to the same location changed over time, sometimes to a great extent.

Forty thousand years after the migration started, human groups had evolved very different cultural practices in their now widely dispersed hunter-gatherer societies. Cultural evolution continued during the era of settlement, which started ten thousand years ago, and continues to the present day. If the members of the founding tribe could visit the planet today, they would be astonished and a little overwhelmed by the cultural diversity they would encounter. It is unlikely they could communicate or identify with any of their contemporary relatives.

Scope of Cultural Variations

As a result of fifty thousand years of cultural evolution within widely dispersed and isolated communities, human societies today are a mosaic of thousands of cultures and sub-cultures. Each of these is composed of many elements which, in turn, can have many variations. The diversity of just one common cultural element, religion, illustrates this nicely.

It is estimated that there are currently more than four thousand religions/faith communities with one theme in common: some type of belief in supernatural forces that influence human affairs.[13] However, despite this basic commonality, there is great diversity in the doctrines, rituals, and disciplines embraced by adherents of any particular religion. Here are a few examples of religions, their geographic epicenters, and the estimated total number of adherents (Figure 4-7).

Religion	Location	Adherents
Shinto	Japan	2,700,000
Hinduism	India	950,000,000
Mormonism	United States	15,000,000
Mandaeism	Middle East	70,000
Judaism	Israel	12,000,000
Zen Buddhism	Japan	9,600,000
Lutheranism	Europe	80,000,000
Roman Catholicism	Worldwide	1,250,000,000
Yoruba	Africa	20,000,000
Quakerism	United States	360,000

Figure 4-7. Sample of Religions

Just think of the social differences in communities that arise from this cultural element alone, and the fact that adherents of many different religions may all live in the same geographic region or in close proximity to each other. Add to this the effects of another major cultural element, language—of which there are more than seven thousand (see Chapter 5)—and the variety of cultural options grows even greater. For instance, here's an example of how humans would convey the same phrase in five different languages.

English: Here's how you say it
Swedish: Detta är hur du säger det
Chinese: 这就是你怎么说
Yoruba: Eleyi je bi o so o
Persian: گویند می را آن شما اینجا در

When all the elements of culture and their potential variations are considered, the total number of combinations is very large and is

---

[13] It is uniquely human to develop such belief systems, despite the fact that there are no supernatural forces at work. See more about this impulse and its broader impact on humans in Chapter 9.

reflected in the diversity of cultures found among humans on Earth. What is striking is that all of this variation is largely arbitrary, reflecting the unpredictable interaction of humans with each other and with their environments through the course of history. Any culture is the product of its history (and geography) that has been shaped by many chance events, rather than shaped by any rational design. This arbitrary quality of culture has some important impacts on humans.

Status of Cultural Diversity

Periodically, particularly within the last five thousand years, human migrations (frequently backed with military force) brought different cultures into contact with each other. This worked to reduce cultural differences, at least locally or regionally. In these encounters, the stronger force usually assimilated the weaker one, though a partial fusing of different cultural elements commonly occurred. Examples of this process include:

- The migration of the Bantu peoples in Africa starting about 3,000 years BP.
- The territorial expansion of the Roman Empire in Europe commencing about 2,300 years BP.
- The expansion into Southeast Asia by the Mongols about 800 years BP.
- The colonization of the Americas by Europeans beginning about 500 years BP.

In each case, cultures co-mingled with each other with some mutual adaptation, though indigenous cultures and peoples often suffered some negative outcomes in the process.

Cultural interactions became common and widespread after the initial colonization of the Americas. Mostly European countries, largely driven by economic motives and supported by more advanced military and transportation technologies, established colonies all over the planet, bringing along with them their cultural norms—which were typically imposed on the local populations. From the current perspective, all these interactions tended to reduce cultural diversity, though it is testament to the durability of tradition that the core of many cultures survived even though some of their practices and beliefs were modified.

In very recent times, additional forces have been at work to further reduce cultural diversity on a planetary basis. During the last one hundred years—in part as a result of large-scale "world wars" that crossed cultural lines—cultural isolation has been reduced greatly through the rise of global commercial markets, the worldwide distribution of media, and the widespread use of electronic communications. Commercial air travel has given rise to a small, but growing class of global citizens who are comfortable working and communicating across cultures, and who are spreading multi-cultural norms that link people together through shared goals and expectations. This is still a small minority of humans, but it illustrates, once again, the human capacity for flexibility and adaptation.

Impact of Diversity

Until recently, humans were members of very culturally diverse societies with little knowledge of or contact with each other. Culture continues to be a very powerful and necessary force shaping human behavior. To become human, participation in a culture is required. But the norms imbedded in the culture are very important in determining the patterns of behavior that will emerge. Unfortunately, as a result of the way in which they have customarily developed, cultures promote group cohesion and the, sometimes very overt, exclusion of other humans who don't share the same social norms. This sometimes has made communication and cooperation very challenging, and has even promoted conflict.

As global interconnections continue to build, cultural diversity appears more and more problematic. Population growth and urbanization bring humans with different, sometimes incompatible, norms into close contact with each other. The emergence of environmental problems like global warming affects all cultures and require cross-cultural collaboration to resolve. Economic problems are now often globally interconnected. And military technologies for a few countries now have global reach.

Few, if any, current cultures are well positioned to tackle these kinds of issues. Instead, most cultural norms and practices have a fragmenting effect. Communications splintered into thousands of language variations serves as a prime example. While some humans lament the potential loss of cultural diversity, a greater integration of human efforts looks increasingly essential. All social habitats face circumstances requiring more interdependence.

5 Physical Characteristics

HUMANS ARE UNEXCEPTIONAL from a physical perspective. They are not particularly large, strong, fast, or well-endowed with aggressive or defensive features like sharp teeth or claws. Their senses such as sight and hearing are adequate rather than exceptional. Yet they have a number of adaptations that in combination, have allowed them to out compete all other life forms on the planet. They occupy the highest level of the food chain in every ecological niche and are multiplying rapidly.

MASS

An adult human weighs, on average, about one hundred thirty-seven pounds.[14] Males are, on average, about fifteen percent heavier than females. However, a focus solely on the average human obscures a significant degree of variation. Weight and height correlate strongly with each other. Normal weights range between 91 pounds (height of

---

[14] What is considered a normal weight is based on the Body Mass Index (BMI). This index is obtained by measuring body weight in kilograms and dividing it by the square of height in meters. It is an indicator of the amount of body fat being stored. Higher BMI's indicate more body fat storage. A BMI lower than 18.5 indicates that a person may be underweight; a score between 18.5-24.9 indicates normal or healthy weight; a score between 25-29.9 indicates overweight; and a BMI greater than 30 indicates obesity.

4'10") to about 204 pounds (height of 6'4"). For a male of average height (5'6"), the normal weight range is 118-154 pounds. For a female of average height (5'2"), the normal weight range is 104-135 pounds. These normal weight ranges assume adequate health and nutrition.

As will be discussed in more detail in Chapter 6, many humans in the modern world have access to more food than they need to maintain a normal level of activity and body weight. As a result of easy access to foodstuffs and a general genetic impulse to store fat as a hedge against times when food is scarce (which it rarely is for most people), many humans are overweight or even obese. Around twenty-five percent of the worldwide human population falls into one of these two categories; at the other extreme, however, perhaps as many as five percent of humans are underweight due to inadequate nutrition.

BODY

Humans follow the normal mammal body plan with a few major differences (Figure 5-1). For instance, they stand upright and walk on their hind limbs, which is a defining characteristic. They range in standing height from about 4'8" to 6'6", though there are rare instances of both shorter and taller heights. The shortest human on record was just 21" tall while the tallest was 8'11". The extremes were due to genetic abnormalities or disease conditions and are outside the heights attained through normal developmental processes. Males are, on average, ten percent taller than females. Average normal height has been increasing over the last five hundred years, due in part to the wider availability of good nutrition and improved living conditions.

At the top of a standing figure is the head, which includes two eyes with protective eyelids facing forward and providing good stereoscopic vision. Each eye includes an iris that comes in a variety of color variations that help distinguish individuals. These colors range from very dark brown, almost black, to light blue or light green. Every human had dark brown eyes until a mutation arose and spread starting around ten thousand years ago.

The head also has two ears, one on either side for receiving sounds; a nose for receiving scents; and a mouth for receiving foodstuffs. The mouth includes a tongue for manipulating items and twenty-eight relatively small, densely packed teeth mounted in opposition to each other, used for reducing foodstuffs to smaller pieces before swallowing. About eighty percent of humans grow four

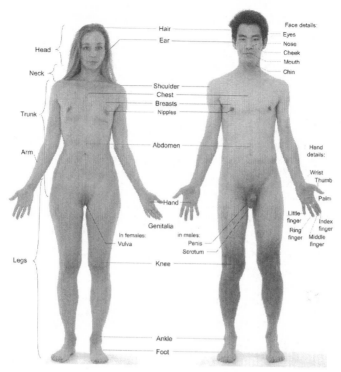

Figure 5-1. External Anatomy

additional molars that erupt in early adulthood. These are vestiges from a point in evolutionary history when jaws were larger and more focused on grinding plant materials. Among modern humans, there is generally not enough room in the jaw to accommodate them and they are typically removed to avoid problems with chronic pain and infections.

The features of the front of the head, taken together, are referred to as the face. It is an important part of the human appearance, as its form is used as a means of identifying individuals and discerning their intentions. To a social animal, like humans, facial details are extremely important. Faces are very expressive and play a significant role in human communications.

Between the head and the torso is the neck, a short, muscular column housing components of the digestive tract, nervous system, the upper backbone, and providing the capacity for head mobility.

The human forelimbs, called arms, hang at the side of the torso and terminate with hands capable of a precise grip of objects. This is facilitated by thumbs that are very flexible and able to make direct and powerful contact with all four of the fingers of a hand. The fingers of the hands are relatively long and flexible and have protective nails.

The torso (trunk) houses the organs used for respiration, blood circulation, digestion, excretion and sex. The hind limbs, called legs, are optimized for locomotion, particularly running. The legs terminate with bony structures called feet that, like the hands, have projections called toes. Unlike the fingers, the toes are shorter and less flexible, optimized to be part of a stable platform for walking and running. They also have protective nails like the fingers.

Human bodies are densely covered with hair follicles, though most of these hairs are very short with light pigmentation, giving the appearance that humans are generally hairless—an unusual characteristic for a mammal. Hair generally only grows thickly on the top of the head (and for males, the face), in the armpits and in the pubic area. In addition, especially among some males, hair can grow rather coarsely on the chest, back, arms and legs. Hair color varies naturally from black to almost white and is another characteristic used to distinguish individuals from each other.

Most humans currently cut the hair on their heads to match whatever norms are typical of the culture within which they reside. Usually there are distinct differences between males and female styles, generally driven by gender identity and sexual selection criteria. In some cultures shaving the head or even removing all body hair is fashionable.

TAIL

Humans don't have tails to assist in balance while in motion, unlike most of their mammalian relatives. What is left of the ancestral tail can be seen in a small bone at the base of the spinal column called the coccyx, commonly and appropriately referred to as the tailbone.

TRACKS

When humans walk barefoot, they leave a distinctive track given their upright posture. Five toes on each foot along with a well-defined heel leave a characteristic impression in soft soil or beach sand (Figure 6-2). The gait is represented by alternating left and right footprints as one leg moves forward followed rhythmically by the other. The distance between footfalls increases when running. Now that many humans

Figure 6-2. Human Tracks

wear shoes, the distinctive toe and heel pattern has been replaced by the appearance of the outsole of the shoe being worn, but the overall shape remains the same. Human tracks are easily identified and are common everywhere.

SCAT

As with other mammals, human metabolic and digestive processes produce waste products that must be eliminated from the body, primarily through urine and feces. Feces are normally continuous or segmented cylinders about two inches in diameter of varying lengths, produced in the rectum and passed voluntarily through the anus. They are normally brown to yellowish-brown in color and composed mostly of water, gut bacteria, indigestible vegetable fiber, and various metabolic products such as cholesterol, that the body seeks to eliminate. The consistency can vary, but generally they have a smooth, soft texture. A typical bowel movement might weight between eight and sixteen ounces. Urine is clear, generally with a yellowish tint, resulting from pigments associated with the breakdown of red blood cells. Urine may be passed several times a day and feces may be eliminated one or two times per day.

Humans generally prefer to excrete their waste products in private and to cover their feces. They have an aversion to the smell of their own excrement, reflecting a reflexive disgust for the health threats posed by the bacteria and the occasional parasites imbedded in it. When they lived in low-density hunter-gatherer groups, the disposal of feces was not much of a problem as long as fresh water supplies were not fouled.

As population densities increased with settlement and agriculture, humans developed increasingly sophisticated technologies for separating excrement from living spaces. The use of shared latrines and privies became common. In recent times, elaborate sewer systems have been constructed in many localities, particularly in areas with high population densities, to remove, decontaminate, and safely dispose of human waste. Poor sanitation practices of people living in close proximity cause humans serious health problems.

Most of the time, humans do not use excrement to mark territory, as do many other mammals. However, males will sometimes use urination as a way of attempting to establish dominance. Such behavior is usually now seen as socially unacceptable.

COLORATION

Because human body hair is so fine, the underlying color of the skin is easily seen. When humans originally dispersed from Africa about fifty thousand years ago, their skin color was a dark brown. However, as a result of geographic isolation of small populations in diverse ecological niches over many millennia, skin pigmentation diversified. Today humans have a range of skin colorations from brown/black to very light pink, depending on their genetic lineage (Figure 5-3). All differences reflect the amount of the skin pigment, melanin, that is present. Skin color has no biological significance other than to denote a propensity for sunburn among those with lighter skin tones.

Along with differences in skin coloration are differences in eye color and shape; hair color and texture; nose, lip, and ear shapes—all of which help humans distinguish individuals and groups (tribes) from each other. Humans are especially sensitive to facial characteristics and use those characteristics to make social status judgments about each other, though such judgments are often unreliable. But in the past, when tribal affiliations were more dominant in shaping social interactions, judgments often had immediate health and safety consequences.

Figure 5-3 Color Variations

SIGN

Unlike more shy animals, humans are not hard to find. Their dwellings are conspicuous and they have taken up the practices of even giving addresses—specific geographical locations—so that they can be more easily found. This is another indication of just how social these animals are.

In addition, they travel in conspicuous ways in wheeled vehicles on well-traveled roadways; they walk on concrete sidewalks and permanent paths, cruise waterways in boats, and fly through the sky in large, easily observed aircraft. But since they have no real predators (with the possible exception of some microorganisms), there is no

obvious reason to be discrete. Now that there are more than seven
billion humans on the planet, it is not hard to find one to observe.

VOCALIZATIONS

Human vocalizations are very distinctive and a key to their success as
a species. They make many kinds of sounds for a variety of purposes.[15]
On average, male vocalizations are about an octave lower than female
vocalizations.

Language

Humans have the ability to finely control their vocal cords to produce
a sequence of precise sounds called speech. Depending on the
language spoken, there twenty to sixty distinct speech sounds that are
combined to form words. Words are combined to form phrases and
sentences using grammar conventions to convey meaning to others
humans. This is a capacity unmatched by any other animal species.
There are four key features of human language worth special note.

(1) Humans have a compulsion to name things. For instance, they
name each other so that individuals can be specifically identified and
lines of descent can be followed. Humans also name plants, other
animals, and physical features of the natural world. Geographic
locations and features are given specific names, too. Foods are named.
Activities and processes are given names. Abstract ideas are given
names. The scope of this activity is immense. There are millions of
words across all languages used just to name things.

(2) Humans use language to describe and differentiate the things
they name. This is where one of their greatest cognitive advantages
becomes apparent. They are masters of describing things using
metaphors—figures of speech that describe one thing through
comparison to certain characteristics of another thing that may not
even have an obvious connection. Here are some examples of
commonly-used metaphors:

- Food for thought.
- Rolling in dough.

---

[15] Here the focus is on spoken language and gestures. Other forms of current
human communication, such as writing and various media, are described in
Chapters 2 and 9.

- Night was falling.
- Sweet smell of success.
- The world is a stage.

The genius here is the ability of humans to build webs of meaning in their languages that connect concrete and abstract ideas with each other. This has the advantage of making ideas, especially abstract ones, more easily (though perhaps only incompletely) understood. Metaphorical thinking has been very important for developing and communicating new knowledge.

(3) An important feature of language is the common practice of trying to describe the relationships among things and events, particularly the cause-and-effect relationships. This is at the core of the human knowledge base, which humans have used to great advantage. Once a relationship has been identified (when the insects hatch on the pond, the fish will feed) it can be shared with others through language and, in turn, it can be used to predict and exploit future events. Of course, this capacity has its challenges. New relationships, at least initially, must be described using existing words, and those words may not provide a perfect means of expression. And sometimes, perhaps even often, the proposed relationships are incorrect (the earth is flat) or imaginary (my guardian angel will protect me).

(4) Language facilitates social interaction, often with the goal of persuading others to act in a certain way. One human might try to convince another to join in an activity, help with a project, share some food, buy an item offered for sale, try a new medicine, or elect a new group leader. Sometimes the appeal is made through "rational" arguments detailing relatively objective costs and benefits. Other times the persuasion might appeal to emotion, describing how the other human would feel if a certain decision was made. Humans are also especially adept at using deceit (exaggeration or lying) to literally fool others into following a certain course of action. Humans routinely use some form of deception with an ulterior motive, in hopes of achieving a personal benefit. Though persuasion is an essential part of human social interaction, the use of deceitful tactics undermines trust and cooperation, and is considered inappropriate.

Despite the strengths of language, humans make cognitive errors in using it that can hinder rather than promote communication. A common error is treating an abstract idea as if it were actually a concrete thing. Consider the word, *nation*, as an example. It is an abstraction referring to a group of people living in a territory within distinct geographic boundaries. Of course, as seen from space, none of the boundaries that define nations actually exist; they are imaginary. However, humans who live within a nation typically act as if they are real, and are often prepared to defend the "homeland" from other humans who reside elsewhere. In this case, language, taken too literally, can amplify territorial impulses (see Chapter 9) and promote conflict. So abstract ideas, expressed through language, can, if treated too concretely, lead to unfortunate consequences.

There are many other instances where humans confuse abstract concepts with concrete ones, influencing a wide range of behaviors and potentially leading to bad outcomes. Some examples of widely held, particularly troublesome abstract concepts include, *race*, *honor*, *enemy*, *mind*, *soul*, *love*, and *sovereignty*. The fact that language is used to communicate does not mean that it automatically conveys a clear and accurate meaning. In fact, the meaning of verbal communication is often unclear, depending a great deal on context rather than just the words themselves.

Full mastery and precise control of a language is not easily achieved, requiring years of disciplined study provided by skilled teachers or mentors. The typical human only attains modest proficiency, and frequently encounters some difficulty communicating effectively with others and understanding the messages received from other speakers. Offense is frequently given or taken through simple misunderstandings. Some tolerate these miscommunications better than others and are able to paraphrase or ask questions of speakers to clarify meanings. Clear communications are difficult to achieve in most cases.

Many language variations have developed over the last fifty thousand years since humans left Africa when the migrants initially shared a common spoken language. These variations have arisen due largely to the geographic separation of small human groups throughout the world. Language not only coveys meaning but also supports group (tribal) cohesion. Those that speak the same language can easily identify each other and work closely to achieve common objectives— like securing and retaining resources. Language is fluid and constantly adapts to new and changing circumstances. Speech sounds are revised, new words are created, and new grammar conventions are adopted. In spoken language, most of this occurs unconsciously and spontaneously within a language community. This process can happen rather quickly, with language changing noticeably even within one generation. No surprise, then, that languages diversified greatly during the human migration.

Presently, just over seven thousand languages still in use have been catalogued. But this number is in decline as geographic isolation has diminished through the efforts of centralized nation-states, modern communication technologies, and the dissemination of mass media (example: popular music and movies). The top ten languages, ranked by an estimated number of native speakers, are shown in Figure 5-4.

Rank	Language	Speakers
1	Mandarin (Chinese)	955 million
2	Spanish	405 million
3	English	360 million
4	Hindi	310 million
5	Arabic	295 million
6	Portuguese	215 million
7	Bengali	205 million
8	Russian	155 million
9	Japanese	125 million
10	Punjabi	100 million

Figure 5-4. Major Languages

The top one hundred languages in use today are spoken by a total of about eighty-five percent of the world's population. All the remaining thousands of languages are spoken only in relatively small, isolated language communities. Unfortunately, most human languages are distinct enough that speakers of different languages can't understand each other without an interpreter. This is somewhat by design, as languages originally emerged to support group cohesion. A distinctive language helped individuals recognize kin and other allies. Today language differences are a constant problem, hindering large-scale cooperation in the modern world.

One final feature of spoken language deserves recognition. When in groups (which they frequently are), humans have a great capacity to focus attention on a particular speaker, even when many individuals are speaking at the same time. For instance, when humans convene in a public place such as a large restaurant, small groups will be having distinct, coherent conversations while the overall effect seems chaotic when considered as a whole. This ability to focus attention on a specific speaker when many others are talking or when there is distracting ambient sound is very important in coordinating efforts and mobilizing actions in a variety of situations. This is another distinctive characteristic of human vocalization.

Emotional Vocalizations

Humans also make a variety of sounds associated with emotional states that are so common they appear to have genetic origins. They scream when frightened or distressed. They laugh when they are happy or amused.[16] They weep when unhappy or fearful. They sigh when frustrated or resigned to circumstances. They gasp when surprised.

A particularly interesting emotional vocalization of humans is singing—a sustained, rhythmic, and often melodic sequence of sounds designed to evoke an emotional state. Sometimes singing just involves the utterance of tones individually or in groups. But more often singing involves vocalizing evocative words and phrases. This behavior has ancient roots dating back well before the beginning of the human migration from Africa. Humans sing together or perform for each other, which clearly promotes group cohesion.

Fairly early on, singers began using non-voice accompaniments; initially, percussion instruments like sticks were banged together in rhythm or drum beats. Later, humans developed many different types of instruments that produced tones to accompany songs. The flute was one of the earliest innovations. Over thousands of years, accompaniments of singing evolved to the point where humans now listen to complex musical compositions played only on instruments. Like singing, this musical form is designed to evoke emotional states, something that almost all humans seek out regularly and find quite entertaining.

Non-Verbal Gestures

In addition to vocalizations, humans use gestures, particularly of the face, arms and fingers to communicate emotional states and give silent instructions. For instance, when an index finger at the end of an

---

[16] Laughing is a response to language that is considered humorous. Humor is a form of communication intended to evoke a pleasant emotional state. It is a form of communication that arose as a means of strengthening group cohesion. It is one of the ways, like stories and myths, that tribes use to reinforce a common identity.

extended arm is pointing in a direction, the message is, "Look over there." Many of these kinds of gestures are universally understood. Sometimes, gestures are simply used to amplify the messages in speech. The waving of arms or the pointing of a finger when a human is talking generally means something like, "Pay attention, this is important!" Gestures can even substitute for spoken language, as is the case with the elaborate system of sign language used by communities of deaf individuals and their associates.

Faces are particularly expressive. Smiles, frowns, furrowed brows, flaring nostrils, and widened eyes all communicate emotional states. Humans are very attuned to these gestures to judge the intents of other humans in their vicinity. They look for evidence of calmness, agitation, happiness, aggression, uncertainty, and more in facial configurations.

Clapping is another hand gesture that is widely practiced. The hands are struck together creating a percussive sound to signify, particularly in groups, that a shared activity has been appreciated. This gesture is common when live entertainments have been provided, though there are many other triggers in social groups as well.

ACTIVITY CYCLES

Humans basically prefer, as a result of long evolutionary development, to be active during daylight hours, though they now use technology to create artificial "daylight" even when the sun is not visible. This allows them to be active for more hours of each day than would otherwise be possible, since their night vision is limited. Humans generally lie down and sleep at night, typically for about eight hours. Sleep is a state of unconsciousness when physiological processes work in the background to perform a variety of important maintenance functions. Sleep patterns vary quite a bit with some individuals needing fewer hours of sleep than others to maintain good health. Some humans prefer to be active at night and to sleep during daylight hours, though this pattern has some long-term adverse health consequences.

There is substantial variation from human to human in the scope and duration of daily activity. Some of this variation comes from differences in genetics and some come from learned preferences. With technological supports like artificial lighting, easy access to foodstuffs and convenient transportation, humans in many parts of the world are relatively free to organize activities to suit their personal preferences.

In addition to daily cycles, humans have annual activity cycles that are more weakly expressed. Responses to seasonal changes were more apparent when humans lived in the wild. Though modern living conditions tend to minimize seasonal effects, many vestiges, often connected to food availability, are still expressed culturally. Seasonal rituals are still widely practiced.

LIFE SPAN

The average life span today for human females is seventy-four years and for males, sixty-nine years. This is the longest average life span in human history, primarily due to reduced infant mortality, better nutrition, and improved healthcare. Historically, individuals living in the wild could easily reach into their sixth decade or longer if they survived childhood. Child mortality rates were relatively high—thirty to fifty percent. Today the average rate is under one percent, though there is variation among different populations.

The maximum lifespan for humans is around one hundred twenty years, though fewer than one percent of the world population lives to age eight-five. Fewer than .01 percent live to age one hundred (Figure 5-5, showing age groups and the approximate percentage of males and females in each group).

The long period of growth and development that occurs after the birth of a new human is described in Chapter 8. Once humans enter adulthood at around age twenty, they typically begin a long adult phase of specialized work, since there are very few humans still practicing the original foraging lifestyle. Work involves performing tasks for a specified period of time each day, under some level of supervision by other humans, in exchange for goods, services, or financial compensation. These arrangements are at the heart of human cooperation across time and space that forms the basis for most modern cultures.

With the onset of sexual maturity, a period of childrearing also frequently begins. Since each offspring requires around twenty years of supervision and support, the period of active parenthood can span three, even four, decades.

Like other animals, humans age. Aging is a gradual decline of vitality that begins slowly around age twenty-five and accelerates over the next four to five decades. This process is largely genetic with some changes timed by genes, while other changes are the result of

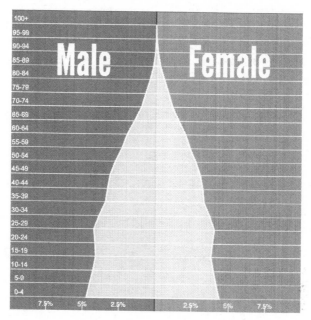

Figure 5-5. Population Pyramid

cumulative errors in the body's repair mechanisms. Lifestyle and environmental factors also play a role. By about the sixth decade, the effects of aging become more prominent. Hair begins to lose its pigment and gradually turns gray or white. Skin becomes more dry and wrinkles appear. Bones become more brittle and muscle mass diminishes. Metabolism slows.

Though humans have a capacity to learn throughout their lifespan, cognitive function also changes with advancing age. Memory degrades slowly over time. General information processing slows, becomes more limited in scope, and is more prone to error.[17]

Even in the absence of disease, the normal effects of aging can be debilitating. The quality of life for the many aged can be poor, requiring ample support from other, younger humans. Typically these are family members or others with familial-like ties. Among those with the

---

[17] Most humans have learning capacity that they do not fully exploit. Due to the interaction of a number of cognitive biases, humans often resist learning difficult new domains of knowledge after the end of formal education. This can be problematic given the collective knowledge base is expanding rapidly, replacing incorrect or incomplete information with new and sometimes dramatically revised insights.

necessary financial resources, caregivers may be paid for their services, though this is fairly rare on a global scale.

Like all organisms on Earth, humans eventually die. Human practices related to death are quite interesting. They look after their dead, will go to great lengths to recover corpses, and frequently perform autopsies to determine causes of death, if they are not obvious. They have a variety of group rituals that are performed, particularly for deceased family members, which typically includes burial or the dispersal of cremated remains, and the marking of gravesites. Humans go out of their way to remember the deceased and even, in some cultures, venerate them.

Much of this activity follows religious rituals that are associated with a hoped-for transition, after death, into an afterlife. Of course, since death is just the biological end of an animal's life cycle, this line of thinking is fanciful—apparently intended to reduce the fear of death among the survivors, because all humans recognize death as inevitable. Their treatment of death is another clear indicator of the social nature of humans and their dependence on shared social norms to guide behavior.

VARIABILITY

A human's physical characteristics are the result of the assembly instructions contained in its DNA, an organic molecule in the cells of the body that contains over three billion codes. Of these codes, humans share 99.9 percent in common—which makes them a surprisingly homogeneous species. All the variability of characteristics seen in humans is the result of different configurations of just one tenth of one percent of the human genome, or around three million base pairs. These pieces are rearranged during reproduction to produce humans with distinct characteristics. Within the entire pool of human DNA, there are trillions of possible configurations.

The existing genetic variability is, along with ongoing mutations in DNA, the basis for evolutionary change in the species. The "average" human DNA template is constantly shifting as new individuals with new configurations are born and older individuals die. Furthermore, since the human population is composed of distinct, mostly separate breeding groups, DNA configurations tend to be limited despite the overall variability present in the species. In general, humans have been becoming more diverse in their physical characteristics as their gene pools have been geographically isolated, while dramatically increasing in population size. Recently, however, migrations and relatively easy access to long-range travel have worked to spread some genes more widely.

Humans are only now coming to understand their own variability from a genetics point of view. A complete human genome was sequenced for the first time just over ten years ago. Since then, technology has reduced the cost and decreased the time needed to compile a full genetic profile. As a result, the genomes for a few hundred thousand individuals are now known. Tens of thousands more genomes, selectively sampled from populations from all over the planet, are needed before the underlying patterns of variability will begin to fully emerge. Humans are just now at the start of a project to understand genetic variability within the species, but it should accelerate quickly from this point and be completed within a couple of decades.

6 Diet and Health

HUMANS MUST CONSUME nutrients on a regular basis to survive and prosper. Though their biology includes many physiological processes designed to maintain good health, humans are also subject to diseases that can threaten vitality, both short and long term. A great deal of time and effort is expended in securing food and drink, pursuing good health, and responding to diseases.

DIET

Like all other animals, humans must ingest food to provide energy and raw materials to the cells that make up their bodies. Foodstuffs of various kinds must periodically be placed in the mouth, chewed, swallowed and digested so that various nutrients can be absorbed. Without ingesting food, a healthy adult human can't survive longer than about sixty days.

Humans also require the regular intake of fresh water[18] to maintain several internal processes and to replace water lost through breathing,

---

[18] Water containing any significant amount of dissolved salt is toxic to humans, so the vast volumes of water in the planet's oceans, which have an average salt concentration of thirty-five parts per thousand, can't be consumed. Fortunately, rainwater is free of dissolved salts so humans have access in most places to adequate freshwater in streams, rivers, lakes, and underground aquifers.

perspiration, and excretion. Without drinking water, a healthy adult human can't survive more than six or seven days.

These facts may make it seem as if humans are particularly fragile. But generally, humans have adequate access to food and water, and, even though the quality may sometimes be somewhat poor, they have physical adaptations that promote survival under adverse conditions.

Digestive Biology

The human digestive system is broadly similar to that of other mammals. It employs both mechanical and chemical processes to render nutrients that can be absorbed into the body. Its major component, the gastrointestinal tract (sometimes simply called the "gut"), is an internal muscular tube about thirty feet long, with various zones that accomplish specific digestive functions. Digestion is the process that converts complex organic material into simpler forms that can be used by the human body to power and repair its various physiological systems.

Figure 6-1. Process of Eating

Foodstuffs that are placed into the mouth (Figure 6-1) are chewed to reduce particle size and to mix with saliva, which contains enzymes that start the digestive process. Once swallowed, the moistened food mass travels to the stomach where the components of the foodstuffs are further broken down into component parts through chemical digestion in an acid environment. In the stomach, original food particles are turned into a creamy paste that is passed in doses to the small intestine.

Chemical processing continues in the next foot or so of the small intestine, including the addition of more liquid to the partially digested mass. As the now liquefied matter passes through the remainder of the small intestine, nutrients are absorbed into the blood stream and eventually routed to cells where they are needed.

In the next step of digestion, the remaining organic matter enters the large intestine, which is the home of a colony of microorganisms, mostly bacteria.[19] This colony is made up of as many as five hundred different species of these single-celled organisms. It is a very large colony: there are generally more microorganisms in the human gut than there are cells in the rest of the human body. It is also a dynamic colony, continuously reproducing itself and losing members through excretion.

The bacteria, in particular, play an important digestive role in fermenting residual organic materials, producing additional useful nutrients that can be absorbed by the human body. In turn, the microorganisms benefit from being able to live in a warm, moist environment with a steady source of food. So the colony and the human have a symbiotic relationship, both benefiting from the presence of the other.[20]

In addition to completing the digestion process, the large intestine absorbs more fluid back into the body and forms and stores feces in the rectum at the end of the gastrointestinal tract for later excretion. Most of the water that humans obtain from drinking and foodstuffs is absorbed in the large intestine. At the end of the digestive process, about sixty percent of fecal matter to be excreted is bacteria and the rest is water and partially digested or indigestible material, such as fiber.

---

[19] A gut bacterium is much smaller than the average human body cell, typically only about a tenth as large (3 microns versus 30 microns). Depending on the size of the human, the gut colony weighs between one and two pounds.

[20] It is a beneficial relationship most of the time. Under certain conditions, the excessive growth of microorganisms can cause illness or even the death of the host. Some bacteria, such as E. coli, are particularly dangerous after they have been excreted, if accidently re-ingested.

It typically takes about 24–72 hours for a meal to travel the full length of the gastrointestinal tract. Overall, the digestive system is normally quite efficient, extracting more than ninety percent of the nutrients available from the foodstuffs that are ingested.

The digestive system is rather complex, having been honed by millions of years of evolution. It is a hybrid system that has characteristics of both animals that eat only plant material (herbivores) and those that eat only meat (carnivores), thus allowing the human digestion of a large variety of foodstuffs. It is also particularly well adapted to cooked food—foodstuffs that have been prepared for easier digestion before they are eaten. Humans are the only animals that cook their foods.

Nutrients

The human body is a biological engine that needs a supply of raw materials obtained from the environment to power its life functions and to supply building blocks for the repair and replacement of tissues. These raw materials are called nutrients and come in several major forms.

Carbohydrates. These are organic compounds that are obtained from plant material. They provide much of the energy used in the human body. Typically, a human gets about half of the energy needed each day from these compounds. In addition to the nutrient value of carbohydrates, humans also get fiber, that, though not digestible, is important to the smooth operation of the digestive system.

Fats. These are also organic compounds, but have the distinction of not dissolving in water. They are available from both plant and animal foodstuffs. In addition to providing a form of concentrated energy, they play important roles in various internal biochemical processes. Two fatty acids (Omega-3 and Omega-6) are essential and must be obtained from foodstuffs. Humans get about a third of their daily energy requirements from these compounds.

Proteins. These are another class of organic compounds that provide important structural building blocks for the body; support other critical biochemical processes, including gene regulation; and also provide energy when needed. Proteins are absorbed as amino acids, of which nine different varieties are indispensable, and must be obtained from foodstuffs. Among adequately nourished humans, protein provides between ten and fifteen percent of the daily energy requirements.

Vitamins. These are also organic compounds that are needed, generally in small amounts, by the body to carry out a number of physiological processes. They don't provide a source of energy or structural building blocks. At least thirteen of these compounds can only be obtained from plant or animal foodstuffs (or to a somewhat limited degree by ingesting manufactured substitutes).[21]

Minerals. These are inorganic elements that provide important building blocks (for bones and teeth, for example), in addition to supporting many important physiological processes. All seventeen essential minerals must be obtained through foodstuffs, which can be plant or animal, though absorption is most effectively achieved from animal sources. Seven of the essential minerals are needed in relatively large amounts on a daily basis, while the remainder only need be obtained in trace amounts.

Water. Though not a nutrient per se, water is an essential medium for life processes within the human body. It is heavily involved in the transport of nutrients and waste products, provides structure to tissues, and plays a role in the formation of many large organic molecules. About sixty percent of adult body weight is water. The human body regulates its water supply very carefully. Water can be obtained from foodstuffs or directly through drinking. Regular consumption (about a total of three quarts per day) is essential to survival and good health.

With the exception of minerals and water, nutrients can be thought of as processed sunlight. Plants that turn sunlight into organic material through photosynthesis are at the bottom of the Earth's food chain and support all other life forms that lack the capability to convert sunlight to food. Therefore, humans, the top predators, eat plants that produce energy from sunlight, and eat many other animal life forms that have processed and further concentrated the energy originally sourced from plants.

The digestive tract is responsible for breaking down foodstuffs into component parts that can be absorbed. This is in preparation for

---

[21] One vitamin, B_{12}, is only available from animal foodstuffs or in a synthetic form.

further processing by organs such as the liver, in a biochemical chain that eventually delivers molecules useable by individual cells. Food is broken down into many different component parts that are eventually used as fuel or employed in repair and rebuilding operations.

Energy Requirements

About sixty percent of human daily energy use supports basic metabolic activities such as breathing, pumping blood, maintaining body temperature, thinking, repairing tissues, and replacing cells on a regular basis.[22] Around ten percent of daily energy is used to support digestion. Finally, about thirty percent of daily energy is used for physical activity, such as moving about. These proportions vary somewhat depending on various environmental conditions.

When human ancestors lived in the wild as hunters and gatherers, men used about 3,000 calories of energy a day, and women about 2,300, varying somewhat based on body size. The foraging lifestyle was an active one that provided lots of exercise and demanded plenty of food energy. The good news is that hunter-gatherers only had to expend about one calorie of energy to reap an average return of ten calories from foodstuffs. The key was to achieve this consistently enough to stave off starvation.

Interestingly, the daily energy demands for moderately active humans in the present day haven't changed much—still about 3,000 calories for men and 2,300 calories for women.[23] However, particularly in the industrialized world, the environment and activity patterns are much different than they were in the wild. As discussed earlier, most humans are no longer directly involved in food production. They simply obtain foodstuffs from other humans who produce ample supplies. Modern agriculture is currently able to produce hundreds of calories of food energy for every calorie invested by a farmer who uses

---

[22] For instance, the cells that line the digestive tract are replaced every three or four days, red blood cells about every 120 days, and connective tissues every few years. By the time a human reaches about age 60, all the cells of the body have been completely replaced about three times. The only major exception to this replacement cycle is the neuron, which largely remains intact from birth to death, unless a disease condition intervenes.

[23] "Moderately active" means of average height and at the top of the normal weight range: sleeping eight hours a day, sitting four hours a day, and involved in non-strenuous moving around for twelve hours a day.

machines to accomplish most tasks. The modern day problem is not producing enough food calories, but getting them to some of the people who need them.

Assuming that a reasonably varied diet of plant and animal foodstuffs is consumed, energy needs for a moderately active human can be met by eating about a pound of food per day. But not all humans are moderately active.

Presently, many humans, perhaps as many as twenty-five percent in the United States alone, are almost completely sedentary with energy requirements not significantly above those required to run their basic metabolic processes. For men, this is about 1,700 calories and for women, about 1,300 calories. Problems can arise when humans, especially sedentary humans, consistently consume more (sometimes, many more) calories than needed.

One evolutionary defense mechanism of the human body is to store excess energy, usually in the form of fat, when the opportunity presents itself.[24] This was a clear advantage when humans lived in the wild and might have experienced periods when food was not readily available. So consistently eating even as few as fifty more calories per day can lead to significant weight gains over relatively short periods of time. Worldwide, around fifteen percent of humans are overweight (BMI between 25 and 29.9) and ten percent are obese (BMI between 30 and 49.9). This concern will be discussed further in the upcoming section on health.

On the other hand, some humans obtain too few calories in their diets and/or too few of the essential nutrients. Historically, mass starvations have occurred in several populations around the planet. For instance, in China around one hundred fifty years BP, four successive rice crop failures resulted in the starvation deaths of around forty-five million people. Even in the present, when sufficient calories from foodstuffs are available, starvation-related deaths still occur. And millions more humans are malnourished. Worldwide, around ten percent of humans experience insufficient nourishment. Of course, this is a significant public health concern.

---

[24] A commonly used measure of fat storage is the Body Mass Index (BMI), which is based on the relationship between an individual's height and weight. The greater the BMI, the greater the body weight associated with a given height. A BMI of between 18.5 and 24.9 is considered a body mass with a normal amount of stored fat. (See Chapter 5, Physical Characteristics, Footnote 15.)

Foodstuffs

The human diet is composed of different foodstuffs. Humans are very adaptable in their dietary choices, accommodating a very wide range of foods. Humans will eat just about anything that isn't poisonous or (too) spoiled. Evolution has made them true omnivores, with one exception: they can't digest cellulose, which is a common part of plants and predominate in grasses, leaves, and woody tissues. Despite the fact that it is indigestible, humans require the ingestion of some cellulose to support smooth digestion.

Of course availability of foodstuffs, differing personal tastes, and cultural preferences may limit what any given individual eats. Also of importance is the fact that humans have had a preference for cooked food, which has had a big impact on their dietary choices. Many raw foodstuffs can be and are eaten, but the vast majority of foods are eaten cooked, individually or in combination with other foods.

The human diet has changed substantially throughout the course of history. When humans lived in the wild as hunters, gatherers, and scavengers, about sixty percent of their calories were obtained from animals and about forty percent from plant materials. The sources within these categories were quite varied and based on what was available locally and seasonally. Perhaps a third of the energy they obtained was from wild (and healthful) animal and plant fats. Humans in the wild generally ate when the opportunity arose, though the preference for processing foods (pounding, slicing, and cooking) certainly influenced the timing of meals to some degree. Periodic gatherings around the campfire were common.

The human diet began to change dramatically with the invention of agriculture. Domesticated plants and animals became ever-greater components of the food supply, eventually almost totally replacing the consumption of wild varieties. Humans put ever greater reliance on a small number of cereal grains and animal species, ironically putting themselves at greater risk for starvation due to potential crop failures. The rapidly increasing human population that accompanied settlement compounded this potential.

Food Groups

In the present day, humans eat foods from several food groups, nearly all of which have an agricultural origin, and/or now involve industrial-scale processing of some form. In fact, some foods humans consume are now mostly synthetic, products of chemical and taste engineering.

Cereals. These are the products of grasses that have been bred over millennia to produce large seeds. Rice, wheat and corn are most common, with rice and wheat accounting for sixty percent of all the calories consumed worldwide. Grains have been very important to humans because once harvested, they could be stored for long periods of time to be used in seasons when natural food was less abundant. (Though with the advent of modern food preservation technologies such as refrigerators, storage has become less of an issue for some populations.) Grains typically must be cooked in some manner to make them palatable.

Legumes. Various kinds of beans and peas are the product of plants that have also been domesticated to produce large seeds, generally in pods. Other common examples include lentils, peanuts, and soybeans. Legumes, like other plant-based foods are typically cooked in some way before consumption.

Starchy Roots. These are the fleshy tubers of plants that humans have, in some form, included in their diets throughout history. The most common current domesticate is the potato, which comes in several forms. Cooking is generally required to improve palatability.

Sugars. While sugars occur naturally, in fruits and honey, and certainly would have been part of an ancestral diet, the consumption of sugars has risen dramatically in the modern world. Easily refined from sugar cane and cornstarch, sugars are used as an ingredient in many food products and as an effective preservative, particularly of fruits. Because humans find the taste satisfying, its use has expanded in the overall diet and now accounts for more than ten percent of the total calories consumed planet-wide, even though sugars have very little nutritional value.

Vegetables and Fruits. Edible plants and the fruits of trees and shrubs have been part of the diet of humans since before they evolved to their current form. The modern varieties of vegetables such as lettuces, peppers, onions, carrots, herbs, and fruits such as apples, oranges, and various berries have gone through substantial domestication to improve size and flavor. Vegetables and fruits are often eaten raw, but are also cooked using a variety of methods.

Seeds and Nuts. Many plants produce seeds and/or nuts as part of their reproductive processes. Like vegetables and fruits, humans have always consumed seeds and nuts as part of their regular diet. Common current examples include peas, lentils, almonds, walnuts, cashews, and pecans. Seeds and nuts are nutrient dense and are typically eaten raw or roasted.

Oils. There are several plants from which oils, which are plant-derived fats, can be extracted. Among the most common of these in the human diet are olive, peanut, and soybean oils. They are typically not consumed alone, but used in cooking methods and combined with other foods to create dressings, sauces and marinades.

Meat, Fish and Eggs. Animal flesh has also been part of the human diet since the beginning, though the sources have changed dramatically. Though humans still hunt wild game, most meat and, increasingly fish, come from domesticated stocks managed through large industrial processes.[25] Common meats include beef, pork, lamb, goat, and chicken. Shelled eggs, primarily from domesticated chickens and waterfowl, are widely consumed. Like other foodstuffs, most (but not all) meat, fish, and eggs are cooked prior to consumption.

Milk and Milk Products. Interestingly, some humans have developed a tolerance for consuming milk after weaning, which is unusual for mammals. A gene mutation that appeared in northern European populations a few thousand years ago spread rather widely, allowing about forty-five percent of humans to continue drinking animal milk through adulthood. The primary source of drinking milk is now domesticated cattle, whose milk is collected almost continually through large-scale, industrialized processes. Milk is also converted into secondary products such as yogurt (soured milk) and cheese (preserved milk) and are consumed in large quantities. Milk is usually heated (pasteurized) before consumption or before it is used in secondary products, to kill pathogens that are common in raw milk.

---

[25] In wealthier societies, the hunting of wild game (and fishing) is not generally undertaken as a means of subsistence. Instead it is considered a sport or a form of recreation accompanied by a range of social rituals, including the attainment and display of trophies. It is an activity deeply rooted in the human hunter-gatherer past when hunting prowess was a mark of status within tribal groups. It illustrates well the persistence of an ancient impulse that has become somewhat irrelevant in the conditions of modern life in much of the world.

Fats. Animal fats, including beef fat (suet), pork fat (lard), fish oils, and butter, are all part of the human diet. Red meat is often laced with intramuscular fat and is a primary means of ingesting animal fat. Unfortunately, the fats associated with domesticated animals are of a kind generally harmful to humans if consumed regularly.

Soft Drinks. Humans often drink fresh water directly. But very often they consume water-based liquids that may be extracted from fruits (apple and orange juice are common) or infused with flavors from plants (coffee or tea). These may all be sweetened with sugars or enhanced with milk. In addition, carbonated, flavored water, usually sweetened with sugars, is manufactured and consumed in large quantities worldwide.

Alcoholic Drinks. Several thousand years ago humans discovered that plant juices could be fermented, yielding drinks that contained ethyl alcohol—both a preservative and a moderately potent intoxicant. Such beverages made from grapes (wine) and cereal grains (beer), are very popular and consumed in large amounts. Distillation of plant-based mashes can concentrate the alcohol and produce very alcoholic fluids that are normally mixed with other liquids as part of social rituals in many cultures. Though the moderate use of alcoholic drinks appears benign, excess alcohol consumption and addiction is fairly common (more than seven percent of Americans, for example, have alcohol addiction) and presents significant health issues.

Manufactured Foods. In recent times, humans have learned how to manufacture food-like products through chemical engineering. Often starting with a processed animal or plant product, flavor, texture, and preservative enhancements will be added and then further processed. As an example, various chemical constituents are mixed together to make a slurry, which is then extruded and heated to make crunchy, orange, tube-like snacks. Because fat is a key constituent, they have ample calories, but few nutrients. Humans refer to foods like this as "nutritionally empty," though they have been engineered to taste good. Another term that is sometimes used for foods that taste good but lack nutritional value is "junk food." Consumption of low nutrition, high-calorie foods has contributed to the problem of excess weight gain experienced by many humans.

Preserved Foods. Not all manufactured or heavily-processed foods are of poor nutritional quality. Some heavily-processed foods have been engineered to be resistant to spoilage and are fortified with additional nutrients, such as vitamins and minerals. Preparation methods such as dehydrating and canning, along with the inclusion of chemical preservatives, can insure that foods not otherwise available can be obtained and eaten in regions where spoilage occurs swiftly, such as in the tropics where around forty percent of humans currently live. For some, access to these kinds of industrially-processed foods is important in securing adequate nutrition.

Patterns of Consumption

Humans are generally healthiest when their calorie intakes and expenditures match each other over time and if they consume a balanced diet. While there is substantial variation in what is eaten by humans, an overall balanced diet is generally one that includes the following components and proportions:[26]

- Fruits and vegetables provide about half of the volume of food eaten each day.

- Grains, preferably whole grains, provide about one quarter of the volume.

- Proteins, which include fish, shellfish, poultry, meat, dry beans, eggs and nuts, provide about one quarter of the food volume consumed.[27]

In addition to these basic components, other foodstuffs may be included in the diet in somewhat limited quantities to enhance the eating experience:

- A small portion of low-fat dairy products may be consumed daily.

- When cooking with fats, vegetable oils are preferred, while animal fats are kept to a minimum.

---

[26] Remember that the average healthy adult human consumes about a pound of food a day, if there is an adequate supply available.

[27] Meats such as those from cattle, pigs, and sheep should only be eaten occasionally with a focus on lower-fat cuts. Preserved, heavily processed meats like bacon, sausage, and ham, should generally be avoided or used only as an occasional garnish.

- Refined sugars, particularly as found in drinks and desserts, are best limited to occasional use.

- Alcohol, if consumed at all, should be limited to very moderate portions.

- The intake of salt, which is a common condiment, should be kept to a minimum.

While these guidelines apply broadly across human populations, there is wide tolerance for variation in diet. Some humans are more sensitive to dietary imbalance than others, probably for a variety of genetic reasons. But as a rule of thumb, this basic pattern of consumption seems to be beneficial to most humans, promoting health and longevity. With a varied, nutrient-rich diet, humans do not normally need to ingest any synthetic vitamins or other dietary supplements, as all necessary nutrients can be obtained from foodstuffs.

Regardless of availability, humans have food preferences driven largely by their sense of taste and cultural expectations. Some foodstuffs are preferred and sought after and some are disliked. Some humans have very broad interests, while others restrict their food intake to a narrow range of options. The scope of dietary choices is relatively unimportant as long as individual energy and nutrient needs are met.

Interestingly, some humans don't eat meat protein, even when it is available, though there is no biological reason for avoiding it. In fact, to the contrary, meat is a dense source of nutrients and the human digestive system is well-adapted to it. However, there may be good ecological reasons to reduce overall consumption. As discussed in the chapter on habitat, through agriculture humans have domesticated several animals specifically as sources of food. And growing animal protein consumes a lot of resources and generates toxic waste products. For instance, a pound of corn-fed beef requires far more energy to produce than it yields in food energy. As the planetary population grows, the sustainability of food production will become more of an issue, requiring thoughtful choices in the allocation of resources.

Overall, relatively few humans appear to adhere strictly to the health-focused patterns of consumption that have been described, often because they do not have access to sufficient quantities of all the food groups, or because they have access to an overabundance of tasty, but unhealthy food choices.

The human diet has changed quite dramatically from the days of hunting, gathering, and scavenging in the wild, primarily as a result of the wide-scale adoption of agriculture. About seventy percent of the calories consumed by modern humans (refined sugars, for instance) were not even available to humans living in the wild. And the foods that are similar (meat, for instance), have been widely modified by selective breeding to produce very different tastes and textures of the end products. A human from fifty thousand years ago wouldn't recognize much of what a modern human eats.

Cuisines

Historically, the types and availability of foodstuffs has varied dramatically across geographic areas due largely to climatic differences in growing conditions and limited means of transporting food over long distances.

Humans are fond of combining foodstuffs and adding seasonings of various types—salt is a favorite—to create specific flavors. When these combinations are standardized and replicated, they are called recipes. Combinations of recipes, when traditionally served together, form a cuisine. Humans have passed recipes from generation to generation so that in the modern world there are distinctive diets in different localities.

This is another way in which culture powerfully affects human lifestyles. Through the course of the migration out of Africa, eating tastes and habits evolved into regional cuisines in many different isolated communities. These differences can still be seen today, despite global food supply chains that make ingredients of all kinds widely available, and the recipes characteristic of different cuisines easily obtained. Just as with languages and clothing styles, food preferences and eating styles vary substantially around the planet.

Food is often prepared in family homes, but it is not uncommon, especially in urban areas, for food to be prepared by commercial vendors and served at carts, stalls, or in restaurants. Humans normally eat food from a plate or bowl and use eating implements such as a knife and fork or chopsticks to move the food into the mouth. This was originally done as a way of avoiding disease pathogens, but is now primarily dictated by cultural custom. There are many different varieties of eating times, number of courses served, orders of presentation, and consumption rituals, again displaying the human capacity for behavioral flexibility.

HEALTH

A human is healthy when able to function effectively in the normal environment, handling the routine stresses that are encountered. Humans are equipped with a range of biological defenses that are intended to maintain a state of good health. These include mechanisms like blood clotting to stanch bleeding and an immune system intended to stop invasions from microorganisms.

Hygiene

Humans undertake a range of practices intended to support and maintain good health. Among these are activities intended to reduce exposure to harmful microorganisms and to reduce the spread of acquired infections. Cultures vary in their expectations for hygiene, but occasional cleansing of the body—especially the hands—is common, especially when associated with excretion. Securing unpolluted sources of fresh water is important for disease prevention. Safe food preparation and storage practices also have a large health impact, though there are substantial local variations.

Sanitizing eating utensils, clothes washing, and household cleaning are widespread practices designed to reduce exposure to harmful germs. There are well-documented practices for those with communicable diseases to help reduce the spread of illness to others. Since humans generally live in close proximity to each other, such efforts are necessary to maintain and protect the well-being of local communities.

Some cultural hygiene practices are more cosmetic than practical, such as the use of deodorants, which are intended to limit the growth of skin bacteria. But norms like this are fairly common features of local cultures, which also typically include expectations for attire and social manners.

For modern humans, there is a relatively simple formula for maintaining good health:

1. Eat a balanced diet with just enough calories consumed to offset the calories used each day.

2. Get about thirty minutes of aerobic and weight-bearing exercise three to five times a week.

3. Get an adequate amount of sustained, high quality sleep each night.

4. Limit the amount of refined sugar, added salt, and alcohol consumed regularly.

5. Actively manage stress.

6. Abstain from smoking tobacco or dependence on drugs (either pharmaceutical or recreational).

7. Practice regular dental hygiene.

8. Participate in immunization programs to defend against contagious diseases.

Despite being a short, seemingly straightforward list, implementing it consistently proves to be challenging for many humans. As with other issues that depend on learning, there is substantial variation in the perceived importance of following these guidelines. However, most humans would experience health benefits from adopting these practices that reflect their own evolutionary histories. They should listen more carefully to their genes.

Disease

Like other animals, humans are susceptible to disease, a deviation from normal biological form or function. But, unlike other animals, humans seek systematic methods to minimize the damage, speed the recovery from injury, and to prevent or cure other types of diseases. Sometimes these strategies work well; other times their interventions are not successful.

There are many causes of disease, some of which are well understood while others remain unknown or are poorly understood.

Genetic Disorders. Genetic (DNA) malfunctions give rise to many diseases. Several thousand have been identified and catalogued. These malfunctions can include inherited genes with coding errors (cystic fibrosis, sickle-cell anemia); coding errors that arise from nonhereditary mutations during development (Down's Syndrome);

mutations in cell growth genes induced by age; environmental forces (radiation, virus infections, and chemical exposures); and for reasons not yet known (many cancers).

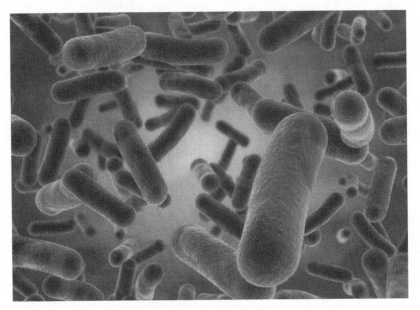

Figure 6-2. Bacteria

Microorganism Infections. Very small, single celled organisms (Figure 6-2) such as viruses, bacteria, and some types of fungi are everywhere in the environment and live on and in humans in vast numbers.[28] Most of these organisms are harmless or even beneficial (the gut bacteria, for instance). But some are very problematic if they successfully gain entry to a human and reproduce rapidly. If the human biological defense system is ineffective in purging them from the system quickly, illness can result. Severity can range from mildly annoying, such as the common cold, to life threatening, such as Ebola Hemorrhagic Fever. A special area of concern for modern humans is the impact of bacteria in the mouth causing tooth decay associated with the consumption of refined sugars.

---

[28] A typical bacterium may only be 3 microns long, an organism so small it can't be seen with the unaided eye. Viruses are typically significantly smaller than bacteria. A common single celled fungi, such as a yeast cell, is about the same size as a bacterium.

Metabolic Imbalances. Good health depends on maintaining balance in many, related physiological processes that are important for the growth and maintenance of body systems. When an imbalance occurs in these chemical processes, for instance the over- or under-production of hormones, a disease occurs. Malfunctions of the pituitary and thyroid glands are often the sources of metabolic diseases.

Physical Injuries. Cuts, bruises, and bone fractures are fairly common among humans. These arise from physical forces applied to the body, such as from a fall, that can exceed the physical limits of the skin, internal organs, muscles, or bones. These kinds of injuries range in severity from trivial to life-threatening. As an example, severely damaged limbs may have to be removed through amputation. Probably every human has experienced some kind of physical injury, as they are a common part of everyday life in all kinds of settings.

Immune System Errors. The immune system, which is essential to maintaining good health, sometimes malfunctions. It can lose its capacity to perform its normal functions (Acquired Immune Deficiency Syndrome, AIDS) or it inappropriately attacks normal body tissues, mistaking these tissues for harmful invaders (asthma, allergies, lupus, rheumatoid arthritis, type 1 diabetes). Diseases arising from immune system errors are fairly common and can be debilitating.

Poisonings. Many substances are harmful to humans. When they lived in the wild, plants were a major source of poisons. In the modern world where chemicals (especially drugs) are manufactured and widely distributed, humans easily come into contact with a variety of potentially poisonous substances. Poisons may be directly ingested, inhaled or, absorbed through the skin. The effects depend on the toxicity of the substance, the amount encountered, and the body's methods for neutralizing them. The effects can range from mild illness to life-threatening.

Aging. As humans age, their biological processes may develop malfunctions resulting in disease. Typical conditions seen in aging are atherosclerosis (hardening of the arteries), hearing loss, deterioration of eyesight, osteoarthritis (inflammation of joints), and cognitive impairments of various kinds. These range in severity from mildly annoying to completely debilitating to life threatening.

Psychological Disorders. Humans are subject to a variety of disorders associated with the function of the brain. Some of these may be transient, others chronic and debilitating. Three of the most common chronic mental illnesses are schizophrenia, depression, and mania. Though they are all believed to be related to neuro-chemical imbalances, their origins are not well understood. Two other relatively common neurological degenerative diseases, which generally appear later in life—Alzheimer's and Parkinson's—arise from abnormalities in the brain, but also have origins that are not well understood.

Nutritional Abnormalities. Humans suffer from diseases associated with both under- and over-nutrition. Aside from the impact of starvation—not obtaining enough calories to sustain life functions—the failure to receive sufficient amounts of some nutrients can also lead to health problems. On the other hand, overconsumption of foodstuffs routinely leads to problems associated with obesity. Having a body mass index (BMI) of 30 or higher typically promotes the onset of atherosclerosis, high blood pressure, chronic oxygen deprivation, and type 2 diabetes.

■ ■ ■

The genetic makeup of each individual human interacts with the environment throughout a lifetime, influencing susceptibility to disease and resilience if a disease is contracted. Differences in DNA sequences affect disease outcomes. For example, some humans have more effective immune systems than others. But the environment also influences the expression of genetic traits. So the environment can affect the immune system too, such as consistent malnutrition, for example. The interplay between genetics and the environment on health is complex and is understood only in broad outlines.

The range of diseases affecting humans is quite great, but they don't all have the same incidence or impact. Some, like the common cold, are very widely experienced, but pass quickly with only minor discomfort. Others are chronic, such as heart disease, potentially causing discomfort and disability for years.

The diseases most likely to eventually cause death planetwide are cardiovascular diseases (heart disease, stroke), cancers, diabetes, and lung diseases (lower respiratory infections, chronic obstructive lung diseases). These are all considered non-communicable diseases in that they are not transmitted from individual to individual. They account for almost seventy percent of human deaths each year.[29]

Deaths from communicable diseases are more rare, with Human Immunodeficiency Virus / Acquired Immune Deficiency Syndrome (HIV/AIDS) the only condition in the top ten causes of death that contributes less than three percent to the total. In contrast, physical injuries account for the other nine percent of total deaths, with the majority of these a result of road traffic accidents (killing around thirty-five hundred humans *per day*).

The prevalence of disease and the severity of its impact varies around the planet. Frequency and effects are greater in poorer countries and less severe in wealthier ones, largely reflecting access to effective healthcare.

Some diseases have increased in frequency in the modern world largely as a function of changes in lifestyle from hunting and gathering days. Chief among these are:

- obesity and diabetes
- heart disease and stroke
- stress, anxiety, and depression
- high blood pressure
- tooth decay
- vision problems

Changes in diet, a more sedentary level of activity, and a more stressful social environment are major contributors. The human practice of smoking tobacco leaves recreationally causes many diseases and leads to many deaths each year. The expanded consumption of refined sugars is another modern phenomenon that has resulted in extensive tooth decay that was not a significant problem when humans lived in the wild. Excessive consumption of alcohol is another contributor to the development of disease. And poor eyesight is a direct result of the human dependence on reading and all kinds of close work that dominates modern life.

---

[29] To put this into perspective, a total of about one percent of the human population alive at the start of a calendar year dies over the course of the next twelve months. Of course, in the same time frame, many more babies are born so that overall population continues to grow at a rapid rate.

Medicine

Long before they began their migration from Africa, humans were attempting to intervene when illness struck a tribal member. Initially this might have involved special pleadings to supernatural forces, or the performance of superstitious rights, or perhaps the use of local herbs that seemed beneficial in treating certain ailments. These were the principle elements of folklore medicine and were largely ineffective, with the possible exception of some herbal remedies. Humans with disease either got better as a result of their own biological resources or they didn't. It was a pretty simple equation.

As cultures evolved during the great migration, so did medical folklore—the beliefs and practices passed down via oral stories from generation to generation. As a result of this divergence, medical traditions developed, sometimes very elaborate in their details. But regardless of their complexity, they were still folklore traditions with little, if any, real medical value.

Such traditional systems of medical thought still persist in the modern world and still have many adherents, despite the rise of evidence-based medicine—the form of medical knowledge produced through the application of the scientific method. As it has in so many areas of the natural world, science has also transformed the diagnosis and treatment of human diseases.[30]

Science-based medicine has emerged only recently in human history. Even a century ago, diagnostic and treatment options were limited and relatively primitive. Slowly and incrementally, diagnostic methods have improved, more effective treatments have been discovered, and effective preventative measures have been more widely put into practice. At present, highly trained medical practitioners use a broad range of pharmacological drugs, sophisticated surgical techniques, complex diagnostic equipment, and specialized care facilities to render treatment to patients (Figure 6-3).

But for all its advances, evidence-based medicine still has great limitations, as not all disease conditions are well-understood, and even when causes are understood, effective treatments have not yet been discovered. The decoding of the human genome only a few years ago

---

[30] Not only has science been applied to human diseases, it has also been successfully applied to diseases affecting other animals and plants. Many humans are now engaged in treating and preventing diseases affecting many other species.

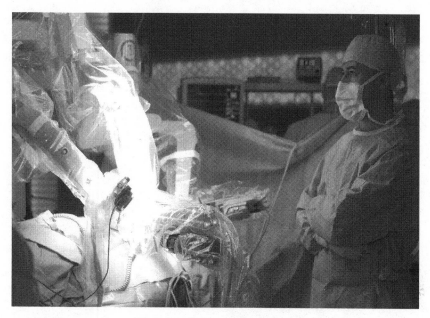

Figure 6-3. Robotic Operating Room

was a tremendous breakthrough in the movement to more specifically tailor individual treatments. Yet practical applications are only slowly emerging, testimony to how complex human biology is on a molecular level.

Another issue with evidence-based medicine is its limited availability. The majority of humans on the planet don't have access to modern healthcare, and as a result there is substantial suffering and early death that could be prevented. Like other inequalities in the distribution of resources around the planet, inadequate access to healthcare presents human society with a major problem in search of a workable solution.

As a result of the lack of access to quality healthcare, the incomplete scientific understanding of diseases, and the human penchant for engaging in superstitious behaviors, many people still try to prevent or treat illness with a vast array of ineffective methods. In the United States, alone, around forty percent of humans engage with scientifically unsupported (and sometimes expensive) approaches. These range from taking various kinds of supplements (multi-vitamins, herbal preparations) to participating in "alternative or complementary" therapies (acupuncture, faith-healing, energy therapy) for various conditions.

On a planetwide basis, well over half of humans still rely primarily on folklore-based medical practices in an effort to maintain health and to control or cure diseases, with little to no real benefit. Though humans have made great progress recently, in many ways medical knowledge and practice is still rudimentary.

7 Mating Habits

THIS CHAPTER DESCRIBES how humans arrange for reproduction. It is a process that, though biologically pretty straightforward, manifests much variation due to human behavioral flexibility.

REPRODUCTIVE BIOLOGY

Like other mammals, humans reproduce sexually, meaning that two individuals—one female and one male—must interact to produce offspring. This kind of reproduction is common in the animal kingdom. It was long ago selected through evolution because of its great advantages in rapidly producing new physical forms that could potentially adapt more rapidly to environmental changes.

As has already been described, humans occur in both female and male forms, distinguished genetically by differences in their DNA sex chromosomes (Figure 7-1).[31] Females have two X chromosomes, one inherited from the mother and one from the father. Males have both an X and a Y chromosome, with the X inherited from the mother and the Y from the father. An X chromosome is larger than the Y and codes for about eight hundred genes (about 154,913,754 DNA base

---

[31] The X chromosome is about 2 microns long and the Y chromosome is only about twenty five percent as long, .5 micron. For comparison, a typical human hair has a diameter of about 75 microns.

pairs) in various configurations. The Y chromosome is much smaller and has only about fifty genes (about 57,741,652 DNA base pairs). The XX or XY pairings are the normal DNA configurations for the sexes.

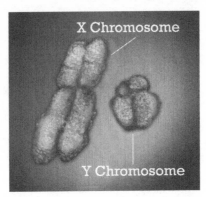

Figure 7-1. Sex Chromosomes

But there are also some other variations that occur rarely that will be discussed later in this chapter.

All newly conceived humans are sexually the same, regardless of whether their DNA includes XX or XY chromosomes. However, once genes are activated, a complex series of changes is set in motion that determines which sex characteristics will emerge. Ultimately, male characteristics will only emerge if a Y chromosome is present to guide differentiation.

Two types of cells are needed for reproduction: an egg and a sperm. The egg is produced by a female who, at birth, already has a lifetime supply in reserve. By the time she reaches mature puberty, her reproductive age (between fifteen to seventeen years of age), the supply has been reduced to about three hundred thousand. Of these, between three to four hundred will be made available for reproduction over a normal lifetime. Somewhat unusual for mammals, human females eventually phase out of egg production at about fifty years of age, when they enter menopause and can no longer bear children.

The major components of the female reproductive system include the ovaries, where the egg cells are stored and periodically matured; the fallopian tubes, where newly released eggs await fertilization; the uterus, where a fertilized egg is incubated; and the vagina which is intended to receive the male's reproductive cells, called sperm. In addition, there is a hormonal system that regulates the female reproductive cycle. Typically, a new egg matures and is released about every twenty-eight days. If fertilization does not occur in a timely fashion, the egg passes through the uterus and out of the body along with the lining of the uterus that had been prepared to support fertilization. This process is called menstruation. The cycle then starts again.

Unlike other primates, the human female does not show any outward sign that one of her eggs is ready for fertilization, and, in fact, may not even be aware of it herself. Hidden fertility has consequences for sexual behavior which will be discussed shortly.

The major components of the male reproductive system include the testicles, which house the testes, and the penis. The male sex cells, the sperm, are produced in the testes when the male reaches full sexual maturity (between ages fourteen to fifteen) and are produced continuously for the rest of his lifetime, though the number and genetic quality decrease with age. Newly produced sperm cells have a lifespan of about three weeks before they die and are reabsorbed, unless ejected from the body through the penis. Males also have a hormonal system that regulates many aspects of sexual behavior, though there is no timing cycle as with the females. Sexual readiness is generally ongoing.

When the male is sexually aroused, the penis fills with blood, becoming enlarged and rigid. It is then inserted in a female's vagina and sexual intercourse begins. When the penis releases sperm, millions of male sex cells swim toward the fallopian tubes in search of a mature egg. If an egg is available, only one of the sperm will be allowed to enter the egg, regardless of the number of sperm cells that are in close proximity. Fertilization, the fusion of the DNA components of the female and male sex cells, will occur.

This then, is the basic reproductive biology of humans. But now the human story gets very interesting because the behaviors associated with reproduction are varied, complex, and occasionally baffling.

Sexual Impulse/Drive

Humans have many genetically-based impulses that guide and shape their behaviors. Among these, the impulse to reproduce is one of the strongest. In fact, humans often refer to themselves as having a sex "drive" to emphasize its motivational strength. Though certainly not an instinct, it is as close to one as humans experience.

The impulse to reproduce is supported by two other very powerful genetics-based mechanisms. First, evolution has encouraged intercourse by making it very pleasurable. Orgasms, intense pleasure responses that can be experienced by both sexes, strongly reinforce sexual behavior. While this mechanism of physical pleasure certainly promotes reproduction, it can also reinforce a wide range of behaviors unrelated to reproduction as well, as will be seen in the upcoming section on sexual variation. In fact, humans (both females and males) frequently engage in personal behavior that produces an orgasm.

The second support mechanism is emotional intimacy. Intercourse promotes feelings of closeness and companionship that are sought by both sexes. It is regarded as a very pleasurable emotional response that generally increases bonding between the participants. This is potentially important for creating supportive conditions in the future for any resulting offspring. As with the physical pleasure mechanism, the intimacy mechanism can also reinforce a wide range of behaviors that are not directly related to reproduction. It is also likely that the intimacy motive is responsible for the fact that humans prefer to have intercourse in private, which is not a preference of other animals.

So the impulse to reproduce is multi-faceted. First and foremost, there is the biological mandate to reproduce. In fact, from a biological perspective, sexual behavior is strictly about reproduction and nothing else. However, the secondary support mechanisms, which are intended to promote intercourse, are much more general in their effects. The additional pleasures associated with intercourse greatly expand the range of sexual behaviors seen in humans.

Very recently, humans have discovered reliable ways to prevent fertilizations that would normally result from intercourse. This has changed sexual behavior in some dramatic ways, though only for the minority of humans that have ready access to the most effective prevention methods. Birth control has given humans more flexibility, so that intercourse has become less about reproduction and more recreational, with an emphasis on pleasure and intimacy. Under these conditions, reproduction can become more of a choice—part of a plan—rather than an inevitable consequence of intercourse. However, based on the rapid increase in world population, it appears that relatively few mated pairs currently manage their reproduction in a planned way.

Gender Identity

The biological sex of a human is determined by inherited DNA, which programs for the development of a specific reproductive system. (Exceptions to this will be discussed later.) But biological sex is one thing, while the development of specific sex-related patterns of

Figure 7-2. Mated Couple

behavior is something quite different. The range of appearances and behaviors associated with a specific sex defines the gender of an individual. In the contemporary world, gender-specific expectations include such things as hair styles, clothing styles, methods of movement, speech mannerisms, play preferences, communication styles, and occupational preferences (Figure 7-2).

Gender-specific expectations are largely determined by the local community (and larger culture) within which an individual is socialized, and are pretty much arbitrary from a biological perspective. In a historical context, gender roles have helped facilitate social interactions by making them more predictable in a world largely inhabited by strangers. Though there may be general behavioral norms, the range of individual variation within the norms can be quite broad. However, outside this range, social sanctions may be invoked to suppress or change what are seen as undesirable behaviors, even though many of these behaviors may be of little significance.

Worldwide, over thousands of years, many different types of gender norms have evolved within human cultures. Some are rather narrow and rigid while others more expansive and flexible. All are subject to change through a variety of social processes. Generally, definitions of femininity and masculinity have tended to reflect the human impulse to patriarchal forms of social organization and tend to promote male interests. Gender roles continue to evolve along with the cultures within which they reside.

PAIR BONDING

Associated with reproduction, females and males frequently pair up as couples and form a family unit for the purpose of rearing offspring. This is called pair bonding and is fairly common among mammals. Humans approach this activity in a surprisingly wide range of ways. This variety reflects the multi-faceted motivations influencing reproduction. Before considering the current state of affairs, it will be helpful to build some historical context.

Historical Perspective

As we have seen, humans lived in the wild in small hunter-gatherer tribes since their migration out of Africa fifty thousand years ago. During this time, evolution continued to shape physical forms and behaviors to optimize reproductive success under the conditions experienced as foraging tribal members. It was under these conditions, which were described in Chapter 2, Origins and History, that human mating habits took shape.

Given that tribes were small, usually not exceeding one hundred fifty members or so, and composed of many related individuals, the pool of potential mates was limited. The incest taboo discouraged close interbreeding as a way of avoiding non-viable offspring. While some mating pairs certainly came from within the tribe, another source of potential mates was also important.

Tribes inhabited large territories and interacted only with adjacent groups, and then only when territorial relations were stable. Territorial conflicts among neighboring tribes were common. But under conditions of peaceful co-existence, two important forms of cooperation took place: trade of goods and exchange of potential mates. Both of these were matters of survival. Particular to the current topic, exchange of mates kept the tribes' gene pools diverse, promoting healthy offspring.

So given the supply of available mates, how were mating pairs formed? We can be sure that the three motives we have already considered—the strong urge to reproduce, the pursuit of orgasms, and the quest for emotional intimacy—were all in play. But the action of these motives would have been channeled within the tribal structure. Very likely, elders played a major role in the formation of mating pairs. It is common in hunter-gatherer groups for mating arrangements to be used to strengthen family relationships and secure resources. In cross-tribal pairings, the emphasis on cementing political alliances was even more pronounced, and persists today in some cultures.

In addition to goals related to social cohesion, other pairing criteria would have been brought to bear. One of these certainly would have been status: the rank and importance of the individuals in their tribe or tribes. Also of importance would have been characteristics and behaviors that would have related to fitness: the ability to succeed in the foraging lifestyle. Robust physical appearance, good health, strength, endurance, mastery of key life skills, and cooperative personality are examples of traits that might have been valued and sought in potential mates.

So, when humans lived in the wild, the pairing of mates was a multi-faceted project. Pairings were done with the support and approval of others, rather than with complete independence for the couple. Certainly, personal preferences may have played a role, but other social forces were probably dominant.

The formation of a new pair was likely acknowledged within the tribe. Given that humans were inclined to believe in supernatural forces, there were undoubtedly some ceremonial activities associated with parings, particularly focused on promoting fertility. Since patriarchy was the norm, females typically left their family group to join the male's clan. Local tribal customs determined how any issues between a mated pair were resolved. These tribal norms for mating behavior prevailed for tens of thousands of years and still prevail in some human cultures today.

Contemporary Mate Selection

As humans transitioned to a settled lifestyle beginning about ten thousand years ago, and lived closer to each other, more mating options became available. This was especially true with the advent of villages and cities, when strangers were frequently encountered. However, there was no rapid change in the mating process, as tribal practices continued to prevail. Mate selection was still local and supervised for the most part.

But in the modern world in some cultures, individuals now have much personal control over the selection of a mate. While close relatives may continue to express opinions, their influence has been reduced significantly. And the reproduction motive has, in some cases, been diminished while the pleasure and intimacy motives have strengthened. But more independent mate selection still shows the impact of the past: humans tend to pair up with individuals who have a similar background and similar prospects.

Status is still important. Both males and females choose displays of clothing, hairstyles, body art, jewelry, physical attributes, and possessions, which are intended to confirm their place in the local social hierarchy and their competitive advantages as potential mates. In fact, substantial cost and effort are expended in these displays.

Fitness criteria are also still important but have been adapted to current conditions. So instead of focusing on the attributes of a successful forager, modern humans of mating age generally look for things like financial stability, intelligence, strong work ethic, loyalty, trustworthiness, cooperativeness, social competence, and good-humor, as well as the traditional indicators of pleasing physical appearance, good health, strong fertility, and well-matched sexuality.

It is common for the male to court the female mating prospect, though cultural practices in this regard seem to change fairly rapidly. It is also common for the female to make the final decision about whether a relatively long-term pairing will take place or not. But there is a lot of variation in the courtship process based on the preferences of the individuals involved. Humans show characteristic flexibility in selecting a mate.

Marriage

Once a pairing has been established, cultural norms typically come into play and attempt to shape the developing relationship. As was noted earlier, tribal groups acknowledged the formation of a new mating pair. This type of acknowledgement has continued into modern times in the form of the marriage ceremony, which, though no longer specifically associated with tribal life, is a public ritual sanctioned now by religious and civil authorities. Though the details of these rituals vary around the world, some form of marriage ceremony is universal in human cultures. Secular authorities generally discourage marriage before a pair reaches the age of eighteen, although there are many exceptions to this.

While marriage is common, there are many relatively long-term parings that are informally established. In the United States specifically, somewhat more than ten percent of all paired couples are unmarried and, of these, about forty percent have children in the household.

Though marriage is mostly symbolic, it sometimes provides some social incentives to form a stable family unit in which offspring can be successfully reared. This is relatively important given that human children mature very slowly over more than two decades, and are unable to care for themselves independently during most of this period.

However, these incentives appear to be relatively weak, as the number of children born to unmarried females is increasing. In the United States, for instance, more than forty percent of all births are now to unmarried females (though some of these females are in a paired, but unmarried, relationship). This may not pose much of a risk to offspring as long as a single parent has access to the resources needed to create a stable rearing environment. Unfortunately, this is not always the case, and some children receive less than optimal care and support. It is important to note that some children of paired couples are also mistreated, so the fact that a household has both parents is no guarantee of child rearing success.

Mating Stability

A pair-bonded male and female involves two individuals with different preferences, expectations, personalities, and socialization. When you add to this genetic predispositions and gender role conditioning that are sex specific, it's not surprising that mated relationships can be challenging to sustain. It generally takes congenial personalities, effective cooperators, skillful compromisers, and mutual supporters to keep relationships thriving. And even then, humans in close relationships have their ups and downs.

With a few exceptions, humans don't mate for life, particularly given the behavior of young adults who may engage in many liaisons during the mate selection process. Overall, pairings tend to be relatively fluid and in some cases are not established at all, despite a generally strong biological impulse to do so. Again, using my example of the United States, currently half its population over eighteen is not married. Though, as we have seen, a proportion of these are unmarried individuals in long-term relationships, individuals who have not yet found a mate, or individuals who are between marriages. In the Earth's wealthier countries, around ninety percent of all individuals will have married at least once by age fifty.

Of those who never marry, some simply have a temperament or have mental health issues that make it challenging for them to attract a mate or to sustain a relationship, despite an interest in being involved in one. Others simply prefer the autonomy of remaining unattached. In any case, formal marriage appears to be increasingly less popular.

Of those who do marry, around half will at some point permanently separate from (legally divorce) their mate. A significant number marry and divorce several times over a lifetime. Of all current married couples, perhaps twenty to thirty percent form stable, strong family units for extended periods of time. Another thirty to forty percent establish functional family units, where the female and male maintain a rather indifferent relationship with each other and ultimately drift apart. About twenty percent engage in periodic verbal hostilities with each other and maintain a strained relationship that can go on for years. And finally, perhaps another twenty percent perpetrate periodic violence (typically initiated by the male) against the mate, including psychological and physical harm, up to and including causing significant injuries or even death. Since the divorce rate is about fifty percent, many marriages are, at any given time, experiencing some degree of discord, dysfunction, and unhappiness.

Infidelity among marriage partners is common. About twenty to forty percent of married males become involved sexually with another partner, while twenty to twenty-five percent of married females also participate in extramarital affairs. Consequently, between twenty and thirty percent of the children born to married couples are not fathered by the male mate. For obvious reasons, infidelity is frowned on by the affected mate and by the larger community with varying degrees of sanction—from shunning and verbal disapproval to execution of the offending mate (usually the female), in extreme cases. There are various degrees of infidelity ranging from one-time events with no emotional attachment, to serial affairs with repeated romantic entanglements. Infidelity is one important cause for ending a marriage relationship.

Though this does not paint a very positive picture of human mating practices, humans are, nonetheless, reproductively very successful (though follow-on child rearing, discussed elsewhere, sometimes is problematic). So pair bonding is a generally fragile activity, offering a broad range of potential outcomes. It is also an activity that preoccupies humans for much of their lifetimes. Even after reproduction is no longer biologically possible, most mates maintain a keen interest in the quality of their relationship.

VARIATIONS

The typical human mating scenario involves a male and a female forming a pair bond and establishing a family unit. But humans display a lot of variation around this activity, driven by basic biology and the three different motives already mentioned: the drive to reproduce, the pleasures of the orgasm, and the desire for intimacy.

Biological Differences

As previously noted, the biological norm for humans includes two different forms: a female individual with two X chromosomes and a male individual with an X and a Y chromosome. But there are other biological variations, too. For instance, some individuals have three sex chromosomes instead of two. Though rare, perhaps one in one thousand births, configurations of XXX, XXY, XYY and others do occur, with varying developmental and health effects.

In addition, rare DNA coding errors (another one in one thousand births) can affect the development of reproductive systems in individuals with normal XX or XY configurations, potentially leading to ambiguities in sex identity. Some affected individuals may have characteristics of both sexes and are considered to be intersexual rather than either female or male. The effects of these developmental differences vary widely, from no impact on daily function to significant disability.

Overall, the human development process is subject to error with the reproduction system being no exception. If the aggregate rate of abnormal genetic processes is perhaps two per thousand births, the total number of affected individuals in a population of one billion is around two million. So while the frequency of occurrence may be low, the actual number of affected individuals can be significant, and so can be the health and psychological impacts—and the need for various kinds of support throughout life.

Impulse Strength

The impulse for humans to reproduce is very strong, along with the desire to obtain sexual pleasure and to achieve intimacy with a mate. The intensity of each of these motivators can vary greatly from human to human. The range of intensity is from little to no impulse strength to very great, even obsessive. Of course, the vast majority of humans fall in the middle of the range. But those toward the outer edges of the distribution account for some interesting variation in sexual behaviors or the lack thereof, especially when combined with life experiences that amplify genetically-based impulses.

At one extreme, there are humans with little or no interest in reproduction, sexual activity, or taking a mate. At the other end of the spectrum are individuals who are obsessed with reproduction and who produce large numbers of offspring. Others at this end of the sexual spectrum are obsessed by the desire to achieve orgasms and seek frequent opportunities for sexual liaisons. Still others are obsessed by the pursuit of intimate relationships, and spend inordinate amounts of time and energy pursing romantic connections with potential mates. Some may even express some combination of all these tendencies. Generally, cultures view the extremes with some level of concern and will often try to temper the most excessive behaviors.

Reproductive Redirection

Overall, humans are very flexible in their sexuality and could be said to be multi-sexual. From a biological point of view, sex has only one purpose: reproduction. However, because humans are so social and so dependent on learned behavior, redirection of reproductive behavior is quite common. Redirection means that sexual behaviors that would normally be directed toward reproduction are channeled to other social ends, sometimes ends that have no relationship to reproduction at all.

The reinforcing properties of orgasms and the strong desire to establish intimate relationships, though important supports for reproduction, are very general motives that also support quite a range of other behaviors. One of the more common reproductive redirections is an exclusive sexual attraction to members of the same sex. Around 1.7 percent of humans, including both males and females, direct their sexual interests in this way. This often, though not always, leads to the formation of pair bonded couples that form family units just like any other, though they cannot reproduce without extraordinary medical interventions (or through adoption).

Human attraction to members of the same sex appears to be largely a product of learned behavior, though there may be some genetically-based temperaments that nudge the development of sexual behavior in that direction. Same-sex orientation can't be driven strongly by a genetic component, since the inability to reproduce in same-sex couples would quickly remove any such genes from the human gene pool.

Although historically, sexual attraction to members of the same sex has been socially stigmatized to varying degrees, there doesn't seem to be any rational basis for this at the present time. The motives of those with same-sex orientation, especially the motive to achieve intimacy with another person, are genuine and heartfelt. And given the population issues facing humans, sexual relationships that reduce reproduction are strategically beneficial.

Compared with those who have a same-sex orientation, there are other humans that have a broader range of sexual interests than normal. About 1.8 percent of humans are bisexual; that is, willing to engage in sexual activities with members of either sex. The interest in bi-sexual liaisons may vary substantially over a lifetime. This is another example of human behavioral flexibility and is generally tolerated socially, unless promiscuity or infidelity are involved.

A quite different example of reproductive redirection involves the voluntary commitment not to engage in sexual behavior at all. This is most often seen in a religious context, where an adherent believes that foregoing sexual relations is a sign of devotion. Thousands of biologically normal humans forego sexual activity (at least most of the time) for this reason. It exemplifies the human capacity to fixate on practices that have an emotional rather than a purely biological rationale.

There are hundreds of other examples of less common reproductive redirections, ranging from wearing clothing normally associated with members of the other sex as a means of achieving sexual arousal, to a fixation on female shoes so strong that a male's orgasm is only possible if footwear is present during intercourse. While a full exploration of these variations is beyond the scope of this guide, it is important to remember that the behavioral flexibility of humans is clearly illustrated in their creative sexual lives.

Deviance

Not all human sexual behavior is positive, though the line between what is acceptable and unacceptable varies from culture to culture. Deviance in this context means that some sexual practice significantly differs from commonly acceptable or typical sexual behavior. Though humans socially define the idea of deviance, it generally refers to behaviors that interfere significantly with normal intimacy relationships or are actually physically or psychologically damaging to another person.

A very common example is the perpetration of rape, usually by males, where intercourse is undertaken without the consent of the partner. It is found in all cultures and, though generally condemned, evokes punishments of widely varying severity. On average, around fifteen percent of females worldwide will experience one or more rapes during a lifetime, though the range of variation can be quite large based on the locality—from perhaps half as many as the average in one society, to more than double the incidence in another. Generally, humans expect their sexual relationships to be conducted between consenting adults, though this ideal is yet far from being universally achieved.

Another form of deviance that has been problematic for humans has been the sexual abuse of children—again, generally perpetrated by males. As many as twenty percent of female children and eight percent of male children have experienced one or more incidents of sex abuse before the age of eighteen. Some perpetrators of child sex abuse have a form of reproductive redirection where all sexual interest is directed toward children. Other perpetrators simply include children in a more diverse range of sexual interests. There is universal condemnation of child sexual abuse with strong community sanctions aimed at preventing and punishing it. However, humans have not succeeded in bringing this form of sexual deviance under control, and the practice is still quite widespread.

Incest is the practice of having intercourse between humans that are closely related genetically. It is considered deviant particularly because of the potential for producing non-viable offspring. Humans generally have a genetic impulse that leads to the avoidance of these kinds of sexual relationships. However, since it is just an impulse, social learning can override it. Incest is normally initiated by males toward female relatives. If the victim is young, incest is considered a form of child abuse. The worldwide prevalence is not known with confidence, though it could be that as many as ten percent of the global female population has had one or more such experiences. Incest is universally condemned and subject to strict punishments.

A wide range of other human sexual deviations occur on a relatively rare basis, including inflicting pain on oneself or others to achieve sexual arousal, engaging in intercourse with members of other species (a practice unique to the human species), obtaining sexual arousal by covertly watching others engaging in sexual behaviors, displaying genitals or other body parts to others when unwelcome, and even engaging in sexual activity with human corpses. All these practices are deemed unacceptable and subject to strong social condemnation and severe legal sanctions.

So the scope of human sexual redirection is truly vast and is often completely unrelated to the original mission of producing offspring.

8 Offspring

HUMAN OFFSPRING ARE somewhat unique in the Earth's animal kingdom due to their long period of physical development after birth. Lasting about twenty-five years, it is the longest period of growth and development leading to maturity of any animal species. In addition, human offspring are born somewhat prematurely, unable to survive independently for an extended period of time. This poses some real challenges for parents (or others) who must devote significant time and material resources to childrearing.

PRENATAL DEVELOPMENT

Once an egg and a sperm fuse (Figure 8-1) after intercourse between a male and a female, biological processes are set in motion that, if successful, culminate in the development of a new member of the human species. All humans start as a single fertilized egg cell about the size of the period at the end of this sentence (the egg has a diameter of about 100 microns). The new and unique DNA pattern in the fertilized egg cell guides development of a new body that will eventually be composed of more than three billion differentiated, yet fully integrated, cells in an adult organism.

The process of cell division and differentiation is well understood and unfolds in a predictable manner in phases. In the first two weeks, the cell mass, referred to as a *zygote*, starts a process of cell division and implants into the wall of the uterus. In the next six weeks, the main

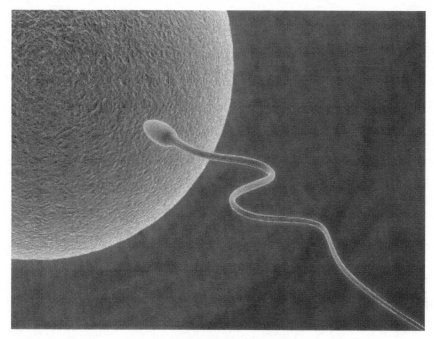

Figure 8-1. Egg Fertilization

elements of the new body plan begin to differentiate, creating an embryo that is about an inch long by the end of this phase and weighs less than an ounce.

Once the main elements of the body plan are in place, by about the beginning of week nine, the final phase begins in which the tissues and organs of what is now called a *fetus* mature, and the body grows rapidly. Not all components of the body plan develop at the same rate. For instance, the brain does not get assembled immediately. The basic structure of the brain forms after about three months (twelve weeks) but is not switched on until after about six months (twenty-four weeks). The maturation process continues through about thirty-eight weeks, when the fetus is normally ready to be born.

The genetically-programmed body assembly process is complex and, as a result, subject to error. Fortunately, DNA has built-in quality control and repair functions that attempt to spot and fix problems that arise during assembly. But this is a daunting biological challenge given the scope and complexity of the project. Failure rates are high.

About two-thirds of fertilized eggs never result in a viable birth. Most of these critical assembly problems are detected early, further development is suspended, and the cell mass is discarded unobtrusively. However, as assembly proceeds, less severe assembly errors, genetic coding problems, disease, or environmental traumas can bring development to a stop, and a pregnancy will end in a miscarriage or stillbirth with the abnormal fetus expelled from the uterus.

Typically, humans only have one child at a time. Twins occur at the rate of about thirteen or fourteen births per thousand (1.3–1.4 percent). Of these, three to four births per thousand are identical twins who share the same DNA, and the rest are fraternal twins who develop from separately fertilized eggs. Rarely, more than two children will be carried in the same pregnancy, though some medical fertility treatments increase the probability of multiple births. In very rare circumstances (perhaps one in one hundred thousand births), identical twins may be conjoined, sharing various organs and other body parts. This condition is considered a birth defect and is always accompanied by severe health problems, which are in most cases fatal at birth or in infancy. Without expert medical intervention, quality of life and longevity are almost always compromised.

ABNORMALITIES

The human reproductive process is imperfect, even though there are formidable quality control and repair systems at the cellular level. As already noted, around two-thirds of fertilized eggs do not result in the birth of a viable offspring. Of the remaining live births, one in fourteen infants (a little over seven percent) suffer from a physical abnormality of some sort, and half of these have more than one malformation. These malformations take several forms with internal abnormalities more common than external ones. Some of the problems are caused by the configuration of genes inherited from parents. More than ten thousand congenital disorders have been catalogued, though most are very rare. Examples include Down syndrome, hemophilia, cystic fibrosis, epilepsy, severe food allergies, and predisposition to the development of cancers. Among these is a range of severity from life threatening to mildly troublesome.

Some genetic abnormalities don't manifest themselves until humans become much older. For instance, Huntington's disease, a degenerative and always fatal neurological disorder caused by a specific genetic mutation in chromosome four, generally does not become active until the third or fourth decade of life, depending on the scope of the inherited malformation. Another abnormality, schizophrenia, does not normally get expressed until around the beginning of the second decade of life. The time when various genetic abnormalities become active or apparent can vary widely among humans.

Other abnormalities can arise from environmental factors experienced by the fetus during development, such as nutrient deprivation, exposure to certain chemical substances, disease pathogens, and irradiation.

If various forms of mild-to-severe cognitive impairment that humans identify as worthy of intervention are also considered as malformations, then the total number of live births with physiological problems approaches fifteen percent or more. Cognitive impairments include a range of mild to severe conditions such as autism, attention deficit hyperactivity disorder (ADHD), various learning disabilities, speech and language impairments, and emotional disturbance. Typically, both genetic and environmental factors are involved in the expression of these conditions. It's not surprising that humans are concerned about cognitive impairments because, as a species, they are completely dependent on learning to acquire the competencies needed in adult life. Any condition that interferes with smooth and timely learning is a concern for them.

It is likely that some humans who are identified as suffering from a disability are really within the normal range of genetic expression, but simply outside cultural norms or expectations, which then triggers social interventions. The difference between normal and abnormal function is not absolutely clear, so at the margins, labeling seems somewhat arbitrary.

BIRTH

A relatively early birth is required because a human head is so large that females often have difficulty passing the newborn through the birth canal. As a result, birthing a child is a painful experience for females, as well as somewhat dangerous. Without medical interventions the maternal death rate for women as a result of childbirth is about 1.5 percent. Serious, but not life threatening, physical complications occur in the range of one in ten births.

On average, pregnant females typically give birth to their offspring around thirty-eight weeks (9.2 months) after fertilization (Figure 8-2). But there is a normal range from around thirty weeks to forty weeks or longer for births of healthy offspring. However, at the extremes of this range, health risks increase for both mother and child. The birth process lasts, on average, around eight hours, though there is quite a

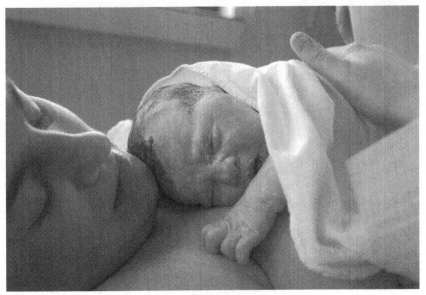

Figure 8-2. Newborn Child

range of normal variation. Average birth weight is around seven and one-half pounds, with a normal range of five and one-half to ten pounds.

Though there are challenges, human reproduction is remarkably successful, reflected in the population growth described in Chapter 3. At least in some populations, the availability of good nutrition for women and their fetuses, and medical interventions, have increased the proportion of live births. And, again through medical interventions, infant mortality has dropped significantly in many populations compared with historical outcomes.

Many genetic abnormalities can be identified early using medical technologies, thus creating an opportunity to limit the number of live births with severe abnormalities. Tay-Sachs disease is a good example. It is a degenerative genetic disease that adversely affects the development of the nervous system, generally in infants. It is caused by an inherited malformation of a gene on chromosome fifteen. Its effects are irreversible and always fatal. It runs in family lineages and can be detected prenatally.

Through genetic screening, prenatal testing, and therapeutic abortion, the number of infants born with this condition has significantly diminished. The deliberate management of genetic diseases, though relatively recent, is an example of how humans can improve the health prospects for their offspring.

Some humans have misconceptions and misgivings about this process of genetic manipulation, believing that a fertilized egg is immediately imbued with a supernatural spirit or soul. This is, of course, a cultural fiction, generally perpetuated through religious traditions, but with no basis in the processes of reproductive biology. However, like other beliefs grounded in supernatural systems of thought, reproductive biology is often a domain of strong and opposing viewpoints. Hopefully, a consensus can emerge focused on assuring good health prospects for all offspring who join the species.

CHILDHOOD

This stage covers the period from birth to about age ten for females and age eleven for males. During this period learning and physical growth are dramatic, yet human offspring during this period are very dependent on adults for support. Overall, children are unable to independently make decisions and successfully navigate most novel situations that they may face.

Infancy

Infancy is the first period of life for human offspring. It somewhat arbitrarily lasts from birth to about age one. During this time, the human child is completely helpless. It can't feed on its own, stand up, walk or communicate through language. It relies completely on parents or other humans to survive.

But it is a period of tremendous physical growth, with birth weight tripling, assuming that adequate nutrition is available. Initially, reflexes guide behavior focused primarily on feeding and self-defense. Like other mammals, when humans lived in the wild, their infants relied exclusively on breast milk for nutrition. However, today in wealthier countries there are a variety of nutritional formulas or supplements, available as substitutes so that some females can avoid suckling their young altogether.

During infancy the senses continue to develop and adapt to the environment. For instance, infants are born with poor eyesight, generally around 20/800 (which in adults is considered legal blindness), to a much-improved 20/70 within the first six months.[32] Vocalizations are limited to crying and babbling, creating meaningless speech-like sounds that are part of the process of acquiring spoken language. Motor activity improves, but is still rudimentary. Crawling on hands and knees becomes the main way of moving about. Handgrip strength and precision improves. Hearing develops with particularly increased attention to speech sounds.

Social learning proceeds through the mechanisms of reward and punishment as the infant explores the immediate environment. Emotional states are evident, but undeveloped. Some aspects of the environment become differentiated, particularly faces of others who attract and hold the infants attention. The infant's mother or other primary caregiver becomes specifically identified.

Early Childhood

Early childhood proceeds from about age one to about age seven. There are several physical and cognitive milestones during this period. A key event in physical development is the emergence of the ability to stand upright and walk. This happens early in this stage and is fully accomplished generally by age two. Coordination of movement and grip improve. By the end of this stage, height and weight have increased substantially. The typical seven-year-old is around seventy percent of adult height, but only thirty percent (males) and forty percent (females) of initial adult weight.

Another important physical milestone is the eruption of primary teeth at around the beginning of this stage. Teeth are necessary for the transition from breast milk (or its equivalent) to a more standard (initially tender) diet. The full development of the first of two sets of human teeth takes about four years.

A final physical milestone in this stage is learning voluntary control of urination and defecation. This training usually starts around

---

[32] Normal vision (20/20) is not fully developed until around age 5, though in a substantial number of humans this level of acuity is never achieved. About forty percent of humans have some degree of near- or farsightedness where objects, either close at hand or in the distance, do not come into full focus. Most instances are the result of inherited genetic variation in the shape of the eyes. Impaired vision is normally corrected by wearing glasses or contact lenses.

age two and is completed by age three. Toileting self-control is an important social skill in all human cultures.

A very important first cognitive milestone is the acquisition of spoken language, which consolidates generally between ages two and three. By the end of this stage, children are able to speak and understand others using relatively complex syntax and grammar, through a powerful interaction between genetic impulse and cultural training. Remember that the language that is learned is completely dependent on the culture in which an offspring is raised. Learning a language is a very impressive accomplishment and is the foundation for all adult human performance. The failure to acquire language skills is seen as a pathology.

New cognitive skills develop in parallel with language acquisition, such as the ability to think symbolically. Simple metaphors are comprehended and manipulated. For instance, a simple toy like a block of wood, can be waved through the air during play as if it were a bird. By the end of this stage, children are beginning to display the rudiments of conceptual reasoning—the ability to see relationships between parts and wholes, and to classify concrete objects based on their characteristics.

Another major milestone of early childhood is the initial attainment of empathy—the realization that others also think and share common emotions. This achievement is fundamental to one of the most important of human capacities: the ability to cooperate with each other, even without direct interpersonal contact. The failure to develop empathy, which happens occasionally, is also seen as a problem needing intervention and correction.

Once the use of language is achieved, adults in the child's community undertake intensive educational efforts. At first, parents generally provide education in the form of socialization. Once language use is initiated or even a bit before, adult *storytelling* commences (see Special Feature at the end of this chapter).

Young children spend much of their time engaged with play activities, alone and with other children. Play is a form of practice and experimentation, often guided by imagination, where offspring develop their motor, cognitive and social skills.

By about age five or six, it is common for children who live in proximity to each other to be grouped together for more formal education, usually supported by an adult with experience and training as a teacher. A great deal of initial emphasis is placed on laying the groundwork for the verbal skills of reading and writing.

During this stage, adults introduce various kinds of fantasies to their offspring, presumably to promote the development of the imagination. Examples of these in the western world are characters like Santa Claus, the Easter Bunny, and the Tooth Fairy. These are largely holdovers from the era of oral story telling that have been converted to multi-media forms for consumption by young children—without revealing that they are imaginary characters. This unusual behavior is also rooted in the long tradition of human belief that there are spirits that animate the world.

It is also in early childhood that most children are introduced to the religious beliefs and practices of their parents and local communities. Cultures seek to take advantage of the cognitive malleability of children at this age to lay the common foundations that support tribal loyalties and social cohesion later on in life.

By the end of this stage, human offspring are still dependent on their parents or other adults, though they can now communicate wants and needs with language and perform some basic tasks independently. However, their abilities are still quite limited.

Late Childhood

This period of development extends from about age seven to the beginning of puberty—the physiological and cognitive changes signaling the beginning of the adolescent stage. Puberty begins around age eleven or twelve. During late childhood, height and weight continue to increase, though the pace is relatively slow. Males and females remain similar to each other in size and body shape. By the end of this stage, the typical child has attained about eighty-five percent of adult height and about sixty percent of adult weight.

Another important physical milestone is the replacement of primary teeth by permanent teeth, which will be retained through adulthood if they are well-maintained. This replacement process, where primary teeth loosen and are shed, begins at about age seven and continues through to about age twelve.

Late childhood begins with the development of one of the most important of all cognitive milestones: learning to read and comprehend written text in the local language. Reading is one of the most formidable of humans skills, and leads to the ability to engage with vast amounts of knowledge that have been accumulated. But since reading is such a recent historical phenomenon, it is not yet supported by genetic programming, as is oral language. As a result, almost all children require sustained and intensive instruction to acquire the skill. Some children experience significant difficulty in reaching this milestone, requiring additional intervention from adults to achieve even basic proficiency. But proficiency in reading is an important element of human success as adults, where it greatly facilitates cooperation, problem solving, and task performance.

Another important cognitive skill is initiated and developed during this phase: learning to write. Humans use writing to communicate with each other without speaking or being in close proximity. As with reading, this is a relatively new skill in evolutionary terms without special genetic programming to support it. And, like reading, some children have difficulty acquiring even the basics of the skill. To help children learn to write, humans provide years of sustained instruction to build the competence expected of adults.

In general, conceptual thinking becomes increasingly complex. Still, most children in this stage of development are still working primarily with concrete concepts. In addition to mastering more complex verbal concepts comes the capacity to understand numbers and perform arithmetic operations. This is another domain requiring substantial instruction as humans are, by nature, very limited in their intuitive grasp of mathematics.

Also, during this stage, and in large part due to their increasing general conceptual understanding, children begin to see and understand themselves in relationship to others. This is an important development for members of a very social species. The formation of a self-image involves being able to assess various personal attributes and to classify them in relationship to the local social hierarchy. Some of these attributes are physical characteristics like height, weight, strength, and endurance, while others are more intangible like intelligence, friendliness, aggressiveness, cooperativeness, or self-control. Part of this image includes gender identity and role learning, the nature of which varies from culture to culture.

A relatively accurate self-image provides a foundation for selecting and attaining personal goals, and influences a variety of human behaviors. The formation of a self-image is subject to error, with significant detrimental emotional side effects that may require the intervention and support of adults.

Finally, late childhood includes the development of a moral sense. The underlying human moral impulse (see Chapter 9) is shaped to align with the local culture. The social controls of guilt and shame are developed in line with socially accepted norms. A failure to develop these moral sentiments is seen as pathological and requires efforts to reinforce compliance.

By the end of this stage, independence has increased, but offspring still require guidance from adults to successfully navigate many situations in the more complex social environment of the modern world. They also normally continue to reside within the family unit.

ADOLESCENCE

Childhood ends with the onset of puberty. Puberty is the name humans give to a genetically programmed biological process leading to sexual maturity. During this process, the body releases hormones that have several effects, depending on the sex of the individual. There is normally a growth spurt that leads to the attainment of adult height and initial adult weight. Secondary sex characteristics emerge. Females develop breasts, their hips widen and round, and menstruation begins. Males add muscle mass, their voices lower, facial hair grows, and the capacity for ejaculation develops.

Females achieve the full sexual maturity characteristic of adulthood generally between ages fifteen to seventeen, and males achieve it between the ages sixteen to seventeen. However, cognitive development continues well into the mid-twenties, when the human brain completes its full physical maturation (though learning continues even through old age). The end of adolescence is not clearly marked physiologically, though it may be culturally determined. Adults appear to have a strong interest in having their progeny move into adult roles after twenty or more years of close supervision. Childrearing is not easy, though it does have its rewards, judging from the reports of parents. Evolution has equipped parents with an emotional impulse to nurture and support their children, though sometimes this impulse is not especially strong or may be absent altogether.

Adolescents continue to receive formal instruction under the supervision of adults. Each adolescent's knowledge base expands and cognitive skills become more sophisticated. The biggest cognitive milestone during adolescence is the emergence and development of abstract thinking. This involves being able to understand and manipulate concepts that have no concrete reference point in physical experience. This is an important capacity because the human knowledge base is full of abstractions connected with each other in interrelated webs. Successful adult performance depends to a large extent on understanding and applying these abstractions to a wide range of problems. This is how humans benefit from the experience of others, both past and present, that transcends their own.

The universe of abstractions includes both verbal and numerical components. By adolescence, instruction from adults is critical in developing proficiency with abstract thinking. Reading emphasizes abstract comprehension; writing provides a means for organizing and expressing abstract ideas; and mathematics shifts from arithmetic to more abstract forms, beginning with algebra. Other subject matter domains, like science and social studies, introduce complex webs of abstract ideas with which offspring are expected to develop some level of proficiency.

Another important cognitive development is the appearance and cultivation of critical thinking. This is the process of evaluating situations (often presented in the form of claims) in a systematic way using relevant evidence. Several intellectual tools, including the mathematical evaluation of data sets, must be learned and mastered through application to increasingly complex and subtle problems. Critical thinking is another contributor to successful adult performance.

Expectations for cognitive performance have risen significantly since humans lived in the wild. Despite the adult investment of substantial time and effort in the modern world to teach their children, outcomes vary widely. Part of this is due to genetic differences in brain function (discussed in greater depth in the Chapter 9) and part is due to uneven learning opportunities within and across cultures. The end result is that some children move through adolescence without fully mastering the elements of abstract thinking. This is generally viewed as a problem that threatens success as an adult, with the level of concern varying with cultural context.

Morality continues to receive attention in this stage with an ever-greater emphasis on compliance with cultural norms. This is sometimes a challenging process for adolescents and their success as adults is uneven; though, in general, the norms of the community are adequately instilled to maintain social continuity across generations.

The emerging sense of self-identity is further consolidated with rank and status becoming more consistent.

Depending on position in the local community, this can be a benefit or a detriment—the cause of a variety of social and personal problems. Humans tend to have distinct identities, even though they are social animals. They act as individuals, but come to align themselves with tribe-like groups, beginning with whatever family unit they are associated with—whether genetically related or not. However, it is common for humans to form links with many different groups with which they cooperate to achieve social goals. Such groups have varying degrees of influence and may have prosocial (e.g., supporting a charity) or antisocial (e.g., joining a gang) motives.

Adolescents experiment with adult roles, including the process of mate selection. Peer group relationships are particularly important. They generally become a dominant reference point for behavior, diminishing the supervisory role of parents to some degree. Though independence is increasing during this stage, adult guidance is still required periodically, particularly when adolescents are faced with unfamiliar problems and situations.

TRANSITION TO ADULTHOOD

As already mentioned, there is no clear physiological marker for the transition from adolescence to adulthood. However, most cultures arrange for some sort of symbolic event signaling when they expect adolescents to begin assuming adult roles. This event usually occurs during the late teenage years, though there is variability. In industrialized cultures, the end of compulsory education, usually around age eighteen, often signals the adult transition. Sometimes this transition is acknowledged earlier if an adolescent enters the workforce on a full-time basis. Or it may be a later transition for adolescents who pursue higher education. Legal systems typically define the rights, responsibilities, and protections that pertain to adolescents and adults.

In a few remnant hunter-gather or subsistence agriculture societies, a rite-of-passage may be a specific and sometimes challenging physical ceremony, the completion of which signals acceptance into adult company. Examples include tests of physical endurance or stylized scarring or tattooing. These kinds of rites typically occur around the same time that sexual maturity is attained.

Once the passage has been completed, young adults are expected to be mostly independent of parents and to no longer live with them or to use their resources. This degree of separation is particularly noticed after mating occurs and new family units are being established. However, there is much variation in the timing and degree of independence that is achieved.

Human offspring develop slowly through predicable steps or stages. Yet the process is remarkably variable. Growth and development are shaped both by the genetic makeup of the individual and by the unique experiences that unfold over the twenty-plus years required to reach adult status. The resulting range of adult competence is rather broad and significant.

SPECIAL FEATURE: STORYTELLING

Until writing was invented, oral storytelling was the principle means of transferring cultural (social) knowledge. It was, and still is, a powerful and effective communication technique, but subject to errors in interpretation. Some of these errors are the result of the limits of language to represent reality, some are due to factual misconceptions possessed by the storytellers, and some are due to inherent cognitive biases of the human brain. The informal teaching process is far from perfect, transmitting errors, and even delusions, from generation to generation.

Storytelling is a key feature of human social life, with origins long pre-dating the start of human history fifty thousand years ago. During the long period dominated by the oral tradition, stories were memorized and passed down from generation to generation. The best storytellers were held in high esteem in tribal groups. The tribe's knowledge and folklore were important for group cohesion and success in daily life.

Writing and, later, book publishing greatly expanded the spread of stories so that today there are many thousands of stories available that are aimed at audiences of various ages, including books for children. Stories are generally intended to both entertain and edify. They generally have a moral purpose; that is, they are intended to teach something specific about some aspect of human behavior. Humans refer to these lessons as the "moral of the story." Such morals may provide models of good behavior or be cautionary tales describing the consequences of bad behavior.

Most stories are fictional, the product of the robust human imagination. Of course fiction is not reality, so the morals may not really be valid. Though a story may be entertaining and emotionally satisfying, it may not provide sound guidance for personal behavior. This is potentially a uniquely difficult human problem because of their behavioral flexibility. Separating reality from the imaginary is sometimes a struggle.

Stories also use standard themes that are repeated over and over again in different contexts. The standard form for stories of any length include a beginning, middle and end—setup, development, and resolution. The themes typically include protagonists, antagonists, family (tribal) relationships, good, evil, life, death, hope, fear, love, hate, revenge, winners, losers, greed, envy, joy, and sorrow. These are just a few of the standard themes (and imbedded dichotomies) woven routinely into stories.

Of particular interest in stories written specifically for children is the use of animal characters that substitute for humans. Thus animals are given human qualities and characteristics and are used to deliver messages (morals) about human behavior. Children seem to find these types of stories entertaining, and thus are more apt to attend to them. This approach does have the, perhaps unintended, effect of imbuing animals (and even inanimate objects) with characteristics they do not actually have. This is an ancient tradition for humans, dating back to their origins when they perceived spirits in many features of the natural world that could help or harm—and who then created religious rites to solicit the support of or protection from such spirits.

In the modern world, stories are packaged into a variety of media including television, movies, video games, and audio books, as well as into paper books and magazines. The oral tradition has been largely replaced in most cultures by forms based on the written word.

Stories and storytelling are deeply ingrained in humans and may even be partially hard-wired into the human brain. Throughout history, individuals who easily and quickly understood stories, had ample capacity to remember the key messages, and could faithfully share the stories with others, may well have been relatively more successful than others, producing more offspring through many generations until their "storytelling" genes became common.

9 Behavior

UNDERSTANDING HUMAN BEHAVIOR is the key to understanding why humans are the dominant life form on Earth. Humans have, by far, the most complex and flexible behaviors of any animal on the planet. In addition, unlike any other animal, they have the ability to collectively save and pass along their behavioral innovations from generation to generation, creating an ever-growing storehouse of useful knowledge and skills that they use to meet their needs, including modifying their environments.

Though the range of behavioral options has grown to enormous proportions in the modern world, the behaviors actually acquired by individuals, primarily through learning, are shaped by multiple forces. Some of these are genetic and others are cultural, but they all have the effect of channeling behavior in certain directions following imperatives established in the distant past. As a result, while human behavior is in general flexible, it is sometimes poorly adapted for current conditions.

NERVOUS SYSTEM BIOLOGY

Behavior is a product of biology. The nervous system is the part of human physiology that controls behavior. Core components of this system, the brain, the spinal cord, an extended network of nerve fibers, and the senses make possible the complexity of human behavior.

The Brain

Humans are not physically exceptional. They're not big, fast, strong, or particularly agile. But they do have one exceptional attribute: their brains. It is an organ with some special qualities.

First, humans have large brains in relationship to their bodies, averaging about 72.6 in³ in volume and weighing about three pounds. This is about the size and weight of a small cantaloupe melon (Figure 9-1). Like other animal brains, the human brain is based on specialized neuron cells that transmit and process information electrochemically through a complex network of connections. There are around eighty-

Figure 9-1. Brain Size Illustration

six billion neuron cells and roughly an equal number of glial cells (which provide support and protection for neurons) in a typical brain. Each neuron has around seven thousand connections to other neurons. Multiplying the number of neurons by the number of connections per neuron yields an astonishing total of over sixty trillion potential interconnections. The human brain is the most complex of any animal, by a wide margin, and quite possibly the most complex single system on the planet.

Second, the human brain is made up of several different structural components that are common to all mammal brains. But what is particularly different about human brains is the large size of the cerebral cortex, which is associated with self-control, abstract reasoning, and planning. Humans have a lot of brainpower devoted to these activities.

Third, the human brain requires a substantial amount of energy to sustain it. While it comprises only about two percent of human body weight, it uses about twenty percent of the body's energy supply. This turns out to have important consequences for how the brain functions, as energy conservation was an important contributor to the brain's evolution.

It might be tempting to explain human behavior based solely on the brain's physical characteristics. But structural differences are only part of the story. To understand the unusual capabilities of humans, more perspective is needed, including the role of the senses and the key elements of the brain's functions.

The Senses and Perception

The human brain is isolated inside the skull and has no direct way of accessing the environment. The only way the brain can encounter the outside world is though the human body's major senses, which include vision, hearing, smell, taste, and touch.[33] While the major systems are overall very good at passing information to the brain, they and the brain's processing circuits do make some consequential mistakes. The brain uses the signals provided by the senses to form perceptions of the outside world.

Vision. Human vision is very good at offering images of the world in both color and in three dimensions. While it is limited to a fairly narrow range of the energy frequencies present in the environment, given the conditions that humans regularly have to navigate, their vision works well for them. But one feature of the vision system can cause problems. When a human looks at something in the environment, only a portion of the visual information available is actually considered. To speed up processing, the brain only samples the scene and then constructs an image. Since this sampling is incomplete, the brain's guess about reality can also be incomplete or even completely wrong.

---

[33] Humans also have some other specialized internal sensory systems that monitor what's going on within the body, but in this chapter, the focus is on sensing what is happening in the external environment.

Optical illusions, failure to see changes in a scene, and missing important details are all symptoms of the limitations of the vision system. They happen all the time and can cause problems based on what is missed or misidentified.

The brain works together with the vision system to find patterns in the environment and attempt to identify them. This is beneficial in most circumstances but is a source of error when the brain thinks it sees something that doesn't exist. This is particularly common when scanning other human faces, because the vision system is particularly attuned to keeping track of the presence and intents of other people.

There are many examples of humans thinking they see faces in clouds or cloth or even items of food, where the observed pattern is completely random but where the brain sees an abstract resemblance to a human face (Figure 9-2). The image in the lower right was taken by a low-resolution camera on a spacecraft in orbit around Mars. Many observers of this image thought they were looking at a human face. The larger image was taken later by a higher resolution camera and reveals the actual geological surface features. Humans, unfortunately, don't always see this sensory error as a perceptual mistake. Perhaps a particularly extreme example of the human brain misinterpreting visual information is the widespread human tendency to see ghosts, apparitions of dead people, often claimed to be seen in poorly lit rooms at night—a completely imaginary sensory event.

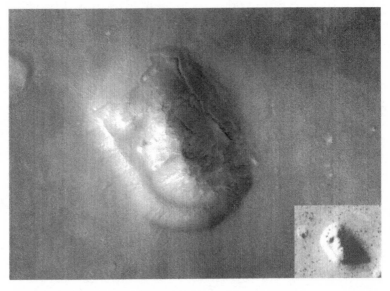

Figure 9-2. Face on Mars

Hearing. Human hearing, the detection of sound waves in the environment, is sensitive and directional. Though not as good as many other animals, it is adequately sensitive to the sounds typically encountered when humans lived in the wild. One of its most important functions is hearing human speech sounds and being able to understand all their subtle details. Though interpretative errors sometimes occur for those with normal hearing, most of these mistakes are minor and are resolved by simply focusing attention and listening again.

Part of the hearing system (the vestibular subsystem) is devoted to providing information about the body's position in the space around it and the direction and intensity of movement. This kind of information is a very important part of voluntarily controlling muscles to achieve specific actions.

Smell. While the human sense of smell, which is based on chemical recognition, is also somewhat limited compared with other animals, it is still quite good with the ability to distinguish among millions of different scents. The system is very good at identifying both useful odors (that food smells good) and potentially harmful ones (that infected wound doesn't).

Taste. Taste is another sense relying on chemical recognition. For humans, taste is a part of the eating process and helps them decide whether a potential foodstuff is edible or not. There are six basic taste receptors that can be activated to varying degrees to produce different flavors. Taste buds in the mouth work in concert with the sense of smell to produce the effect experienced while eating. Unfortunately, the system is far from infallible in detecting inedible substances.

Taste is a sense that has become an object of manipulation in the modern world. Food scientists have learned how to manufacture foodstuffs that contain chemical compounds engineered to mimic natural flavors. Using this technology, commercial enterprises sell a range of food products designed to have great taste appeal, but sometimes without much nutritional value.

Touch. Touch is the sense that lets the body know when it's in contact with anything in the environment. There are several types of receptors involved that sense pressure, vibrations, texture, temperature, pain and the position of body parts. These all help the brain get a sense of what's going on in the environment. There is little evidence that they provide bad information except when they have been damaged in some way.

Perception of Time. Humans perceive time, though not directly as a sense. The brain processes the sequence of information coming from the senses to build an internal chronology. The perception of time is affected by the duration of events. Humans can only perceive short events if they last long enough. For vision, this is a duration of about a tenth of a second, and for hearing, about a hundredth of a second. Anything of shorter duration is perceived as instantaneous. Watching a movie, which is made up a series of individual images, is a good example of how very short individual events merge to form a smooth sense of continuity.

The concrete perception of longer time intervals is deeply rooted in evolutionary experience from the many millennia spent living in the wild. Humans are very conscious of daily cycles, partially because of their need for periodic sleep. They also are sensitive to annual cycles with seasonal variation as these strongly influenced the availability of food sources and weather events. But the perception of even longer time intervals diminishes. Environmental cycles beyond just a few years are largely invisible. Given the life span of humans, an interval of one hundred years is just an abstraction with little capacity to influence planning in the present. And biological (organic evolution) and geological (crustal plate movements) processes, which occur over long periods—millions of years—are well beyond the scope of human time perception.

Very short and very long time intervals can now be accurately measured, but only understood abstractly. Because of its limited scope, the perception of time creates some planning problems for humans. If an event, even a significant one, is expected to occur in the distant future (perhaps ten years from the present), humans have a difficult time mobilizing to respond. For instance, if a very large earthquake is predicted with a ninety percent probability to strike a region where many people live within two decades, the daily or even yearly activities of the humans who live in the area are likely to change very little, if at all. The event is perceived as being too far in the future to be of any great concern to a human brain that has a much shorter-term focus.

There is one way in which the human perception of time has been culturally modified, with problematic results. Past events, particularly those with strong emotional content, would normally be forgotten with the death of those directly involved with them. But with oral storytelling (and more recently through various other kinds of media), events from the past can be revisited, sometimes repeatedly over many generations. These stories from the past, which often become heavily modified through repetition, can prompt actions generations later.

For example, a relatively trivial tribal leadership dispute hundreds of years ago is still remembered and continues to act as a divisive wedge separating two major sects, the Sunni and Shia, of the Islamic religion. Millions of people have been and continue to be adversely affected by the animosities perpetrated by a collective remembrance. Human history is littered with multigenerational feuds and grudges sustained by stories of questionable accuracy.

Finally, the perception of time varies somewhat from person to person and changes with age. Children generally observe that time passes slowly, while the elderly observe that time passes quickly. Changes in metabolism and accumulated experience may partially account for these differences. Regardless, the perception of time is not a constant, regulated by an objective internal clock. Time perception is important to human activity, but has limitations of which humans should be mindful.

■ ■ ■

The senses are essential to human behavior, but fallible—especially the sight system. It's important for humans to understand how their own senses work and can be distorted. Using techniques to defend against errors is important to everyday success. Example strategies include using data-gathering aides like checklists when undertaking observations, performing an observation more than once, or using multiple observers. This helps improve objectivity and reduces errors.

Some humans, as a result of genetic abnormalities, are born without one or more senses. Others, born with normal sensations may, as a consequence of subsequent trauma, lose one or more of their senses. Without any specific intervention, the brain seems to adapt and provide some compensation for these losses. However, the internal compensations may be far from complete. As a result, humans have invented various compensatory technologies like braille, sign language, hearing aids, and cochlear implants.

Memory

Humans have the ability to remember past events or at least an approximation of them. Their brains have several different memory systems which are separate from each other, including short-term memory where impressions of activities and events are stored for a few minutes; working memory where various memories are called out to help perform a specific task; and long-term memory where memories are stored for days, months, and years.

No memory is an exact copy of the event or activity that triggered it. All memories are constructed in the human brain with various degrees of fidelity. In addition, over time human memories are subject to change through combination, loss of detail, and revision. In fact creative revision is quite common. Where details of a story are missing, the brain is more than happy to invent them and integrate them into the story as if they were part of the original event.

Human memory has evolved to strongly support the story format where a remembered narrative has a beginning, a middle where the storyline is developed, and an end where, typically, the moral of the story is revealed. This format has been incredibly important to humans who, for tens of thousands of years, passed information from generation to generation, relying exclusively on memory to accomplish this task. Even after writing was invented, the story format persisted as a dominant form of human communication.

Human memories should always be treated with some skepticism when an accurate, complete description of an event is needed. Testimony from other disinterested observers and physical evidence are regularly required to substantiate accounts from an individual's personal account. Of course, photographic records are now available to help confirm historical events, though such records are often unavailable or are ambiguous.

THINKING ABILITIES

The human brain has some powerful capabilities that are expressed through the activity of thinking. This is an internal cognitive process involving the manipulation of symbols to frame and solve problems, evaluate alternatives, and develop action plans. Three features of thinking are particularly important.

Intelligence

Humans are intelligent. Of course this is, in part, why they are the dominant form of life on the planet. But intelligence is a complex concept, so an understanding of it requires the exploration of several interrelated components.

The first component of intelligence is language fluency. Language plays a big role in human affairs. Being able to understand and use language effectively is generally important. But the ability to work particularly well with the abstractions imbedded in language has been critical to human success.

For instance, there's practical power in knowing how a bacterium interacts with a human immune system to affect human health. Or in knowing with precision what course an object will follow when launched into the air. Or in being able to predict in advance if and when a strong storm will strike. Or in knowing how the decay of a radioactive atom can be used to make electricity. There are countless other examples of how an understanding of abstract relationships, conveyed through verbal and mathematical symbols, are important.

But there's more to intelligence than just the fluent use of language. Another aspect of intelligence is the ability to reason effectively. Reasoning involves reaching logical conclusions based on evidence. When humans reason, they reach conclusions by applying rules of logic. Consider the following reasoning problems that illustrate this process (Figure 9-3). The answers are available on page 170.

These problems, which use a variety of symbol systems, illustrate how the human brain can logically process information to manipulate abstractions and reach appropriate conclusions. But daily life for humans is far from abstract, so reasoning generally has a real world context. Here are some examples of situations where reasoning can help produce positive results:

- Decide if an herbal supplement should be used to improve a medical condition.
- Determine the best candidate to vote for in a political election based on policy positions.
- Develop a plan to allocate resources to achieve a specific future financial goal.
- Propose a solution to a conflict between two associates.

1. A REASONING PROBLEM USING VERBAL CUES

In a certain code ADVENTURES is written as TDRESAUVEN. How is SURPRISING written in that code?

A. IUIPGSSRNP
B. IUIPGSRSNR
C. UINGSSRRP
D. IRIPGSSNRR

2. A REASONING PROBLEM USING NON-VERBAL CUES:

There is some relationship between diagrams A & B. The same relationship persists between C & D. Find the right diagrams for D from the alternatives.

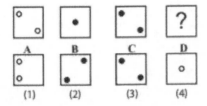

A. 1
B. 2
C. 3
D. 4

3. A REASONING PROBLEM USING NUMBER CUES:

Look at this series:
70, 71, 76, ___, 81, 86, 70, 91 ...
What number should fill in the blank?

A. 70
B. 71
C. 80
D. 96

Figure 9-3. Reasoning Problems

- Select the most appropriate tool to perform a specific task.
- Use clues to solve a crime.

Humans are the only animals that can apply reasoning to solve problems like these.

A third aspect of human intelligence is related to the effectiveness of working memory, a type of memory system introduced earlier. Working memory involves the ability to hold several different pieces of information in mind at the same time and to be able to manipulate them in some way. So for instance, when presented with a sequence of numbers, a human can recall the numbers and repeat them back in reverse order. The human brain can perform this kind of work quite easily as long as only a relatively few digits are involved.

The fourth and final dimension of intelligence is processing speed. This refers to how fast a human brain can perform a sequence of mental actions. This is also referred to as mental agility. When given a set of tasks to perform, thinking takes some amount of time to sort through and process all the necessary steps. Humans have generally rapid processing times compared with other animals.

Intelligence is important because simply stated, language fluency, effective reasoning, ample working memory capacity, and high processing speed contribute to success in daily life. This was true when humans lived in the wild and has become even more important over the last one hundred years, when the human living environment has grown vastly more complex. The human knowledge base has grown very large and the overall pace of life has increased, as most humans now interact with each other in many different ways every day. Intelligent behavior is necessary to not only survive, but also to thrive.

A new, recently emerging dimension of intelligence deserves mention. Humans have invented computer software that has made it simpler to perform a wide range of previously complicated tasks. In effect, the software acts as a thought amplifier that makes it possible for humans who use it to act more intelligently. This is a promising development, though the worldwide use of computers and software is still limited.

Modes of Thought

The human brain has two thinking modes, one that might be referred to as *everyday mode* and the other referred to as *premium mode*. When a human wakes up in the morning, the brain automatically starts in everyday mode, its default autopilot. It is not unusual to stay in this mode all day. It is an energy saving mode that conserves resources. Evolution has equipped humans to save energy because when they lived in the wild, finding the next full meal was not predictable. So the human body became very good at saving energy in many ways. Keeping the brain in a kind of standby mode was part of this energy conservation strategy.

In everyday mode, the brain makes lots of assumptions about what is going on in the immediate environment and doesn't pay much attention unless something really unexpected is encountered. This is efficient and reduces the thinking required to cope with the constant flood of detailed sensory input humans experience.

Humans sometimes call everyday thinking "intuition." This is the idea that something just feels right internally without much thinking and, therefore, must be right. It's also called "going with your gut feeling," to emphasize the sense of being automatic and confirmed emotionally. This is the everyday thinking mode at work. Quick, easy, decisive, and, unfortunately, sometimes wrong.

The everyday mode of thinking developed over tens of thousands of years while human ancestors lived in the wild, hunting and gathering. However, it can cause problems because it is tuned to experiences quite different from those of the modern world. Living conditions have changed, but the autopilot does not recognize these changes. This mismatch can cause problems in daily life, some of which can be potentially serious. Humans may encounter a variety of problems for which the autopilot has no ready solutions, so it substitutes something inappropriate or just plain wrong.

For instance, in a human-made environment like a city, the sensory inputs are very different than they were in the savannahs of the ancestral homelands. But the autopilot mode still looks for traditional danger signals, like rustling grass, which is in short supply. However, the autopilot is not tuned to watch for a moving city bus at a crosswalk, even though this is a real danger and the failure to detect it could be catastrophic. Another example is found in social relationships. In the wild, the autopilot was tuned to watch for and quickly check the intent of strangers in a territory. Wariness was the default. But in the modern world, strangers are everywhere, and though some wariness may still be warranted, a defensive posture may often be counterproductive to efficient cooperation.

Fortunately, humans have another mode of thinking at their disposal: premium mode. In this slower, more deliberate mode, humans clarify the problem that needs attention, gather relevant information, weigh alternatives, select an option that seems best, and plan a course of action. This is good old problem solving, at which humans excel when they focus on it.

But there are two drawbacks to this problem-solving mode. First, it takes some time to work through all the process steps—sometimes a lot of time. In reality, some problems demand quick reactions. Second, premium thinking requires a lot of energy, so the brain resists jumping into and staying in this mode. Humans describe this kind of thinking as generally requiring a lot of effort.

Premium thinking is the mode that has made humans so successful as a species. About three hundred years ago they discovered a very disciplined version of this type of thinking, which they called the *scientific method*. Using this method, humans have made many important discoveries about how the natural world works, and have developed many techniques and technologies based on this knowledge that has transformed daily life for many (but far from all) humans on earth.

One of the great human challenges has been to make premium thinking their standard mode, or to at least dramatically increase the amount of time that individuals spend using it. Of course many, if not most, humans have enough energy available to stay in premium mode all the time. More problematic is the brain's tendency to want to exit premium mode as soon as possible. Practice appears to be a key in making premium mode easier to access and sustain. So do "rules of thumb" (heuristics), such as applying a standard process of elimination method as a useful thinking shortcut. Humans have shown the capacity to get comfortable and efficient with premium thinking, though widespread adoption is still not the norm.

Cognitive Modules

Humans report that they are often conflicted about what to do when faced with a problem. This reflects an underlying feature of human brains. When it comes to thinking, humans are not of one mind. The brain is made up of parts or modules that have different functions and priorities shaped through the forces of evolution. These modules communicate with each other but don't always arrive at the same conclusion.

So for instance: (1) the centers of the brain that process incoming perceptions might report that something is going on that needs attention, the memory centers might try to cross-reference to previous similar encounters, (2) the planning centers might start weighing alternatives, (3) the physiological centers might be trying to decide whether to increase heart and breathing rates in preparation for an escape, and (4) the emotion centers might be getting ready to respond. These activities are not perfectly coordinated, which increases the possibility of a less-than-effective response. An individual human may end up getting contradictory or even bad advice from various members of its decision-making committee.

Complicating matters more is the fact that some of this processing is going on in the background and is not accessible. Only after the brain has done substantial work do signals reach the level of conscious thinking. As a result, some of what is happening in a decision-making process appears to be a complete mystery. The details of some of the brain's mixed messages can't be reviewed for reasonableness.

Most of the time this is not especially problematic; humans adjust in real time and muddle through. But from time to time it can lead to unfavorable, if not fatal, results. Fortunately, just like with mode switching, muddled thinking can be improved through the practice of disciplined strategies, especially those associated with premium thinking. This can help the brain focus on priorities well matched to various types of situations it faces in the modern world; for instance, how to respond to unhappy people, how to solve multi-step problems, how to avoid potentially dangerous situations, or how to negotiate a positive outcome when working with a group of people.

Problem 1, Answer: **A**—The first and sixth, third and eighth, fifth and tenth letters of the word interchange places in the code.

Problem 2, Answer: **D**—Diagrams C and D repeat the same pattern as A and B, but the dot fills are reversed.

Problem 3, Answer: **A**—In this series, 5 is added to the previous number; the number 70 is inserted as every third number.

AUTOMATIC THINKING BIASES

A human brain is not simply a neutral processor of incoming information about the environment. It has a number of built-in shortcuts and simplifications it uses to make sense of events, to speed up routine processing, and to make prudent decisions. These automatic routines evolved over tens of thousands of years while humans lived in the wild, propagated because they provided a survival edge. Their continued use today is largely unconscious and habitual across many different decision-making situations. Unfortunately, many of these built-in shortcuts don't work so well in modern, complex cultures. The following sections provide a few examples of inherent thinking strategies that are part of the standard operating systems of the human brain (Figure 9-4).

Examples of Automatic Thinking	
1	Confirmation Bias
2	Anchoring Bias
3	Availability Bias
4	Commitment Bias
5	Representativeness Bias
6	Attribution Bias

Figure 9-4. Thinking Biases

Confirmation Bias

The confirmation bias is very widely shared and frequently used by humans. It involves searching for and paying most attention to new information that confirms an existing idea or expectation. For instance, suppose a human has heard that a particular natural remedy is particularly effective at relieving the symptoms of an illness (though in reality it has none of the desired beneficial effects and some troubling side effects). The desire to relieve the symptoms of the illness is highly motivating. Quite naturally then, confirmation of a positive benefit is sought through methods such as conversation with others who have used the product and by reviewing online testimonials. The positive reviews receive special attention, while neutral to negative reviews are typically devalued.

Even when a newspaper report of a clinical study denies the remedy's effectiveness, an effort is made to explain away the discrepancy rather than to change the trajectory of the decision-making process. For instance, the report might be perceived as invalid because the report's sponsor, a drug company, has a vested interest in limiting the use of natural remedies. After further deliberation, the human begins to use the remedy at some expense and with no real benefit. The confirmation bias has channeled behavior in a predictable way.

Anchoring Bias

Anchoring is the tendency to focus on only one aspect of a complex situation and put too much emphasis on a single dimension in making a decision. For instance, a human might want to buy an automobile and focus primarily on how much horsepower the various alternative models have, even though another criterion, such as gas mileage might also be worth considering. As another example, a human might go to a grocery store and see a display offering three pounds of meat for a discounted price per pound. The advertised special price becomes the anchor influencing the shopper to purchase all three pounds, perceived as a "good deal," when only half a pound of the product was actually needed.

If the wrong anchor is selected in a problem-solving situation, an inadequate or ineffective solution may get implemented.

Availability Bias

When a human starts thinking about a problem, some personal anecdote almost always comes to mind, especially if it occurred recently or there was some sort of emotional connection to the memory. The availability bias, or shortcut, involves giving the information that came to mind more weight than is called for just because the information was easily available. For example, a human might be faced with giving a friend some advice on a troubling matter. In considering this task, what comes to mind is a story told by another friend about actions taken in a similar situation. This story then becomes the model for action, though the outcome was not especially positive. Due to this bias, other options are under-valued or ignored as alternatives.

Commitment Bias

When a human makes a decision, especially one that took lots of time and effort, he or she tends to stick with the decision, even when there is substantial evidence that the long-term outcome may not be good. For example, a human considers buying a house in a particular neighborhood, and attends several open houses, and secures financing for a mortgage. However, just before making an offer on a particular house, she learns that it is on the nighttime flight path of a nearby airport. But she minimizes the potential concern and proceeds with the purchase, only to be frequently awakened by aircraft sounds in the middle of the night.

Representativeness Bias

When humans use this shortcut, they observe a few characteristics of a particular situation and then automatically assume that it is a member of a general class of situations seen before. For example, a human sees a neatly dressed adolescent wearing glasses, quietly reading a book, and assumes the presence of a good student. It might turn out that the student is completely uninterested in school and is just waiting for a friend.

This is an example of the mechanism of stereotyping—using one or two (possibly irrelevant) characteristics to reach a conclusion (racism, for instance). While identifying and applying patterns in the environment can be useful, misclassification is common and can lead to flawed decisions and inappropriate behaviors.

Attribution Bias

Humans have a tendency to attribute the observed behaviors of others as caused by personality traits rather than situational factors, and to describe their own behaviors in just the opposite way. For instance, a man might hear that another person has accepted some form of social welfare, and describe that person as lazy and underserving of help. While if the same man needs similar help at some point, the choice to accept assistance will be described as the result of circumstances such as having been unfairly fired from a job by an incompetent supervisor, or as simply being the recipient of bad luck.

This bias can lead to inaccurate perceptions of the motives of others. When this happens, cooperation can be reduced and result in poor, even unjust, decisions.

■ ■ ■

The brain uses these kinds of automatic shortcuts and others in routine forms of decision making, particularly when it is operating in everyday mode. Sometimes the resulting decisions are not impaired, but these shortcuts are the source of many mistakes in judgment. This is especially true in complex environments where shortcuts and oversimplification can be troublesome.

Thinking in premium mode can reduce the problems caused by automatic biases. And knowledge of the shortcuts themselves can help humans spot potential trouble spots where their use would be especially ineffective. Inserting mental reminders seems to interrupt the flow of automatic shortcuts. For example, the reminder to "always check the evidence" is useful to control the confirmation bias.

■ ■ ■

The human brain is the key to understanding how humans have become the dominant species on Earth—not physical size, strength, agility, or any other physical characteristic. It's not just the physical attributes of the brain that are important. The physiological components work together in unexpected ways to make humans capable of exceptional behavior.

First, the senses inform the brain about conditions in the outside world to which it has no direct access. These senses, though finely tuned to the original, natural environment occupied by humans for millennia, take some shortcuts that produce perception errors. These errors, in turn, contribute to errors in judgment, which are amplified by the complex conditions of the modern world.

Second, the brain's intelligence is a key part of the human success story. Intelligence has made possible the creation of an ever expanding knowledge base and a level of complex problem solving never before seen in the animal kingdom.

Third, evolution has equipped the brain with two operating modes, one that is efficient but error prone, and the other that provides the capacity for reasoned problem solving. Switching modes at the right time is an ongoing challenge for humans.

Fourth, as another layer of complexity, the brain is divided into loosely cooperating cognitive modules that compete with each other rather than working together smoothly. Only a keen self-awareness and mental discipline can successfully coordinate these competing elements of thought.

Lastly, the brain has some inherent biases that it uses as defaults when making decisions. These shortcuts, shaped by evolution, reduce processing time and are honed for the problems typically encountered when humans lived in the wild. However, they are not especially effective for problem solving more complex situations like those found in the modern world.

The brain, which is the foundation of human exceptionalism, is powerful, but in some important ways fallible. Without self-awareness and the use of some thinking strategies that counteract routine processing, the human brain can make significant errors in judgment. But the picture of human behavior is not yet complete. Other forces are also at work.

INHERITED IMPULSES

Humans aren't born with a blank slate of behavioral options. Their genetic codes push the development of behavior in certain directions as already introduced in the discussion of their vocalizations and mating habits. A built-in genetic template facilitates spoken language. And the urge to engage in sexual activity is a very powerful, genetically-inspired motivation, even when reproduction is not the desired outcome. But, unlike other animals, humans have no rigid behavioral instincts governing interactions with the environment—that is, specific behaviors that are automatically triggered by specific events in the outside world.

Inherited Impulses	
1	Social
2	Tribal
3	Territorial
4	Hierarchical
5	Patriarchal
6	Communicative
7	Cooperative
8	Emotional
9	Aggressive
10	Moralistic
11	Imaginative
12	Religious
13	Adaptive
14	Willful

Figure 9-5. Impulses

This section will bring attention to more examples of behavioral impulses—genetics-based hardwiring in the brain that channels human behavior in a general direction. Though templates promote a range of behaviors, culture and personal experience shape the final form of the behavior that is expressed by an individual.

While there are many and varied hardwired impulses affecting humans, the focus here will be on a subset of impulses that has a very great impact both on individuals and social groups (Figure 9-5).

Much of human behavior is driven by these impulses. They reflect a long evolutionary history where they were shaped by natural selection over thousands of generations, leading to the current version of the human species. [34]

Social

Humans seek out and want to be in the company of other humans. They generally live in close proximity, they work together, they socialize together, and they play together. They build facilities like stadiums that will hold thousands of them at the same time. A few hundred will climb aboard an aircraft and fly together for hours. Several million will congregate in the same city. At the present time, the largest city on Earth, Tokyo, Japan, has a population of over thirty-eight million. Humans not only tolerate living in proximity to other humans, but they actively seek out other members of their species to interact with on a regular basis.

Tribal

The tribal unit has been the center of human life from well before the start of the migration from Africa. The core of the tribe is the family unit, generally including grandparents (maternal and paternal), parents, and their children (brothers and sisters). This lineage is often expanded to include aunts and uncles, nieces and nephews, first cousins and even second cousins. The tribe also typically includes the families of the husbands and wives that marry into the group. The bonds within this tribe are typically exceptionally strong.

But tribal sentiments may not be limited just to family members. Humans like to form or join groups of many kinds that are tribal

---

[34] Humans do have many, internal processes that respond to external stimulation but are part of the autonomic nervous system. The regular contraction of the heart muscle and frequent respiration are good examples. These automatic physiological responses require no conscious effort and are controlled by genetically determined processes.

extensions. They may form tribal attachments to members of their local community, their religious congregations, their political parties, their sports teams, their ethnic groups, and even to their nationalities, even though nationalism is mostly arbitrary.

Humans are extraordinary in their commitments to these tribal groups, and equally extraordinary in their disregard for those who are not members of their tribe-like groups. Humans have a hard-wired distrust of other humans that are not within one of their tribal affiliations.

Territorial

Personal space is important to humans. When humans lived in the wild, hunting and gathering grounds were defined and defended from other tribal groups. In more recent times, humans have implemented extensive systems of property rights that define personal territories. This might range from private ownership of thousands of acres of ranch land, to a small condominium on the 74th floor of a high-rise building in a large city. What these examples have in common, along with all other property owners, is a willingness to vigorously defend their property rights and the fundamental belief that they are entitled to their own piece of territory.

Though humans have tried a number of communal living arrangements of various types, they have not proved sustainable, in part because of the territorial impulse. On the other hand, wars—a particularly distinctive trademark of humans—are fought on a regular basis to expand territory and gain control of resources. The desire for personal and collective territories is strong.

Hierarchical

Human groups have always been organized in ranks with individuals having different responsibilities and privileges. Everywhere you look there are presidents, prime ministers, CEOs, dictators, kings and queens, tribal chiefs, popes, generals and heads of households. Groups expect leadership and will arrange for it because of the impulse for hierarchy.

In addition, humans go out of their way to find and recognize those who are good at doing something, often regardless of the social value. They have all sorts of sports contests, (soccer, beach volley ball, track and field, softball, handball, baseball, surfboarding, basketball, tennis, wrestling, jai alai, etc.), musical competitions, movie awards, poker playing championships, pie eating contests, top student awards, science research awards, dog breeding competitions, and marble tournaments, to name a few. These contests are driven in part by the hierarchy impulse, where humans naturally assume that individuals will be ranked and rated in their social groups.

Wealth is a very common basis for establishing a hierarchy, where the wealthy are accorded more status and prestige than those who are not. All manner of status symbols are acquired and displayed to reinforce social rank. These vary from culture to culture, but generally include fine clothing; jewelry; works of art; large and lavishly decorated dwellings (by local standards); consumption of expensive foods and beverages (by local standards); buying large numbers of anything considered valuable, such as dairy cows or automobiles; and engaging in conspicuous leisure time activities like expensive vacations to exotic destinations (by local standards).

Humans are extremely status conscious and expend substantial effort to elevate their rankings in the various groups of which they are members.

Patriarchal

Patriarchy is the impulse to organize social relationships to reflect male dominance. This has been a common pattern throughout human history and is still the primary organizer of social relationships today. As observed in the chapter on mating habits, the patriarchal impulse is noticeably present in pair bonding. Husbands and wives worldwide rarely share equal status in their relationships, though patriarchal privilege is not always strongly expressed in all cultures.

Other social relationships also show a strong preference for male influence. Political, business, military, and religious leaders are all generally males, though there is no obvious reason for this based on competence. Generally older males have the highest status in organizations, even though they may be well past their peak physical and mental powers.

It has only been in the last fifty years or so that the role of patriarchy has been challenged to any significant degree, especially in more wealthy cultures. As with some other hard-wired impulses, the tendency to grant males special status makes little sense in the modern world. Their roles as effective hunters and defenders of the tribe are largely irrelevant today. There is a growing readiness among at least some humans to mute the impact of this impulse.

Communicative

Humans are prolific communicators. First and foremost, they love to talk to each other, to gossip about the lives of their tribal members, to tell stories about the past, to describe how to perform tasks, and to discuss plans for the future. They seem to have an endless capacity for this activity. It's an impulse that really lubricates their social relationships. In fact, for the long period of living in the wild, talking was the only means of communication.

Humans use communications to achieve a variety of purposes, from sharing information to promoting deceptions—exaggerations or outright falsehoods intended to persuade or fool others into accepting an assertion or into taking a course of action. Deceptive communication is common and presents humans with a difficult interpersonal problem—detecting and gauging the magnitude of lies. Communications with new acquaintances, in particular, are often subject to scrutiny until a reputation for truthfulness is established.

With the invention of writing, the ability to communicate changed fundamentally. No longer did one human have to be in the same place as another to communicate. Communication was freed from constraints of time and place. Next, only about five hundred years ago, humans invented books to more easily share communications.

Of course, writing and reading took a long time to spread through all human populations. But reading is now a dominant means of communication for humans worldwide (about eighty-five percent of humans are literate in their native language). Even more recently, in parts of the world, electronic means of communication like television, email, and social media have created even more communication options that humans have quickly adopted. For instance, there are around 1.5 billion people around the world communicating via a computer application called Facebook.

The impulse to communicate has been and continues to be a major driver of human technological evolution. Once humans found a way to share information with each other on a broad scale, innovation really took off. After writing was invented, knowledge accumulation greatly increased. One generation could build on the work of the previous one without having to rediscover or reinvent past innovations.

Though not all communications are of equal importance (in fact most appear to be trivial), the communication impulse has been one of the key drivers contributing to human dominance.

Cooperative

Cooperation is another hallmark of humans. They have an exceptional ability to work together, even in circumstances where they don't communicate directly or even know each other. This has been true since the beginning of human history when teams initially formed hunting parties. In the modern world, cooperation is broad and complex, making it possible to undertake a huge range of sophisticated activities.

Commercial air transportation offers a good example. Aircraft are designed, meticulously built, and, once in service, maintained according to rigorous specifications; flights are booked and paid for using electronic communications networks; facilities are constructed and operated to coordinate the departures and arrivals of passengers and planes; pilots navigate using a satellite-based global positioning system; and computers track everything from schedule changes to the location of luggage. Literally thousands of humans are or have been involved in making a single flight on an airplane possible.[35]

Underlying this kind of cooperation, which is found in every sphere of human activity, is a fundamental trust that other humans will participate when needed to make all the pieces work together. Humans have an exceptional ability to make very complex systems work effectively through very long sequences of commitment over long periods of time. Trust and the willingness to cooperate have been, and continue to be, essential for continued human success.

To facilitate cooperation a number of cultural supports have been devised, such as specialized labor roles, work schedules, work rules,

---

[35] Another common example of cooperation is citizenship, where people who live in political jurisdictions contribute financial resources (taxes and fees) for government services, some of which may have no direct impact on them. For instance, a government might use collected revenue to provide foreign aid to citizens of another country for humanitarian purposes. While there may be some degree of coercion and unhappiness associated with these contributions to governments, humans have a widespread sense that citizenship comes with obligations and are willing (within limits) to contribute to the common projects.

the formation of work groups with hierarchical management, regulations and contracts, and, perhaps of greatest importance, standards.

Some of the most important of these include methods of exchange (money), ways of keeping time (clocks), ways of uniformly describing objects (weights and measures), and ways of communicating over significant distances (telecommunications). The creation, promotion, and wide-scale use of standards allow humans to drastically expand cooperation through time and space.

While cooperation has been an incredibly important part of human social life, it sometimes breaks down, particularly under the influence of tribal, cultural, religious, and language differences, which have at times been divisive enough to even trigger warfare. There are many examples of failed cooperative efforts, a reminder that cooperation is an impulse that needs support to be maintained and strengthened.

Emotional

Humans are emotional, perhaps exceptionally so. An emotion is a state of mind that seems to arise spontaneously in the human psyche, often accompanied by physical expressions like smiles, tears, or increased alertness. All kinds of circumstances evoke an emotion, including aspects of the outside environment (especially interactions with other humans) as well as internal mental processes, including dreams. Though most emotional responses are clearly shaped by experience, some basic responses have a genetic origin.

The brain's emotion modules are based within the oldest parts of the human brain. They have evolved over a very long period of time and were designed, like all the other impulses, to promote survival. For instance, humans have a generalized fear of snakes shaped by countless encounters with them living in the wild. Avoidance of snakes had a clear survival benefit and became a hardwired aversion.

Circumstances that evoke emotions like happiness, sadness, anger, fear, or anxiety have been shaped by long human experience. For instance, humans associate positive emotions with their affiliations with others, in tribal groups that dominated the social landscape for tens of thousands of years. Yet tribal allegiances can cause significant cooperation problems in the modern world where the nature of social relationships are more varied. Programmed emotional responses can be detrimental. Self-reflection is sometimes needed to keep an immediate emotional response in perspective.

Humans are subject to emotional instability. Stress, for example, is a physiological response to difficult or complex circumstances that can be debilitating if the response is severe or prolonged. But stress is a chronic aspect of the human condition, so most humans will experience it and manage it in some form, such as through relaxation techniques.

Over the course of their lifetimes, around forty percent of humans will experience short- or long-term emotional dysfunctions so severe that they significantly interfere with the activities of daily life and require active intervention by other humans.

Interestingly, humans go out of their way to evoke emotions. They have created all kinds of entertainments like music, song, dance, written stories, movies, and comedy clubs to trigger emotional responses. They also use various community ceremonies like weddings, funerals, religious services, and holidays, specifically for the emotional impact that they cause.

Though emotional impulses are genetic in origin they are strongly influenced by learning. For instance, designating a specific day on a calendar as a holiday has no inherent emotional significance. The cultural meanings and appropriate emotional responses associated with such an event have to be learned and reinforced, often through shared rituals. A holiday like Thanksgiving, celebrated in various (but far from all) countries, provides an opportunity to give thanks for a successful harvest, reflecting an earlier time when harvests were less certain and the solicitation of support from supernatural forces was common. Associated customs like a day off from labor, the assembly of tribal or clan members, and the preparation of a large meal are typically employed to evoke a positive, shared emotional event.

For humans, emotions are constant companions. Anything they do is tinged with an emotional component of varying intensity. Emotions are ancient, strong, pervasive, and the source of great pleasures. But they are also a source of profound misdirection. As a result, human behavior influenced by an emotional response can be unpredictable and counterproductive. One of the challenges facing humans is harnessing emotional impulses in a world with constantly changing conditions.

Aggressive

Humans are not always peaceful in their interactions with each other. In the right circumstances, they can be aggressive both mentally and physically, and will even injure or kill other humans with seemingly little provocation. Aggression takes many forms, both individually and collectively.

From the beginning of human history, groups of humans have aggressively defended hunting and gathering territories with the same ferocity that they displayed in cooperatively hunting large game. In groups organized around tribal affiliations, they have also used violence to expand territories and obtain resources from others. Their history is regularly punctuated with wars, both small and large.

The tribal impulse combines with aggression tendencies to channel violence toward other groups. Humans have the ability to easily distance themselves from others with whom they are not affiliated, and to stereotype out-groups as enemies who deserve harsh treatment. They have mostly unsuccessfully struggled to control the expression of this collective impulse. And the invention of ever more lethal killing technologies has only heightened the concern about managing aggression.

Humans, especially males, will display aggression in varying degrees, up to and including the killing of others, sometimes for even minor affronts. Domestic violence, gang warfare, criminal enterprises, political protesters, and the disenfranchised and deranged are all examples of individuals and groups that can be motivated to act out aggressively.

Though this impulse is strong and pervasive, there is evidence that the rate of violence has diminished over the last thousand years. Several factors, including the broader application of the rule of law, the globalization of commerce, and the societal adoption of feminine values likely have all contributed to this outcome.

In addition, cultural redirections of aggression have become more common and popular. For instance, movies and books portraying violence are common and are thought to provide some relief from aggressive tensions. This is also the case with organized sports, where a wide range of activities—from football to cage fighting—allow the release of aggression under relatively controlled circumstances. The vicarious participation of spectators allows for a release of pent up aggressiveness.

It is also possible that lethal wars over the last several hundred years reduced the population of the most aggressive young males before they had a chance to reproduce, thus eliminating some of the most aggressive genes from the human gene pool.

Moral

A basic moral code is built into human genes, guiding the development of relationships with others. One of these hardwired moral principles is to avoid intentionally harming other humans (tempering innate aggressiveness). But this moral sense is not universal. Instead it is contextual and generally applies mostly to humans that are members of the same (tribal) group. Humans who are not in the group, especially if they are perceived as threats or appear and behave differently, may not be included in the prohibition.

Another important moral principle is reciprocity—returning a favor for one rendered by another human. For example, if an individual asks another person to help with a project, like moving a heavy object, an expectation is established that the person seeking the favor will, at some time in the future, willingly lend assistance of a similar magnitude to the helper. The expectation for reciprocity is central to human social relationships and is a mechanism that underlies effective cooperation.

Altruism, the willingness to sacrifice some personal benefit for a greater social good, is another hardwired moral impulse. It strengthens group cohesion and success. This principal applies most strongly within a specific (tribal) group, and is especially strong in families where one relative may even risk death to protect another close family member. Individuals will generally only perform altruistic deeds consistently within the confines of the group setting. As a consequence, altruism, which is an ally of cooperation, unfortunately does not have a broad native sphere of application.

Humans are acutely attuned to cheating, in social relationships and in the distribution of resources. Free riders, those who use group resources without contributing their fair share, are identified and typically sanctioned with the goal of getting them to participate fairly in the future. If cheating behavior is persistent, an offender may be permanently banished. Long-term group (tribal) success depends on fair contributions from all members.

Building on the basic, hardwired moral principles, humans have developed very elaborate systems for classifying behaviors as either right or wrong, and then establishing forms of reward and punishment to promote compliance. These classification systems started as religious codes that put a supernatural god in the role of enforcer— promising justice in the next life if it was not available in this one. More recently, moral codes have been established through secular means, including the development of laws, enforcement mechanisms, processes for determining innocence or guilt, and penal systems designed to segregate the most serious offenders.

Though contemporary moral codes have arisen from the same genetic wellspring, they differ widely, having evolved like other features of culture, reflecting different local conditions. As a result, social norms vary greatly, making wide-scale cooperation more challenging from cultural jurisdiction to jurisdiction. Often the differences among codes can seem irrelevant or arbitrary in a modern context. For instance, in one culture women may cast votes in an election of leaders, while in another they can't.

Moral codes, especially those based on religious traditions, can be slow to adapt to changing social conditions, thus sometimes retaining rules that have been obsolete for generations.[36] Secular moral codes, though often an incomplete patchwork, seem better suited to the modern world because, unlike religion-based systems that rely on supernatural authority, they are intended to be modified as social conditions change.

Imaginative

Humans have vivid imaginations that they constantly use to envision new concepts and relationships. For instance, they have imagined characters like blood–sucking vampires, talking animals of all kinds, and super-heroes with exceptional abilities. They have also invented relationships like horoscopes to predict the future, magical spells that

---

[36] Rules from the written Jewish religious literature (also subsequently adopted as part of the Christian tradition) written around 2,500 BP: (1) Don't wear clothes made with more than one fabric. (2) Psychics, wizards, and so on are to be stoned to death. (3) Don't eat shellfish. (4) Don't make graven images. For literalists, these rules are still in force because of their supposedly divine origins.

are supposed to cure disease, and a wide variety of superstitions that purport to link ritual behaviors with specific effects.

This impulse is largely a consequence of language, the flexible symbol system that offers nearly infinite possibilities for conveying meaning. But their imaginations are not limited to language alone. Many mediums provide an opportunity for expressing and sharing novel ideas. Expressions can range from hyper-realistic forms, like a meticulously crafted sculpture of an animal, to highly abstract ones, such as splatters of paint spread across a canvas. Millions of humans around the planet are employed as artists to use their creative imaginations in fields as diverse as dance, musical performance, crafts production, novel writing, acting, sculpture and graphic design.

But imagination goes well beyond the realms of entertainment and esthetic experience. It is a key component of the most powerful knowledge production system yet invented: science. With imagination, scientists are able to express new discoveries in understandable ways, often linking new ideas with ideas that are already known. For instance, as the idea of an atom was being formulated a century ago, its structure was compared to that of a solar system, an idea that had already been established. Such metaphorical thinking is fundamental to the scientific enterprise and facilitates rapid, clear communication with others. Human knowledge has advanced rapidly through the clever use of imaginative thinking.

Yet, many problems arise from imaginative thinking. The boundary between the real and the imaginary is often blurred. All too frequently humans behave as if imaginary ideas were real, leading to poor decisions and outcomes. For instance, the (imaginary) belief that a special diet can cure cancer could cause an individual to delay a more proven form of medical treatment, resulting in an early or unnecessary death. Or an unhappy person might seek advice from a person claiming (imaginary) psychic powers instead of pursuing a more evidence-based form of psychological treatment. Or a person might pray to an (imaginary) supernatural being to resolve a conflict rather than engage with a form of mediation.

The imaginative impulse needs to be channeled and disciplined to ensure that fact and fiction remain clearly separate from each other (at least as much as possible). The tools of critical thinking, such as seeking and verifying evidence, developing and applying relevant criteria, working systematically toward a solution, and evaluating alternatives are all effective foils for countering imaginary beliefs.

Religious

One of the strongest human impulses is the urge to be religious. That is, to believe that supernatural forces of one kind or another are at work influencing the lives of humans and that, through various rituals, these forces can be harnessed for personal and group benefit. This impulse arises from a normal psychological process, the routine search for the causes of events in daily life.

The capability to find cause-and-effect relationships, to describe them with language, and to pass them on from generation to generation has been essential to human success. But the process for finding cause-and-effect relationships is difficult and subject to significant errors. One important type of error comes from the human bias to attribute actions to supernatural forces. In the absence of good information to explain an event, humans will use their imaginations to invent possible causes.

Vivid imaginations find supernatural causes all too easily in random, unconnected events. This tendency is a kind of built-in cognitive malfunction widely shared by humans. In fact, it is so common that it is perceived to be the normal state. Humans with weak or no religious impulse are considered abnormal. In reality, since there are no supernatural forces at work, all such proposed relationships are always incorrect. Humans are faced only with natural forces, however awe inspiring, interesting, and mysterious as they may be.

The basic religious impulse is very general, much like the impulse to learn spoken language. The exact form it takes is dependent on local culture. As there are thousands of languages, so there are thousands of religions, all of which are the product of cultural evolution within separate populations spread all over the planet, sometimes acting over millennia. In its most common form, religion is a group activity with shared beliefs and rituals. As a shared system, it has been and continues to work to increase group cohesion—but generally only within the group sharing the same supernatural beliefs.

The community of believers and their religious stories may provide emotional support for some practitioners as they struggle with the uncertainties of life and mortality. But, otherwise, religious practice is ineffective in affecting the course of real events. Rather, great time, energy, and resources have been and continue to be unproductively invested in the practice of religions. And, at times, religion in its collective expression even acts as a significant catalyst for conflict among human groups.

The religious impulse is normally expressed in human behavior but it is not inevitable. Because it's the result of a cognitive malfunction, it needs to be carefully redirected or minimized to avoid decision-making errors of one kind or another. The enormous energy currently devoted to religious practice might be better invested in other effective means of personal improvement (e.g., stress management or regular exercise) and collective efforts to enhance social welfare (e.g., philanthropy or political action).

Adaptive

Humans are curious; they like to explore the unknown and are quick to adapt to new circumstances. They are not passive consumers of the status quo. This adaptive impulse was clearly evident from the time they started the migration out of Africa, radiating around the planet and filling every ecological niche. They developed tools and technologies that made it possible not only to survive in new environments, but to thrive. Their history is one of continuous and accelerating cultural and technological innovation.

With the invention of the scientific method, this underlying impulse to explore and adapt to diverse environments gained enormous new power. The scope and range of their adaptations have become extraordinary, including the foods they eat (domesticated plants and animals), their variety of shelters, their sophisticated tools, their means of industrial production, their forms of transportation, and their networks of electronic communications, citing just a few examples. Now, they not only adapt effectively to new conditions, they can modify their environments to suit their (generally short-term) goals. They are now even making changes on a planetary scale (though tinkering with climate, for instance, is more accidental than planned).

From a strictly human perspective, their strong, adaptive impulse has been extraordinarily successful. But it's not been beneficial to many other plant and animal species with which humans have shared ecosystems. As humans colonized the planet, they hunted and gathered other species relentlessly, contributing to many extinctions, particularly of large land mammals and birds they encountered along the way. Ground sloths, mastodons, cave bears, moa, and dodos were among the species known to have been driven to extinction in association with the arrival of humans into their native territories. (To be fair, climate changes over the course of human history may have played a supporting role in reducing some populations.) Over the last fifty thousand years, more than one hundred genera of large land mammals alone have gone extinct.

The habitat pressures exerted by humans continue to endanger other species. Though originally this pressure was experienced primarily as predation, today habitat destruction is playing a very large role in affecting populations of other species. Humans are sometimes not even consciously aware of many of their impacts on the environment.[37] But wholesale changes to the web of life on the planet will eventually create problems for the human species as well. The adaptive impulse needs to be tempered with a sense of environmental stewardship to ensure that the planet remains habitable.

Willful

Humans are willful, having an impulse to persist in the pursuit of goals. This reflects their long reliance on the hunting and gathering lifestyle, when persistent effort on a daily basis was required to obtain adequate supplies of food. The hunting of big game animals illustrates this very well. Humans rarely brought down a large animal with a single spear thrust, so hunting involved a lot of running after wounded prey, quite often for hours over difficult terrain. Hunting, therefore, generally required difficult, sustained effort. Those who didn't persist in the hunt, didn't eat.

Later, after the invention of agriculture, humans planted crops that needed tending over a whole growing season. Attaining a good harvest required sustained effort (and a fair amount of good luck). Farmers had to tend to their crops through a regular routine over weeks and months, and those that were most persistent, in general, were more successful.

In recent times, human goals have become more diverse, but the ancient impulse to persist remains. The pursuit of a goal can be completely independent of the nature of the goal itself. Goals can

---

[37] As one example, humans, worldwide, produce around three trillion pounds of garbage a year, with much of this concentrated in and around urban areas. More than half of the waste material is non-biodegradable. Yet among most consumers, the massive accumulation of waste and its significant environmental impacts receives little notice.

support positive personal and social outcomes, like pursuing a lengthy formal education, or negative ones, like robbing a bank or compulsive gambling. Once humans identify goals, they tend to persist in efforts to achieve them. All that's required to motivate persistence is that the outcome be meaningful to the individual involved.

In general, humans don't like being told what to do or that their goals are unrealistic or counterproductive, though they will tolerate this to varying degrees based on the status of the person delivering the message. For instance, an individual may become convinced, despite advice from others and a lack of clinical evidence, that a form of expensive therapy may solve a health problem. Feedback that is critical of a planned course of action is rarely received well, typically eliciting defensiveness and even hostility. When interacting with humans, it's wise to pay attention to their goals and be mindful of the resistance to change that will be encountered once a strong emotional attachment has been firmly established.

Willfulness applies to the pursuit of collective goals as well. Once a human group reaches consensus about achieving a goal, the group can be extraordinarily persistent in pursuing it. And just as with individuals, goals can have positive or negative consequences. For instance, a group might set a collective goal of protecting its most vulnerable members or, conversely, might set a goal of repressing them. In another case, a group might decide to attempt to resolve a resource dispute through negotiation and compromise, or conversely, might launch an attack resulting in substantial injury and death on both sides. Willfulness, like other impulses, is flexible, supporting both positive and negative goals, and, like other impulses, must be channeled to produce beneficial personal or collective effects.

■ ■ ■

Genetically-coded human impulses guide the development of human behavior. These impulses are varied and interact with each other in interesting ways. For instance, the religious impulse integrates with and reinforces the tribal, hierarchical and patriarchal impulses.

It is also easy to see how the impulses lead to specific individual and collective behaviors that form common themes throughout human history. The tribal, territorial, and aggressive impulses have frequently contributed (and still contribute) to conflict between individuals and groups. On the other hand, the social, cooperative, and imaginative impulses create the conditions for the invention and spread of new innovations.

Not all impulses have the same behavioral trajectories. They may be mutually reinforcing, unconnected to each other, or even incompatible. For instance, the territorial and cooperative impulses can push behavior in contradictory directions, while territorial and tribal impulses often reinforce each other. This makes sense given that impulses arose somewhat independently as adaptations to the variety of human experience.

The impulses are the product of deep evolutionary processes shaped by historical conditions, many of which are no longer relevant in the modern world. Patriarchy is a good example. Not all expressions of impulses are beneficial in the modern world. Fortunately, while impulses may guide the development of behavior, they don't rigidly determine its final form. By selectively strengthening some impulses and diminishing or re-directing others through a disciplined program of learning, humans have the capacity to change the effects of impulses on their behavior.

LEARNED BEHAVIOR

Humans start learning while they are still in the womb and continue learning throughout their lifetimes. Learning means acquiring relatively long-term changes in behavior that result from interactions with the environment. Here are a range of simple examples of learned behaviors: being able to identify a rabbit, solving a differential equation, sweeping a floor, driving a car, fearing dogs, singing a lullaby, identifying a safe mushroom, getting along with a sibling, always wearing a lucky hat to a local team's soccer game, feeling stressed at work, cooking an octopus, writing a letter to the editor, and kissing a potential mate. Yes, humans have to learn how to do all these things. And this is just a miniscule sample of the very large repertoire of behaviors a typical human acquires.

Humans get all kinds of feedback, both positive and negative, as they actively interact with the world around them. These interactions result in changes in behavior that are cumulative. Thus, as humans get older, their behaviors generally become increasingly more complex and better adapted to their surroundings (though plateauing and even some regression are not uncommon).

Collective Knowledge Base

Without prescriptive instincts, humans rely completely on learning to acquire the knowledge they need to survive and prosper. Given that the total human knowledge base has grown dramatically and that societies have become very complex, the role of learning has become supremely important.

Through the vast majority of human history, information was passed from one generation to the next orally, and it focused primarily on how things were presumably related to each other (folk knowledge) and how to perform tasks (craft knowledge). Examples of folk knowledge from the days of living in the wild include knowing: where game animals liked to congregate, which berries were edible, sources of fresh water, whether a stranger meant harm, and the moods of a local deity. Examples of craft knowledge include knowing how to: track a deer, throw a clay pot, cook a tough root, tan a hide, make a spear point, or prepare for a change in the seasons.

From the start of human history, knowledge that accumulated through collective experience continuously increased in scope and complexity, though initially access to the whole body of knowledge was very limited. Until only very recently, language differences and geographic isolation significantly constrained the spread of new knowledge.

With the invention of writing and the eventual mass production of books, collective knowledge became more widely available. But it was not until the invention of the scientific method, about five hundred years ago, that the knowledge base began to expand at a much higher rate. At the same time, often-unreliable folk knowledge began to be replaced with empirical knowledge that more accurately described real world causes and effects.

Using this science-based knowledge, humans were also able to go beyond traditional craft methods of innovation and invent new technologies by applying scientific principles. For example, humans used knowledge of physics principles to invent and then perfect a mechanical steam engine in the nineteenth century that ushered in an industrial revolution. This kind of theoretical and technical knowledge has only recently exploded across all domains of human activity. Computers, software, and networks have further transformed the creation and distribution of new knowledge, though these innovations are not yet available to most people on the planet.

Though humans share a common collective knowledge base, they must learn about it individually, generation after generation. Fortunately, they are generally able learners and older humans have made arrangements to support the transfer of knowledge to their offspring.

Structure of Individual Learning

Across their lifespans, individuals learn in different contexts, at different rates, and to different levels of attainment. Early learning, from birth to around age five, is centered within the family where young children acquire many kinds of useful knowledge and skills through mostly unstructured personal experience, including play. This process is called socialization, and, though it changes character over time, it literally continues as a mode of learning for the rest of an individual's lifetime as a consequence of ongoing personal experiences. Socialization is the dominate mode of learning until formal instruction is introduced, usually around age five or six.

At this point, children are generally required to participate in organized instructional activities—they enter a period of compulsory education. Most societies around the world generally require the young to congregate together (in schools) for a few hours most days where teachers provide instruction. The age at which required instruction begins and its duration varies a bit across societies, but there is a near universal acknowledgement that formal instruction for offspring is needed and desirable.

This reliance on formal education is another aspect of humans that is unique in the animal kingdom. Adult humans determine what should be learned, and provide specific experiences for their young to support the acquisition of the desired knowledge and skills. No other species devotes so much time and energy to the behavioral development of their young.

Primary Education. The first period of formal instruction is referred to as primary education and extends from about age five or six until about age eleven or twelve, a total of six or seven years. At present, around ninety percent of all children in this age range worldwide attend school. Though this may seem like a high rate of participation, it means that more than fifty million school age children are not receiving formal education. Given the importance of formal learning, this level of nonparticipation has significant negative consequences for those affected.

The program of instruction (the curriculum) in primary schools has a few main common targets or goals, referring to the concepts and skills students are expected to learn.

Literacy includes developing proficiency in reading, writing, speaking, and listening in at least an individual's native language. Of these, speaking and listening are skills that are acquired quickly and easily as a result of genetic templates that support them. Oral language has deep roots in human evolutionary history. Because of the ease with which oral language is acquired, relatively little formal education effort is devoted to it, unless communication problems are identified.

On the other hand, substantial time and effort must be devoted to developing reading and writing proficiency, in part, because these skills lack genetic templates. Writing, for instance, has been such a recent human innovation that evolution has not had an opportunity to shape the genome to support its easy acquisition and use. As a consequence, skill levels vary greatly. The central focus of writing instruction is composition. The primary modes are exposition or persuasion, where the writer attempts to explain an idea or procedure, or to convince a reader of the merits of a proposal. Humans highly value clear writing and fluency with conventions (spelling, punctuation, grammar).

The innovation of writing generated the need to be able to read; to be able to independently make sense of abstract visual symbols. Reading instruction focuses on the comprehension of texts of increasing complexity. This skill supports learning of other subjects because of the widespread use of textbooks. Reading is also important in performing many tasks that rely heavily on written instructions. Vocabulary development is another key feature of instruction, as reading vocabulary can be significantly larger than spoken vocabulary.

In many localities, a goal of education is to learn more than one language. Sometimes, this is almost a necessity, as more than one language may be spoken in a local community. At other times, learning another language may be part of a cultural expectation for being well-educated, even though the second language may be rarely used. There are presently no universal expectations for learning a specific second language, though learning English is very common due to its widespread use in commerce, education, scientific research, and entertainment. Sometimes, the acquisition of a second language does not begin until after the completion of primary education.

Humans are not naturally proficient with mathematics. In the wild, they had no need to perform any complicated calculations. In fact, they were generally only fluent processing quantities up to about eight. Since the invention of and subsequent broad application of mathematics, humans have come to rely heavily on mathematical ideas. At present, general adult competence includes mastery of basic mathematical concepts, operations, and calculating tools.

The study of arithmetic—knowledge of the properties and manipulation of numbers—begins at the outset and continues throughout primary education. Addition, subtraction, multiplication, and division using whole numbers, fractions, and decimals, form the core of instruction. In addition, concrete aspects of geometric forms are also woven into instruction.

Through methodical efforts, humans have come to understand a great deal about the natural world. This includes the natural world's scope, its history, the way it's structured, and how its component parts work. It's a very large, complex, still incomplete, and not fully integrated knowledge base that is of central importance to modern human affairs.

It is a knowledge base that is relatively new, mostly discovered within just the last two hundred years through scientific research and theory building. It has extensively replaced previous human conceptions of the natural world, though there has periodically been some resistance to some of the findings that have emerged that conflict with folkways.

In primary education, students are introduced to concrete scientific ideas as they apply to everyday life. For instance, natural history is commonly studied, where students are introduced to plants and animals and physical features of the environment, ranging from earth materials to weather. Emphasis is often on observation and classification skills. By the end of primary education, children are expected to understand that all events in the natural world have scientific explanations, even if the details are not yet fully understood.

Primary education also typically includes instruction in cultural expectations and practices ranging from learning how to participate in the local form of government, to rules for engaging in economic activities, to a review of cultural history (most often told from the ethnocentric point of view of the local tribe). In addition, cultural forms of esthetic expression like art and music may be introduced and developed. In some societies, religious practices may also be taught as part of the program of studies in primary education.

Secondary Education. After primary education is complete, some students continue formal learning by enrolling in a secondary school, which may or may not be compulsory. Typically, programs of study at this level continue on for another six years, from about age twelve to age eighteen. Significantly fewer students complete a full secondary education program—perhaps around forty percent of the worldwide population.

The program of studies at the secondary level is generally more differentiated, with instruction offered in different courses provided by specialized teachers. This specialization occurs because the subject matter becomes more complex, requiring teachers to have more in-depth knowledge.

Instruction continues in literacy with an emphasis on reading comprehension. The study of literature (fiction) is often used to achieve this goal, though the comprehension of non-fiction sources, like instruction manuals, are increasingly used because of their relevance for adult performance. Writing instruction emphasizes composition of more sophisticated explanatory or persuasive works, though creative (fictional) writing is also sometimes the focus of instruction.

Mastery of arithmetic continues as a main emphasis of mathematics instruction. In later secondary education, there is a shift for most students to more abstract mathematics, beginning with algebra and advancing from there to increasingly challenging topics, often with calculus viewed as the capstone course. Topics in geometry, statistics, and probability are also typically included in the course of study.

Secondary science instruction focuses on more specific bodies of knowledge such as biology, physics, chemistry, and the earth sciences. Content becomes increasingly abstract and mathematical tools are introduced and developed as a way of expressing scientific principles. Students diverge in the courses they take, with some students specializing while others pursue more basic concepts and skills.

It is typical for some courses in history and geography to also be required in secondary school. These typically continue to present content from a rather ethnocentric perspective and focus primarily on relatively recent historical events covering no more than the last few thousand years. Often courses in art, music, personal finance, vocational skills, and physical education are offered and sometimes even required to varying degrees. In some schools, religious ideas and practices continue to be taught.

There is substantial variation in the course of studies pursued by secondary school students, though students graduate with essentially the same credential, a high school diploma, for which there are no objective achievement standards. Participation in compulsory education normally ends with the onset of adulthood, in the range of sixteen to eighteen years of age.

Higher Education. After the completion of secondary education, young adults may voluntarily pursue additional formal education. The motives for this are generally economic, as many adult employment options are in specialized fields that command higher compensation than manual or semi-skilled occupations.

As workplace requirements grow more complex and specialization continues to increase, particularly in industrialized societies, there is a growing awareness that the current scope and duration of compulsory education may provide insufficient preparation. As a consequence, after graduating from a secondary school, some students continue their formal education by enrolling in two-year certification programs in regional community colleges or trade schools that provide further preparation for more specialized careers.

Other students voluntarily apply to and are selected for—usually on the basis of demonstrated academic merit—continued learning in colleges and universities that charge fees for their services. Once admitted, students move from local schools that provided compulsory education to schools delivering more advanced programs of study, sometimes far removed from their childhood homes.[38]

Higher education may continue for several years as students develop specialized concepts and skills through participation in a sequence of related classes and regular achievement testing. As a result of successfully completing courses of study, various kinds of certifications are granted that signify different specializations and levels

---

[38] On a worldwide basis, perhaps fifteen to twenty percent of students have the cognitive ability to succeed with a program of rigorous academic study.

of accomplishment. Aside from pursuing economic and educational goals, participation in higher education also has significance for social status. It is another means of marking a higher position in the elaborate human hierarchy system. Of the (full-time) students who begin a four-year baccalaureate degree, only about sixty percent complete a course of study and obtain a degree within six years.

There is a strong expectation among humans that leaders in government, business, research and the professions will be drawn from those who have participated successfully in programs of higher education. So there is a great deal at stake in the quality and availability of opportunities for higher education to support a functional social infrastructure. Presently, higher education is a scarce resource with unequal access and widely varying levels of quality. Only about seven percent of the world population over twenty-five years of age has a college degree, though this percentage is growing slowly.

Lifelong Learning. For the vast majority of humans, formal education rarely extends beyond about the age of thirty. Of course learning continues, but it becomes more informal, unstructured and serendipitous. This is the typical mode for the last several decades of the human lifespan.

However, this pattern is becoming increasingly problematic, especially in industrialized societies, because the collective knowledge base is being revised and expanded at an exponential rate. Previously acquired information rapidly grows obsolete. The knowledge and skills needed for individual success and effective participation in citizenship responsibilities are constantly moving targets. Regular updating is becoming increasingly necessary. This imperative will be discussed further in Chapter 10.

Educational Standards

Institutions around the world providing formal education are mostly very decentralized and fragmented. As a consequence, student participation and achievement vary greatly. Humans have no universally-shared learning goals or measures of student achievement at any level from primary through higher education, despite the fact that some limited efforts have been made to establish them.[39]

---

[39] A few international tests of student achievement have been developed. Perhaps the most notable of these is the PISA (Programme for International Student

Though standards have been widely adopted in many areas of human activity (weights and measures, for instance), the educational enterprise has resisted standardization, even though its mission has universal application—teaching offspring the concepts and skills needed for successful adult performance. All humans share the same cognitive processes that make learning possible, making schooling relevant for all. And teachers can successfully apply the same range of effective instructional methods in any context, though tailoring is required to account for individual student differences.

■ ■ ■

Humans are completely dependent on learning. In response to this need, they organize compulsory formal learning experiences for their offspring. Generally, this takes the form of sending their children to some sort of school where they receive various types of required instruction, typically in reading, writing, mathematics, science, and a variety of cultural norms. A knowledgeable or specially trained adult is usually responsible for providing this instruction.

When compulsory education ends, formal education may continue for many more years for some students. Formal education ends for nearly everyone by about age thirty. For the next several decades, learning continues, but in an informal way, despite the fact that the collective knowledge base quickly makes previous learning obsolete.

The extent and quality of formal education for the young varies greatly around the planet. In addition, humans haven't yet developed a worldwide system of standards and measurements of achievement. But the reliance of humans on learning is absolute and directly related to the success of individuals and the cultures within which they live.

BEHAVIOR VARIABILITY

Human behavior arises from broadly common sources. However, there are substantial individual differences related to each source.

Assessment) test administered every three years to samples of fifteen-year-old students from more than seventy countries or economies around the world. Standard sub-tests include reading, mathematics and science. The results provide an estimate of the achievements of about twenty-eight million students.

Understanding these variations is central to understanding the extensive range of behaviors humans exhibit.

Biological Differences

A review of behavioral variation begins with the basic biological hardware: the brain. While human brains share a similar template, they are not all exactly the same. They vary in physical characteristics and, consequently, in the way they process information. Varied brain configurations come from the assembly instructions provided by the individual's genetic DNA code, as potentially modified by environmental conditions such as physical injury or disease during development.

For instance, some genetic configurations produce faulty neuron maps leading to a condition like epilepsy. In other cases, the wiring instructions may facilitate particularly easy acquisition of languages. In other cases, the wiring may result in deficits in processing social relationships, such as is seen in autism. And in still other cases, the wiring may result in a photographic memory.

Humans also differ somewhat in the way their senses work. All five of the major senses vary in their sensitivities and range of function. In extreme cases one or more senses may not be fully operational due to genetic factors, injury, or disease. Deafness and blindness are relatively common examples. But in a more moderate way, senses may be compromised, such as in color blindness, which generally has a genetic origin. The sense of taste and smell also vary substantially in intensity. For instance, there is a genetic configuration of these two senses that results in a "super taster" where very fine differences in taste can be recognized. The sense of touch is also variable, particularly in the level of sensitivity. For example, some humans have a genetic configuration that produces hypersensitivity, resulting in irritation or pain when objects are touched.

These kinds of core biological differences provide a platform from which other types of human variation arise. Variations in brain configurations, which have implications for behavior, are particularly important.

Thinking Ability Differences

Elements of human thinking also vary within the human population. Intelligence serves as a particularly good example of thinking ability differences because it has been studied extensively. Different brain configurations produce different levels of human intelligence, defined by four interdependent attributes: verbal proficiency, reasoning, working memory capacity, and mental processing speed. The more fluid the verbal proficiency, the more effective the reasoning, the greater the working memory and the faster the processing speed, the higher the intelligence.

If the intelligence level of every human was measured and the results plotted on a graph, it would form a bell-shaped curve, a so-called normal distribution (Figure 9-6).

In such a distribution, most individuals cluster together in the center of the range, while individuals with lower and higher levels are found on the wings of the curve. It is clearly evident from the graph that most humans have similar intelligence. (This pattern is seen in other human characteristics like height and weight, which are also normally distributed.) But it is also clear that some humans have lower or higher levels of intelligence relative to the norm—around twenty percent at each end of the distribution.

Does this general pattern of variation apply to humans universally? The answer is generally affirmative, with qualifications. The total world population is made up of several distinct lineages, each with its own bell-shaped distribution. When these sub-populations are examined closely, the distributions are not identical. Average intelligence varies a bit from group to group and the number of humans at the extremes also varies. However, there is substantial overlap of intelligence scores for all human populations. It is assumed

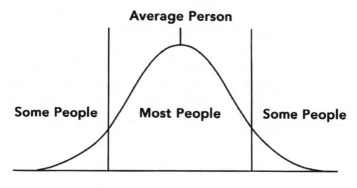

Figure 9-6. Normal Distribution

that the observed differences result from long periods of geographic population isolation that modified the composition of different gene pools.

Another kind of sub-population study has attempted to determine whether there are intelligence differences between males and females. Rather extensive efforts have found no significant differences. Both the male and female distributions are essentially the same as that of the total population.

Because differences in intelligence have been studied rather thoroughly, the range of variation is well understood. Is this variation of any practical consequence for humans? Does the level of intelligence matter? It does seem to matter, quite a lot, especially as it relates to facilitating learning. Intelligence provides the foundation for successful learning. And learning, especially that promoted by formal education, is a cornerstone for adult proficiency. It enables and enhances critical thinking and effective problem solving.

Humans often express the sentiment that every person should be enabled to reach full potential. In this context, potential is largely defined by intelligence and the attainment of full potential relies on a personalized program of formal education. Through education, the potential of intelligence can be realized.

Intelligence is also related to another important element of self-awareness—an appreciation of one's own scope of personal knowledge and understanding. This awareness is important to effective critical thinking. A side effect of modest intelligence is a lack of awareness of what is *not* known. Such individuals don't know what they don't know, so they approach critical thinking and problem solving with a perspective that is often too limited. To some extent, formal education is intended to impart the necessary broader perspective. But sometimes it fails to provide the needed feedback.

The capacity to switch between everyday- and premium-thinking modes, described earlier in this chapter, also varies, as does the way the thinking modules work with each other in making decisions. And, just as with intelligence, variation also appears to be distributed normally for these thinking abilities, too.

Automatic Thinking Differences

Some individuals rely more heavily than others on automatic thinking shortcuts due, in part, to their brain configurations. For these humans, their cognitive hardwiring favors the use of shortcuts when processing information, and because the strategy is automatic, there may be no awareness that a bias is involved. For instance, the confirmation bias can be so strong that even the presentation of strong counter evidence in a situation will be ignored or dismissed.

Other humans rely less on cognitive biases or are able to manage them depending on the context. Though thinking shortcuts are not all bad, they need to be turned off or at least accounted for in many important analysis and decision-making situations. The ability to self-control the use of automatic thinking varies across humans and is another normally-distributed trait.

Impulse Differences

Impulses vary in intensity from person to person. They, like other cognitive features, have a genetic origin and are hardwired into each brain's biological configuration. For instance, for some humans, the impulse to be aggressive is felt very mildly and is easily managed. For others, the impulse is very strong and difficult to control. Some humans who are easily provoked have to take anger management classes or are even removed from the opportunity to interact with others through incarceration.

As another example, the impulse to be religious also varies greatly. Some people are indifferent to religious affiliation while others are completely overwhelmed by the impulse and will spend a lifetime focused on religious matters. Priests, ministers and monks are good examples. Humans have an unusual capacity to devote themselves to systems of belief, even when the systems are largely imaginary.

Consider also the moralistic impulse. Some humans feel this impulse strongly (or at least strongly enough) and can easily adhere to the moral code of the society in which they live. Others feel the impulse much more weakly, and are subject to developing behaviors that deviate from the moral norms. In more extreme cases, criminality can result. This is not a trivial matter. In the United States, more than two million individuals are incarcerated for criminal acts. While criminality has many interrelated causes, a weakness of the moral impulse is surely one of them.

In addition to varying in intensity, impulses interact with each other as was discussed earlier in this chapter. Considering both of these perspectives, it can be useful to create profiles that illustrate their effects. Here are example profiles for three different humans (Figure 10-7). A sliding scale is used to show the relative intensity of an impulse as an individual experiences it. On the left side of the scale, the impulse

Impulse Intensity Examples			
Impulse	Profile A	Profile B	Profile C
Social	------**X**------	------------**X**	------**X**------
Tribal	------**X**------	---**X**---------	------------**X**
Territorial	------**X**------	---**X**---------	------------**X**
Hierarchical	------**X**------	**X**------------	------------**X**
Patriarchal	------**X**------	**X**------------	---------**X**---
Communicative	------**X**------	---------**X**---	---------**X**---
Cooperative	------**X**------	------------**X**	**X**------------
Emotional	------**X**------	---**X**---------	------------**X**
Aggressive	------**X**------	---**X**---------	------------**X**
Moral	------**X**------	------------**X**	---**X**---------
Religious	------**X**------	**X**------------	---------**X**---
Imaginative	------**X**------	------**X**------	---------**X**---
Adaptive	------**X**------	---------**X**---	---**X**---------
Willful	------**X**------	---**X**---------	------------**X**

Figure 10-7 Impulse Profiles

is not felt or expressed strongly. On the right side of the scale the impulse is felt and experienced strongly.

Profile A is fairly typical for most humans. All of the impulses are felt and expressed through behaviors in a moderate way. Profile B has a different configuration and represents a generally strong cooperator and who has quite flexible behaviors appropriate to various situations. The impulse to aggression is low and emotional responses are tempered.

Profile C has a somewhat more problematic configuration. Several related impulses are felt and expressed strongly, but in a way that undermines behavioral flexibility in a variety of situations. This human would be strongly affected by tribal affiliations and may cooperate effectively with others, but only within the group. A strong impulse toward aggression and emotional sensitivity increase the likelihood of defensiveness or a belief that members of outside groups are enemies.

It's also worth considering that the strength of impulses, like intelligence, may vary by human group or population. As humans dispersed from Africa over the past fifty thousand years or so, groups of humans settled in different locations and became reproductively isolated from each other. As a result, over the generations, the populations diverged from each other in both physical and psychological ways through well-understood evolutionary processes. As a result, the average strength of the impulses expressed in different cultures may also vary, which could be contributing to current social problems. For instance, a culture where the impulse to patriarchy is especially strong may experience difficulties in reaping potential contributions from its female members.

Another important example might be related to the impulse to cooperate. The average capacity to cooperate effectively may be lower in some groups than others. If there is a critical mass of poor cooperators in a population, it could make the entire population less able to rally support for resolving social, political or economic problems.

In summary, humans vary a great deal in the extent to which they feel and express impulses. Impulses that evolved and were adapted to human life in the wild may not be well suited to life in complex modern societies. One of the challenges facing humans is how to manage the expression of impulses in a way that makes them work to individual and collective advantage. Up until very recently, humans were largely unaware of these genetic factors, and they have not yet found a way to effectively manage them.

Learned Behavior Differences

No two humans have the same acquired learning because they never have exactly the same experiences in their environments. So acquired learning is, by definition, highly variable. What makes acquired learning interesting is not its range of variety, but the fact that humans in groups learn many of the same things and share many of the same norms of behavior. As already discussed, this happens informally through socialization and also through formal education. Humans send their children to schools to learn the range of concepts and skills thought most important within a given local community. This idea of acquired learning occurring in the context of a local community is important.

Planetwide, there are a wide variety of cultural practices, all of which have to be learned. Spoken language is a prime example. This was discussed extensively in Chapter 5 in the section focused on

Vocalizations. But in addition, there are many kinds of cultural norms, which are more or less widely shared in local human communities. There are norms for communicating with others, preparing food, exchanging goods, settling disputes, pursuing mates, treating illnesses, sanctioning unacceptable behaviors, worshiping a deity, and many, many more. What's key is that all of these norms are learned. For any given individual human, the set of norms acquired through learning is largely an accident of birth.

But even though there are a rich variety of norms around the world, this does not mean that all norms are equally beneficial to individuals or to the human community as a whole. In fact the evidence suggests just the opposite. Cultural traditions are rooted in the past when humans had much less insight into themselves and into the rest of the natural world. Many norms were never beneficial and are only less so in the modern world. A continued reliance on folk or natural remedies for treating illness is a good example. Homeopathy as a purported treatment for various diseases has tens of thousands of adherents worldwide, despite the fact that it is completely ineffective. The persistence of dysfunctional cultural norms is a problem for humans—one that has not yet been addressed very effectively.

Another important aspect of variation in acquired learning is how it interacts with behavioral impulses to shape their final expression. For instance, an individual with a strong impulse to aggression can have the impulse strengthened or weakened by informal or formal learning experiences. Such an individual might receive aggression reduction counseling or simply be surrounded by a community where peaceful values are the norm, and experience a reduction in the aggression impulse. Conversely, the same individual might join a gang or serve in the military, where the aggressive impulse might be valued and strengthened. A key insight is that acquired learning modifies basic behavioral impulses, potentially reducing or strengthening them.

Similarly, acquired learning interacts with thinking abilities and the tendency to use thinking shortcuts. Through learning, humans can display more intelligent behaviors and make better use of their premium-thinking mode. They can also reduce their susceptibility to shortcut errors through disciplined learning activities. Just as with the impulses, acquired learning can modify some basic aspects of human behavior.

Opportunities for formal education vary greatly around the planet. There are also great variations in outcomes, in subjects taught in schools, and in how well they are learned. And, of course, participation is incomplete. Millions of human offspring, mostly in the poorer countries, receive little, if any, formal education at all. These issues have been identified by humans as a problem, and many suggest that variability needs to be reduced and the learning potential for each individual needs to be better realized going forward.

Learned behavior is highly variable, whether attained through informal (socialization) or formal (compulsory education) means. It interacts in very important ways with impulses and the human thinking abilities like intelligence and modes of thought. Acquired learning is also important in understanding social behaviors in human groups where shadows from the past continue to shape the present, sometimes in unfortunate ways. Learning, and the behavioral flexibility it makes possible, are the greatest assets of the human species.

10 Conservation Status

HAVING REVIEWED THE history and characteristics of humans, it is now time to sum up the state of the species and speculate on where they are headed over the relatively short term—over the next one hundred years or so.

CURRENT CONDITIONS

It is undeniable that humans are the dominant species on Earth. In a short fifty thousand years they have risen from a small, rather undistinguished population in Africa with a limited range, to successfully inhabit every landmass on the planet and to expand their population to more than seven billion. With their technologies they have reshaped whole landscapes, created extensive zones of agriculture, invented and produced a vast variety of goods and services, built sprawling cities, and controlled the range and numbers of most other species. Their collective knowledge base is large and expanding rapidly, thanks to the widespread use of the scientific method. They are exceptionally social, using language as a tool to organize and to cooperate on a global scale. They have created elaborate cultures that provide a rich context for expressing an extraordinary range of individual behaviors. Humans are deeply connected to their kin and are emotionally anchored to their various tribal relationships. They are innovative and are relentless problem solvers. This is a species that, in many ways, can be admired.

But there are some concerns, mostly arising from their evolutionary history. Some of these concerns relate to genetic abnormalities that can affect their physical forms. Other, very important concerns relate to the evolution of their cognitive functions—the ways they normally think. Each human alive today is deeply influenced by the evolutionary history of the species of which it is a part. The long reach of the biological past is still felt in the present in ways that can be troublesome. Three different species problems are particularly important.

First, consider the total human gene pool and the individual physical expressions of it. There are great, shared similarities with limited variation in physical forms. But some of these variations in the gene pool are problematic, leading to harmful physical manifestations (see Chapter 6). Humans have identified more than ten thousand genetic configurations that are considered disease conditions, some of which are devastating in their consequences. But these conditions all arise from the normal process of reproduction. (Other disease conditions arise from genetic assembly errors during development, from environmental insults, and from infections by other organisms.) Harmful genes continue to circulate in the total gene pool, and development, guided by DNA, is subject to errors that survive biological quality control and repair measures. As a result, perhaps fifteen percent of humans suffer from some genetic abnormality significant enough to interfere with the routines of daily life.

Second, evolutionary history has shaped a human nervous system that, in some fundamental ways, is mismatched with current conditions on the planet. For instance, humans have an impulse to aggression, especially toward strangers, yet now live in close proximity to millions of other people in cities all over the planet. Regular interaction with strangers is routine and necessary to maintain cooperative activities, but the unending steam of interactions can cause chronic stress and promote acts of aggression.

The human brain is powerful, but flawed. And because the flaws are widely shared, they are not generally perceived as problems. Largely unconscious and unappreciated habits of thinking and behavior can seem completely natural, even when they are often counterproductive. Humans are wonderfully unaware of their own thinking processes. They just act, with little reflection. Ironically, this lack of self-awareness is facilitated by one of their cognitive biases, the tendency to blame outside factors for mistakes.

This bias and others were discussed in Chapter 9. Several thinking biases were highlighted that can lead to reasoning errors. For instance, the commonly employed confirmation bias frequently hinders critical thinking. The human brain makes frequent, predictable errors in processing information that have significant consequences for daily life.

Behavioral impulses that have a genetic foundation can also be channeled in sometimes extreme and unhelpful ways. The human propensities for aggression and territoriality have long caused problems among human groups. And the tribal impulse, one of the strongest of the genetic predispositions, has a constant negative impact on cooperation, which is fundamental to the success of a social species. By nature, when the human brain processes information about the outside world, it makes consistent, predictable mistakes, especially when it is operating in the energy-saving, everyday mode.

The normal human condition of innumeracy is a problem in the modern world where quantitative reasoning is essential for effective problem solving. Even with significant formal learning aimed at strengthening this capacity, a great many humans lack the mathematical literacy tools needed for processing and acting on quantitative information, which is commonly encountered in daily life.

Lastly, humans have not achieved a working balance with the environment in which they live. In many ways they have created, and continue to create, ecologically unsustainable conditions across all of the ecosystems they inhabit. Part of this is due to their sheer population numbers, now more than seven billion. And part is due to their technological practices that allow them to exploit resources for their own use.

For instance, they are extracting finite, non-renewable mineral resources from their planet without regard for how future needs will be met. The same is true for energy resources. They also produce vast amounts of household and industrial waste (more than four million tons per day), much of which is toxic and resistant to decomposition. Humans are also reducing the populations of other species at a rapid rate, impacting the web of life. Currently, they are even modifying climatic conditions on a global scale, the future consequences of which are not clearly understood. As a species, humans are degrading the environments on which they rely. This will have some adverse long-term consequences if not resolved in a timely fashion.

PROSPECTS

Behaving like a standard, genetically-programmed human can be problematic individually and collectively. Three immediate concerns stand out: (1) the continued exercise and possible escalation of violent conflicts among human tribal groups; (2) the inadequate education of most offspring, limiting the potential for effective individual and collective problem solving; and (3) an ongoing decline in the quality of the Earth's environment due to human activities.

Violent Conflicts

In the last thousand years, human violence directed at members of its own species has diminished, but not nearly enough for a positive prognosis going forward. In about the last one hundred years, more than two hundred million humans died through self-inflicted wars, genocides, preventable disease, and starvations, resulting from the failure of the species as a whole to mount credible interventions. The magnitude of these casualties raises some concern for the next hundred years—particularly given that humans have now invented more and more lethal technologies to inflict harm on others.

Many armed conflicts are still underway and more are expected if tribal forces are not reduced. In a worst-case scenario involving the use of nuclear weapons, the results could be catastrophic. Even without a worst-case scenario, a reasonable prediction is that large numbers of humans are going to suffer and die over the next several decades at the hands of other humans.

Inadequate Education

Though worldwide efforts to educate human offspring have improved modestly, significant gaps remain and a new challenge looms. Only around forty percent of humans complete both primary and secondary programs of formal education. Such a low participation rate severely constrains the prospects of millions of people all over the world and reduces the potential for collective efforts to solve persistent problems.

Unfortunately, even the completion of a secondary education program is no guarantee that all necessary skills and concepts have been learned. Weak programs of study (curricula), poor instruction, and distraction-filled schools all reduce the potential for strong achievement. Though it is hard to know with certainty because of the lack of standard achievement measures, it is likely that fewer than ten percent of those with high school diplomas have truly mastered even the minimum competencies in core subjects. Overall, it is likely that more than ninety percent of human offspring receive either no or inadequate levels of education.

To complicate matters further, the human collective knowledge base is expanding and restructuring rapidly. This puts significant pressure on the formal education system to integrate new knowledge and skills into its program of studies to keep it current and relevant. The pace of change is so rapid that the risk of educational obsolescence has become a very real threat. The expansion of the collective knowledge base is even more challenging for adults who are no longer participating in formal education. New insights and perspectives can only be successfully exploited if they are understood and rapidly integrated.

The need to update and spread quality formal education going forward is obvious and daunting, but underpins all efforts to push human progress ahead.

Environmental Deterioration

There are concerns about environmental damage caused by humans. Various kinds of air and water pollution are escalating, the atmosphere is warming, and ocean acidification is increasing. As a result of these factors, and of the spreading presence of humans in all ecosystems, the populations of many other species are in decline.

Continuing human population growth is amplifying these effects. For instance, expanding the food supply to feed the eleven billion humans that are expected to inhabit the Earth in about one hundred years looks like a daunting challenge, especially given that nearly all arable land is already under agriculture. The availability of potable water supplies is also a concern, as is the depletion of fossil fuels that powers most economies.

Conservation Rating

Overall, the prospects going forward look somewhat dim. If past trends remain on the same trajectories, there is a high potential for severe problems for the species. The next hundred years look crucial to longer-term human success. A fairly rapid, and likely difficult, transition to a more peaceful, globally integrated, and ecologically sustainable planetary order appears essential. Whether humans can make this transition is far from assured. However, there are reasons for some optimism, largely based on their demonstrated capacity for behavioral innovation and flexibility, which could be leveraged to support the next phase of their social evolution.

Due to largely self-inflicted risk factors, the human species' conservation status is classified as endangered (EN) (Figure 10-1).[40]

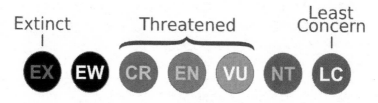

Figure 10-1. Conservation Categories

VIABILITY IMPROVEMENT PROJECTS

Since organic evolution created the fundamental problems that confront humans in the present day, can evolution provide the solutions? Could natural selection reshape the gene pool? Well, of course it is shaping the gene pool even now, though the direction of change is uncertain, and the rate of change is far too slow to have an impact in the near term. Since current human knowledge of genetics is still fairly rudimentary, no technology for actively reshaping the gene pool is or will be possible in the foreseeable future. Humans will have to solve their near-term problems with more or less the same genes that are already in place. (Eventually, humans will be able to genetically modify their brains to largely eliminate the most serious of the inherent cognitive errors, and to reduce the impact of the most harmful impulses).

As an alternative to genetics, could humans invent pharmaceutical products that could address some of their evolutionary issues (for instance, remediate cognitive biases, control behavioral impulses, or increase intelligence)? Doing so would require a knowledge of human

---

[40] International Union for the Conservation of Nature (IUCN). 2012. Status categories include: EX—extinct, EW—extinct in the wild, CR—critically endangered, EN—endangered, VU—vulnerable, NT—near threatened, LC—least concern.

biology, especially of the brain, that is far more advanced than the state of their current understanding. So, again, in the short term, it is unlikely that the manipulation of human biochemistry will provide any quick solutions.

This leaves humans with one primary option for improving their species—modifying what they learn through the course of individual development. As observed throughout this field guide, one of the hallmarks of humans is behavioral flexibility. They change their behaviors and cultural habitats with lighting speed compared with the rates of change of organic evolution.

In fact, this is the capacity that has been most responsible for their ability to out compete other species. Humans learn from collective experience and apply that learning in ever-changing ways *in real time*, while other species mostly change behaviors as a result of natural selection. Humans adapt to changing conditions very rapidly, and now even modify the environmental conditions they encounter, rather than simply adapting their behaviors to those conditions.

All humans must learn the concepts and skills they need to become functioning members of their species. This suggests that modifications to the program of learning may offer a way forward, a way to modify the current trajectory of human history. Learning can drive changes in individual behavior and then enlightened cooperation can drive changes in cultural habitats. Several suggestions for improving the viability of the human species over the next four generations (about one hundred years) are offered below. The emphasis of these suggestions is on the species as a whole and the scope is planetwide.

These recommendations are not so much a menu of options as they are a recipe of ingredients for reducing the possibility of a severe population reduction or even an extinction. Humans should work on all of these recommendations at the same time to produce the best possible future outcome for the species.

Provide Universal Formal Education

All human offspring should participate in compulsory education from about age four or five through about age twenty. The goal is to ensure that each human achieves the maximum potential possible for a given level of cognitive ability.

During the period of compulsory education, every student should pursue the same core curriculum (see the Special Feature at the end of this chapter), which should be centered around the development of critical thinking. Supporting this central goal should be the development of language literacy (reading, writing and speaking) and mathematical literacy (quantitative reasoning). Every student should also learn the basics of a standard second language which would facilitate communications among different language groups. English appears to be a likely candidate because of its already worldwide use as the predominant language of science, commerce and entertainment.

Another key component of the core curriculum should include learning the big ideas from all branches of science, how the scientific method produces new knowledge, and the nature of scientific evidence. Big ideas are broad generalizations about the natural world that rest on an extensive scaffolding of scientific knowledge, often sourced from several disciplines. There are dozens of these ideas that need to be thoroughly developed through a highly organized program of studies. Learning to think like a scientist, especially with regard to judging the quality of evidence for a claim to correctness, also contributes to the development of critical thinking.

Understanding the flow of history from the formation of the universe to the present is another component of the core curriculum. Milestones describing the evolution of the physical, biological, and, eventually, the cultural features of the world as they have unfolded across the seamless stream of time should be highlighted. This dramatically expanded version of the more traditional history of civilizations and their elites should be taught to provide a fuller context for the affairs of modern humans.

Learning the core curriculum to the needed level of depth and sophistication is a big learning project that should occupy students throughout all their years of compulsory learning. Among all of the viability improvement suggestions, this recommendation has the highest priority. It doesn't matter whether an individual lives in North or South America, Asia, Europe, Africa or even the most remote island in the Pacific Ocean. A shared core curriculum is essential for all members of the species, regardless of location, economic status, or lineage.

The world community needs a critical mass of well-educated individuals who share common perspectives in order to organize effectively to solve broad-based problems. While every school-age child should have an opportunity to participate in the same core program of formal learning, special efforts should be made to find highly talented individuals for whom exceptional academic instruction would be provided. While the core curriculum should be the same, instruction should be very personalized.

Promote Lifelong Learning

As knowledge accumulates at a greater rate, individual humans are having more difficulty integrating new insights with previous learning. A gap has opened between what many humans understand and the current information in the collective knowledge base. This is a drag on progress, as cooperative problem solving depends on a shared understanding of problems and their relationships with each other.

To close the knowledge gap, humans need to engage in lifelong learning to regularly update their perspectives and, if necessary, reset their conceptions of the world. A means to accomplish this in a coordinated fashion is needed in every culture. Fortunately, though no such institution exists today, an institution does exist that could be repurposed to be a center for lifelong learning on a very broad scale.

Libraries are ubiquitous with more than 320,000 worldwide and, they could provide the support needed for a program of lifelong learning in a great number of communities. Library staff could monitor changes in the human knowledge base, package the information for distribution, coordinate media outlets, and host local discussion groups. Partnerships with public and private schools, newspapers, radio and television stations, and online resources such as social media could insure consistent communication of important findings in all domains. Multiple channels will be needed to convey new research findings and ideas to a diverse audience with different backgrounds and levels of education.

Another important initiative would focus on constructing a planetwide system of communication; perhaps an enhanced version of the current Internet. Key features would include openness and a relative lack of censorship. In conjunction with this access system should come robust, well-vetted news sources that give all humans access to the same information about current events in as close to real time as possible. Commentaries would be noted as such, and different points of view would have equal time allotments.

Through a program of coordinated efforts, perhaps ninety percent of the population could obtain and process the same updates to the human knowledge base on an ongoing basis. In this way, all humans could continue to learn together through all stages of life.

Shift Energy Production

Human cultures run on energy, most of it currently provided by the combustion of fossil fuels. The total global rate of energy use is about eighteen terawatts and is steadily increasing.[41] Humans are an energy-intensive species, and their current practices for supplying it are unsustainable. Environmental damage is mounting and traditional supplies will eventually be exhausted. To resolve these issues, a massive global project should be undertaken enlisting all of the best physicists and engineers to harness hydrogen fusion to generate a relatively unlimited supply of electricity. Not only would this supply all of the energy needed to power human activities, it would also potentially eliminate competition for resources, which is a current significant source of conflict among tribal groups. With planetwide cooperation, the problem could be solved within a couple of decades.

In the interim, the wealthiest humans—those in the top third of the planetwide income distribution—should take steps to conserve energy, reduce carbon emissions and overall consumption, and reduce the size of dwellings. The intensity of these efforts must increase, the longer it takes to bring full-scale fusion electrical production online. The remaining two-thirds of the human population are already forced, by local economic circumstances, to consume energy supplies very modestly to begin with; for them, energy consumption really only needs to become a priority if personal wealth significantly increases.

Reduce Human Population

The human population is currently unsustainable if sustainability means providing every living human with a standard of living similar to the one enjoyed in the industrialized parts of the world. Since there appears to be no rationale to justify denying a decent global standard of living, human population needs to ratchet down to a more sustainable level. A good start in this direction would be to limit

---

[41] A terawatt is one trillion (10^{12}) watts. This is a rate of energy capable of lighting ten billion, 100 watt, incandescent light bulbs at the same time.

reproduction to one child per couple for each of the next four generations.

By adopting this policy, instead of increasing population to around eleven billion in the next hundred years, the population would be reduced to around two billion. That's still a lot of humans, but it's certainly a lot more sustainable. To achieve this goal, females in particular should be supported through formal education, access to birth control measures, and social policies that promote their financial independence. Governments should also promote policies of reproductive restraint and modify financial incentives accordingly. Though there will be some social challenges associated with a top-heavy population pyramid, careful economic planning, broad cooperation, and increases in productivity should be able to mitigate the downside risks.

In conjunction with population reduction, significant efforts should be made to reduce the number of children born with genetic abnormalities, with the goal of reducing the number of such births to zero by the end of the next hundred years. Medical research aimed at making this goal possible should be a priority, along with building a public consensus recognizing it as a public good. This goal seems clearly in reach as humans increase their knowledge of the genetic mechanisms of reproduction.

Extend the Use of Standards

Standards are important because they facilitate cooperation. Humans have already made some progress in implementing planetwide standards. Time is a good example. A range of intervals have been adopted including seconds, minutes, hours, days, months, and years. Nearly all humans mark the passage of time in a standard way that allows them to synchronize their activities anywhere in the world. Standard time in its present form was put in place only about forty years BP. Humans have adopted Coordinated Universal Time (UTC), which is based on extremely accurate atomic clocks. Written references to time have also been standardized through adoption of ISO 8601, developed by the International Organization for Standards about twenty-five years BP. This standard provides the means for communicating about time in consistent ways.

More work is needed to make the most important standards shared on planetwide basis. For instance, the metric system of decimal measurement is already used in most, but not all societies. In this instance, humans can and should move quickly to make it a universal standard.

Other areas that would benefit from standardization include language (already discussed), electronic communication protocols (the Internet being a good example), and financial currencies. In this last case, humans have around one hundred eighty different currencies in different regions that are used to purchase goods and services and are linked to each other through constantly fluctuating exchange rates. Though electronic transactions can now instantaneously convert one currency to another, having a universal currency would simplify matters. At the present time, because of its widespread use, the US dollar may already be a default universal standard. It is possible that currencies may be completely replaced in the foreseeable future by electronic forms of exchange. Bitcoin is an early example.

Improve Human Health

Poor health has obvious individual consequences, but also wider community impacts. When humans are ill, they are less productive and have to redirect resources to acquire health care, if available. In the United States alone, almost twenty percent of annual economic output (around $3.5 trillion) is devoted to providing healthcare for humans with diseases. Of course, some of this is unavoidable, as aging alone inevitably causes medical issues. However, there is substantial room for improvement in health outcomes for humans that would reduce suffering, enhance productivity, and reduce healthcare costs.

Part of the gain possible here is through medical advances that will improve diagnosis and result in treatments that are effective but less intrusive, shortening recovery times. Another avenue for improvement can come from humans arranging their environments to implement the health maintenance guidelines described in Chapter 6: Diet and Health. Eating healthfully and in moderation, exercising regularly, getting adequate sleep, managing stress (through intentional breathing exercises, for instance) and avoiding substance abuse are all straightforward parts of a healthy lifestyle that are within reach for most humans. Organizing the cultural environment to support these basic principles should be a priority for public policy makers.

Another way to improve health outcomes would be to ensure that all humans have access to adequate nutrition and healthcare services. Currently, there are rather great disparities among various populations.

Expand Meritocracies

All social systems should offer advancement based on merit—demonstrated ability to perform competently. This is a trend already underway in many cultures, but needs a planetwide scope and accelerated schedule. The traditional tribal practices based more on heredity and family connections should be displaced to build broad confidence that upward social mobility is possible and is grounded in competence.

Professionalism should be greatly expanded, such that humans create performance standards for various occupations and activities, and then hold their practitioners to those standards through systems of certification and accountability. This is a particularly healthy form of cooperation that can introduce and spread new practices efficiently and quickly. The principles of professionalism need to be applied to nearly all forms of human social activity to speed up and harmonize all kinds of cooperative activities.

In addition, to support meritocracy, every culture should systematically search for and promote the development of those with significant cognitive abilities, regardless of background and economic status. New scientific discoveries and breakthrough innovations depend on having a large and growing core of highly educated individuals who are constantly pushing forward the human knowledge base. All of the recommended species improvements depend on enlisting and coordinating the efforts of very talented individuals from all over the world.

Though it is an important enabler of competence, having strong cognitive ability is not enough. Intellectually gifted humans are subject to the same cognitive biases and misdirected impulses as anyone else. They are not immune to the forces of basic biology. In fact, the talented and well-educated tend to be especially self-assured. An unfounded sense of certainty can be as problematic as ignorance. Talent must be carefully cultivated to achieve a workable meritocracy.

Diminish the Impact of Patriarchy

Humans are mammals with a preference for male social dominance. This preference has had generally disastrous consequences both in terms of social conflict and in the suppression of contributions from female members of the species. Steps should be taken to remedy both of these adverse effects. As a general strategy, increasing attention to and investment in females is needed.

The same methods recommended to help control population growth also work here to limit the expression of patriarchy. Give women free access to quality education, provide effective means of birth control, and implement policies to give women economic independence, such as through access to meaningful work or through subsidized financing to start businesses (micro-loans, for instance).

In addition, patriarchal laws that restrict women's access to opportunities need to be repealed in all cultures. Examples would include laws that restrict voting rights in political elections, the ability to travel at will, access to certain occupations, and rights to free association. In cases where patriarchal practices are enshrined in religious traditions, adherents must work to diminish them or seek alternative forms of religious expression.

Strengthen Secular Institutions

Institutions are needed to facilitate social cooperation. But they only work well if they operate transparently, are predictable in their actions, employ empirically-derived knowledge, and include strong checks and balances that prevent abuse. Humans have invented many institutions to regulate social affairs. They now need to be strengthened to improve social cohesion.

As an example, consider legal systems. Effective social relationships depend on the operation of a robust, fair system that enforces norms of behavior. Policing needs to be effective and fair, bringing offenders to justice. The criminal justice system must then determine guilt or innocence and assign reasonable punishments. These systems, which employ both force and authority, must have multiple and strong checks and balances to remain credible. They must be transparent and evenhanded in their application of procedures and consequences.

There is, unfortunately, much variation in the quality of the legal institutions around the planet. As part of the process to improve quality, humans should work to establish a global set of standards, a system of consistent funding of these services, and a planet-wide system of performance audits for accountability purposes.

In a related effort, humans should take steps to end corruption, the widespread practice of soliciting compensation for favors. Such practices have a corrosive effect on cooperation. An important step in facilitating this change is the policy of providing adequate compensation to civil servants with strong sanctions for misbehavior. Corruption is deeply rooted in the tribal history of humans. But a better social contract can expand cooperation and confidence in social institutions.

Programs for upgrading and integrating other secular institutions (governments, education, healthcare, military forces, family structures, mass media, industries) should be pursued as a way of enhancing cooperation and creating social stability on a large-scale basis.

Globalize Tribes

Humans have a strong affinity for identifying with various kinds of tribal groups and using these affiliations as a basis for channeling behavior ranging from altruism to aggression. Tribal thinking has long created problems for humans, often leading to various forms of conflict. Going forward, every effort should be made to create some tribal linkages on a global basis so that every member of the species has some tribal affinity with every other member. Though this will not be easy given the human history of cultural fragmentation, many problems have a planetwide scope and require cooperation on the same scale.

To move toward this goal, humans might find opportunities to celebrate common ground. This can be done symbolically by creating new holidays, entertainments, and sporting events that have a global reach. In addition, philanthropic organizations might establish international branches all over the world. Perhaps a period of international public service for all youth, like the Peace Corps in the United States, could promote international relationships. The expansion of international business and scientific organizations would be helpful. And, of course, cross-cultural travel and exchange experiences on a much larger scale would expand a sense of international community.

Perhaps a universal passport could be developed where individuals could qualify for easy travel access to many, if not all, countries. Though given the current state of geo-political affairs, security checks might still be required for some time; the sense of global citizenship conveyed by a universal passport could promote cohesion.

What would set these new efforts apart from those of the past would be some planetwide institutional coordination and support, working systematically to improve communications and identification with others. The tribal impulse should be harnessed to create as much cohesion on a planetwide basis as possible.

Integrate Social Safety Nets

Some humans, perhaps as many as one third of the planet's population, can't thrive without the support of others. As a social species, there is a natural concern for the welfare of others, though this is constrained by tribal thinking. Historically, rather great disparities in living standards have arisen, largely due to geographical isolation and the dynamics of cultural evolution. The current rather wide range of inequalities among humans needs attention, since, on a fundamental level, it contributes to needless suffering and feeds potential conflicts among groups.

At a minimum, every human should have access to adequate nutrition, secure shelter, formal education, basic healthcare, meaningful employment, and personal safety. Planetwide standards should be adopted and international efforts undertaken to achieve these basic lifestyle goals. Existing systems should be integrated and spread planetwide to ensure a minimum standard of living for all, and the opportunity to achieve advances through education and hard work.

As a species, humans are substantially interdependent and all benefit from collective actions to help each other to succeed.

Accelerate Scientific Research

The application of the scientific method has transformed the quality of life for most humans in a very short time. Still more progress is needed on many fronts, and time is of the essence. More public resources should be invested in science, and the scope of scientific inquiry should be broadened.

Many practical problems have yet to be solved in areas such as energy production, information processing, medicine, cognitive science, and environmental systems. Science is the most powerful tool available for developing the knowledge needed to solve these problems.

In addition, the human knowledge base has not yet achieved critical mass and is not adequately integrated. Much of the current knowledge still exists in isolated specialties, yet the underlying features of nature being studied are all seamlessly related. Some of the great advances to come will flow from the efforts to unify all the sciences. For instance, merging the field of psychology with the field of biology will eventually provide new means to effectively address a variety of problematic behaviors. Humans must push forward using science as their principle tool for understanding themselves and changing the trajectory of their own future.

SPECIAL FEATURE: UNIVERSAL CORE CURRICULUM

A universal core curriculum is a description of a program of study that should be made available to every school-age child on the planet. It describes the content areas to be studied and what knowledge and skills students are expected to acquire (learning goals). This core curriculum is designed to prepare students to participate in a complex global environment that relies heavily on effective communication, cooperation, and problem solving. The curriculum should include the following components.

Critical Thinking. Arguably, the most important goal of education is to develop critical thinking, the capacity to make well-reasoned decisions and to systematically solve a broad range of problems. Critical thinking involves:

- Recognizing and compensating for common human perceptual errors and cognitive biases.
- Framing issues and problems clearly.
- Collecting or selecting relevant, accurate data for consideration.
- Choosing the right tools for data analysis.
- Evaluating evidence to find relationships.

- Weighing alternative explanations or choices.
- Checking the process for logical errors.
- Communicating methods and results transparently.

Evaluation of evidence is a particularly important aspect of critical thinking. To develop this capacity, a careful study of the methods and standards used in science to judge the quality of evidence is essential. In addition, the study of the scientific method is helpful in understanding how evidence is produced. Finally, the evaluation of sources of evidence, including the use of mathematical tests, needs to be developed to distinguish quality reporters from more unreliable or especially-biased ones.

Though rarely taught now, the core curriculum should include instruction on the nature of human cognition: promoting a self-awareness of thinking and the development of self-disciplines to control it. Goals include learning about the nature and limits of perception; thinking biases and short cuts, and how to defend against mental errors; human impulses and their roles in guiding behavior; and the features of effective cooperation. These learning goals are important foundations for critical thinking.

Despite frequent appeals to improve critical thinking capabilities, very little time and few resources are currently devoted to develop this capability through formal means. The lack of attention to teaching critical thinking directly is often justified by pointing out that it has an interdisciplinary nature. According to this line of thinking, it doesn't need to be taught directly because it will be indirectly acquired through the study of other subjects. Unfortunately, there is little evidence to support this contention.

Literacy. The emphasis of reading and writing instruction should shift somewhat. More attention should be directed to the comprehension of non-fiction texts, including scientific research studies, technical guides, and instruction manuals. The ability to comprehend these kinds of sources is a fundamental building block of critical thinking, which relies on obtaining accurate information.

The inclusion of literature in the reading curriculum should be largely focused on works that increase empathy for the experiences of others, especially those from different cultural backgrounds. The scope and sophistication of these efforts to build empathy should be systematically developed through a planned sequence of instruction unfolding over many years.

Developing the ability to write clearly and concisely to communicate information, critique an argument, explain a procedure, and convey an informed opinion are all important learning goals. Preparing coherent short informational or persuasive speeches for delivery before groups of various sizes is another important competency. Both writing and speaking are important means to convey the results of critical thinking to others and to mobilize support for collective actions. Quality personal communications support effective cooperation on many levels.

Every student needs to develop a working competence with the language eventually selected as the world standard, English as a possible example. No communication strategy is more powerful than communicating with others in the same language, regardless of where a person resides in the world.

Mathematics. The current goal of developing mastery with arithmetic, including addition, subtraction, multiplication and division should remain in place. But there should be some shifts in emphasis, primarily to support the development of critical thinking.

More effort should be directed at developing concrete understanding of statistics and probability as these are critical for evaluating evidence. More attention would also be focused on the comprehension of very large and very small quantities and how to relate different levels of magnitude through the use of scales. Practical understanding of geometric forms in two and three dimensions (areas and volumes) should also be important points of emphasis.

Understanding the concept of a variable is essential to understanding a key principle of critical thinking—the idea of cause and effect. The logic of independent and dependent variables and how they interact needs to be developed and understood in the context of real life situations.

Science. Effective critical thinking requires an ample supply of accurate knowledge. The knowledge base derived from the sciences is fundamental for analyzing and solving problems. Therefore, the study of scientific knowledge has a prominent place in the core curriculum.

But rather than teach science as just a collection of separate subjects, such as physics, chemistry or biology, it would be better to teach it through a concentration on big ideas about the nature of reality that have been developed through decades of scientific inquiry.

The big ideas that form the basis for instruction are derived from such diverse scientific disciplines as physics, chemistry, biology, geology, meteorology, and such social sciences as psychology and economics. Examples of big ideas that could form the basis for the science curriculum include:

- Atoms are the fundamental building blocks of matter.
- Distinct elements interact and combine with each other through chemical processes.
- The relative motion of objects is predictable, even when very complex.
- Energy can be conserved and transformed, but not created or destroyed.
- The solar system, of which Earth is a member, is only one of billions in just the local galaxy alone.
- The Earth's surface is dynamic and has changed dramatically over its history.
- The cell is the fundamental unit of life.
- Life processes require inputs of energy and raw materials to be sustained.
- All living and extinct organisms are related to each other and are the products of evolution.
- Organisms live in ecosystems with many complex interdependencies.
- Humans are biological forms, just one species among millions on Earth.
- Human behaviors arise from the function of the brain.
- The brain's outputs are shaped both by genetic impulses and environmental interactions.
- Humans are uniquely dependent on learning to acquire the proficiencies needed to be successful organisms.

In addition to the big scientific ideas, humans also need an understanding of key technologies on which they depend to one degree or another: energy, transportation, computing, healthcare, manufacturing, construction, agriculture, as examples. The principles of engineering—the process of converting theoretical knowledge to practical applications—should also be introduced and developed.

History. History, the record of change through time, should also be part of the core curriculum, though the subject in its current form needs to be revised to include a much broader scope and more global perspective. With an expanded timeline, some major themes, in chronological order, should include:

- The origin and early history of the universe.
- The formation of stars and the evolution of matter.
- The formation and geologic history of the Earth.
- The origin and evolution of life.
- The rise of mammals, primates and humans.
- The migration of humans from Africa.
- The human lifestyle shift to settlement and agriculture.
- The formation and impact of villages, towns and cities.
- The invention of science and the spread of industrialization.
- The rise and proliferation of digital technologies.

Big, complex themes like these combine findings from the sciences with insights from traditional history, particularly for events in the last few thousand years. Within the themes are many important milestones that need to be understood individually, but then woven together into a coherent overarching narrative to place current affairs in context.

One of the greatest challenges in mastering history is to develop a perspective with the time scales and evolutionary physical and biological processes involved. Another challenge related specifically to human history, is to develop a full awareness of everyday life through many time periods and cultures. The modern lifestyle, especially in industrialized countries, is very different from the life experiences of most humans who have ever lived. Understanding daily life in the past gives rich perspective on the present.

■ ■ ■

These are the core components of formal education which need to be made available to all school-age youth on the planet and delivered by skillful teachers with the necessary resources to successfully differentiate teaching strategies for students of varying ability levels. Schools can add other subject matter to the local program of studies, as desired, as long as mastery of the core curriculum is the top priority.

Along with the implementation of a core curriculum, a universal achievement test should be developed and administered on an annual basis, at least to a sample of students representing a cross-section of the worldwide school-age population. To be fair, the test should include questions designed to provide a quick assessment of cognitive ability. Achievement test results can then be adjusted to account for such differences. For instance, an average achievement test score for a student with an IQ of around 120 may signal a degree of underachievement, while the same score for a student with an IQ of around 90 may signal very good achievement and substantial academic progress. Raw test scores are difficult to interpret unless the right context is established (and even then must be treated with caution due to various measurement difficulties). Adjusted results should be used to focus specific educational improvements in every context as needed.

For humans, learning is everything—the foundation for self-awareness, personal achievement, strong social relationships, and harmony with the environment. Future prospects depend, in large part, on how well this system of universal education is implemented. It is the strongest hope for a rapid shift in an otherwise problematic human trajectory.

Afterword

WE HUMANS ARE distinctive members of the animal kingdom. We are all part of a single species sharing characteristics and a common heritage. But we also vary from each other in many ways. No two individuals are exactly the same—even identical twins. As a group, we have more biological similarities than differences, yet the differences produce billions of distinct individuals.

We have powerful, yet imperfect, brains which are finely tuned to use language. The ability to create and transmit collective knowledge from generation to generation has provided us with the most powerful tool ever invented: culture. With it, we have transformed and come to dominate the natural world at a rapid pace.

Yet ours has been a troubled journey. As human powers increase, our ability to harness them are constantly challenged by our own cognitive shortcomings and ancient impulses. Fortunately, we have the means, through our complete reliance on learning, to adapt quickly and avoid old mistakes—if what we learn supports effective critical thinking and collective problem solving.

The human story will continue for better or worse. Among all species, we have the unique capacity to positively influence the future through collective, enlightened action. Perhaps we can not only remain the dominant species on Earth, but also truly become the wisest one, as well.

Illustration Credits

FIGURE I-1. Date Conversions. Table by R. Smith.

FIGURE I-2. Scale Model of Quantities. Illustration by R. Smith.

FIGURE I-3. Scale Model of Small Objects. Illustration by R. Smith.

FIGURE I-4. Comparisons of Small Objects. Illustration by R. Smith.

FIGURE 1-1. The Earth Viewed From Space. Photo taken by Apollo 11 crew, 1972, from a distance of about twenty-seven thousand miles. NASA. Public domain.

FIGURE 1-2. Simplified Tree of Life. ©Shutterstock. Used under the terms of the standard license.

FIGURE 2-1. Stages and Periods. Table by R. Smith

FIGURE 2-2. Early Mammal. Megazostrodon. ©Shutterstock. Used under the terms of the standard license.

FIGURE 2-3. Early Primate. Dryopithecus. ©DK Images. Image Credit: Dorling Kindersley, Francisco Gasco. Used under the terms of the DK Images license.

FIGURE 2-4. African Range. ©D-maps.com. Used with permission under terms of D-maps license.

FIGURE 2-5. Migration Process. Graphic prepared by Artist Team based on concept by R. Smith. Used under terms of commercial license.

FIGURE 2-6. Colonization Timeline. Table by R. Smith.

FIGURE 2-7. Cuneiform Writing. Babylonian clay tablet. Wikimedia Commons. Public domain.

FIGURE 2-8. Population Growth. Chart by R. Smith.

FIGURE 2-9. Scientific Method. Simplified version from Wikimedia Commons. Used under the terms of the Creative Commons Attribution-Share Alike 4.0 International license. Image credit: ©ArchonMagnus.

FIGURE 3-1. Population Differences. Two standard distributions with different means. Graphic prepared by Artist Team based on concept by R. Smith. Used under terms of commercial license.

FIGURE 3-2. Human Population Density. Wikimedia Commons. Public domain. Image credit: United States Department of Agriculture.

FIGURE 3-3. Geo-political Boundaries in Europe. Satellite map of Europe with border overlay. Image credit: ©Google Imagery, ©NASA TerraMetrics. Used under the Google Terms of Use.

FIGURE 4-1. Hunter-Gatherer Shelter. Wikimedia Commons. Public domain.

FIGURE 4-2. Mud Brick Home. ©Shutterstock. Used under the terms of the standard license.

FIGURE 4-3. Typical Contemporary Home. ©Shutterstock. Used under the terms of the standard license.

FIGURE 4-4. Mansion. ©Flickr. Used under the terms of the Creative Commons Attribution 4.0 license. Image Credit: Mitchell Friedman.

FIGURE 4-5. Egyptian pyramids. ©Shutterstock Used under the terms of the standard license.

FIGURE 4-6. High Density Cityscape. New York City. ©Shutterstock. Used under the terms of the standard license.

FIGURE 5-1. External Anatomy. These models have had body hair and male facial hair removed and head hair trimmed. The female model is wearing red nail polish on her toenails and a ring. Wikimedia Commons. Public domain.

FIGURE 5-2. Human Tracks. ©Shutterstock. Used under the terms of the standard license.

FIGURE 5-3. Color Variations. ©Shutterstock. Used under the terms of the standard license.

FIGURE 5-4. Major Languages. Table by R. Smith.

FIGURE 5-5. Population Pyramid. Public domain. Image credit: United Nations, Department of Economic and Social Affairs, Population Division. World Population Prospects. The 2015 Revision. (Medium variant)

FIGURE 6-1. Process of Eating. ©Shutterstock. Used under the terms of the standard license.

FIGURE 6-2. Bacteria. ©Shutterstock. Used under the terms of the standard license.

FIGURE 6-3. Robotic operating room. ©Shutterstock. Used under the terms of the standard license.

FIGURE 7-1. Sex Chromosomes. Public domain. Image credit: Jonathon Bailey, National Human Genome Research Institute, National Institute of Health.

FIGURE 7-2. Mated Couple from Thailand. Wikimedia Commons. Used under the terms of the Creative Commons Attribution-Share Alike 2.0 Germany license. Image credit: Manuel Jobi.

FIGURE 8-1. Egg Fertilization. ©Can Stock Photo. Used under the terms of the end user license agreement.

FIGURE 8-2. Newborn Child. Wikimedia Commons. Used under the terms of the Creative Commons Attribution-Share Alike 2.0 Generic license. Image credit: Tom Adriaenssen.

FIGURE 9-1. Brain Size. ©Shutterstock. Used under the terms of the standard license.

FIGURE 9-2. Face on Mars. NASA. Public domain.

FIGURE 9-3 Reasoning Problems. Prepared by R. Smith based on examples from indiabix.com and tamilcube.com.

FIGURE 9-4. Thinking Biases. Table by R. Smith.

FIGURE 9-5. Impulses. Table by R. Smith.

FIGURE 9-6. Normal Distribution. Graphic prepared by Artist Team based on concept by R. Smith. Used under terms of commercial license.

FIGURE 9-7. Impulse Profiles. Table by R. Smith.

FIGURE 10-1. Conservation Categories. From International Union for Conservation of Nature (IUCN). Wikimedia Commons. Used under the terms of Creative Commons Attribution 2.5 Generic license. Image credit: Peter Halasz.

References

Books

Alper, Matthew. 2006. *The God Part of the Brain: A Scientific Interpretation of Human Spirituality and God.* Naperville, IL: Sourcebooks, Inc.

Ariely, Dan. 2009. *Predictably Irrational: The Hidden Forces That Shape Our Decisions.* New York: HarperCollins.

Asbury, Kathryn and Robert Plomin. 2014. *G is for Genes: The Impact of Genetics on Education and Achievement.* Hoboken, NJ: Wiley-Blackwell.

Barton, Nicholas H., et.al. 2007. *Evolution.* Cold Spring Harbor, NY: Cold Spring Harbor Laboratory Press.

Boyer, Pascal. 2001. *Religion Explained: The Evolutionary Origins of Religious Thought.* New York: Basic Books.

Brown, James H. and Mark V. Lomolino. 1998. *Biogeography, Second Edition.* Sunderland, MA: Sinauer Associates, Inc.

Carroll, Sean B. 2005. *Endless Forms Most Beautiful: The New Science of Evo Devo and the Making of the Animal Kingdom.* New York: W. W. Norton & Company.

Cassidy, John. 2009. *How Markets Fail: The Logic of Economic Calamities.* New York: Farrar, Straus and Giroux.

Cowan, Ruth Schwartz. 2008. *Heredity and Hope: The Case for Genetic Screening.* Cambridge, MA: Harvard University Press.

Dawkins, Richard. 2006. *The God Delusion.* Boston: Houghton Mifflin Company.

Dawkins, Richard. 2004. *The Ancestor's Tale: A Pilgrimage to the Dawn of Evolution*. Boston, MA: Mariner Books.

Dawkins, Richard. 1976. *The Selfish Gene*. New York: Oxford University Press.

Dennett, Daniel C. 2017. *From Bacteria to Bach and Back: The Evolution of Minds*. New York: W. W. Norton.

DeSalle, Rob and Ian Tattersall. 2008. *Human Origins: What Bones and Genomes Tell Us About Ourselves*. College Station, TX: Texas A&M University Press.

Diamond, Jared. 2005. *Collapse: How Societies Choose to Fail or Succeed*. New York: Viking.

Diamond, Jared. 1997. *Guns, Germs, and Steel: The Fates of Human Societies*. New York: W. W. Norton & Company.

Diamond, Jared. 1992. *The Third Chimpanzee: The Evolution and Future of the Human Animal*. New York: HarperCollins.

DK Publishing. 2009. *Prehistoric Life*. New York: DK Publishing.

Dutton, Denis. 2009. *The Art Instinct: Beauty, Pleasure and Human Evolution*. New York: Bloomsbury Press.

Enders, Guilia. 2015. *Gut: The Inside Story of Our Body's Most Underrated Organ*. Vancouver, BC: Greystone Books.

Epley, Nicholas. 2014. *Mindwise: How We Understand What Others Think, Believe, Feel and Want*. New York: Alfred J. Knopf.

Fagan, Brian. 2004. *The Long Summer: How Climate Changed Civilization*. New York: Basic Books

Ferguson, Niall. 2008. *The Ascent of Money: A Financial History of the World*. New York: Penguin Books.

Flynn, James R. 2007. *What is Intelligence?: Beyond the Flynn Effect*. New York: Cambridge University Press.

Greene, Joshua. 2013. *Moral Tribes: Emotion, Reason and the Gap Between Us and Them*. New York: The Penguin Press.

Goldman, Lee. 2015. *Too Much of a Good Thing: How Four Key Survival Traits are Now Killing Us*. New York: Little, Brown and Company.

Haidt, Jonathan. 2006. *The Happiness Hypothesis: Finding Modern Truth in Ancient Wisdom*. New York: Basic Books.

Haidt, Jonathan. 2012. *The Righteous Mind: Why Good People are Divided by Politics and Religion*. New York: Pantheon.

Harari, Yuval Noah. 2015. *Sapiens: A Brief History of Humankind*. New York: Harper.

Harris, Sam. 2010. *The Moral Landscape: How Science Can Determine Human Values*. Ney York: Simon and Schuster.

Harris, Sam. 2004. *The End of Faith: Religion, Terror, and the Future of Reason*. New York: W. W. Norton & Company.

Harcourt, Alexander H. 2015. *Humankind: How Biology and Geography Shaped Human Diversity*. New York: Pegasus Books.

Herrnstein, Richard J. and Charles Murray. 1994. *The Bell Curve: Intelligence and Class Struggle in American Life*. New York: Free Press Paperbacks.

Hunt, Earl. 2011. *Human Intelligence*. Cambridge, MA: Cambridge University Press.

Hutson, Matthew. 2012. *The 7 Laws of Magical Thinking: How Irrational Beliefs Keep Us Happy, Healthy and Sane*. New York: Hudson Street Press.

Jablonka, Eva and Marion J. Lamb. 2005. *Evolution in Four Dimensions: Genetic, Epigenetic, Behavioral and Symbolic Variation in the History of Life*. Cambridge, MA: MIT Press.

Jobling, Mark, et.al. 2014. *Human Evolutionary Genetics, Second Edition*. New York: Garland Science.

Kahneman, Daniel. 2011. *Thinking, Fast and Slow*. New York: Farrar, Straus and Giroux.

Lieberman, Daniel E. 2013. *The Story of the Human Body: Evolution, Health and Disease*. New York: Pantheon Books.

Lecointre, Guillaume and Hervé Le Guyader. 2006. *The Tree of Life: A Phylogenetic Classification*. Cambridge, MA: The Belknap Press.

Lynch, Gary and Richard Granger. 2008. *Big Brain: The Origins and Future of Human Intelligence*. New York: Palgrave Macmillan.

Menzel, Peter. 1994. *Material World: A Global Family Portrait*. San Francisco: Sierra Club Books.

Mithen, Steven. 2006. *The Singing Neanderthals: The Origins of Music, Language, Mind and Body*. Cambridge, MA: Harvard University Press.

Nowak, Martin A. and Roger Highfield. 2011. *SuperCooperators: Altruism, Evolution and Why We Need Each Other to Succeed*. New York: Free Press.

Novacek, Michael. 2007. *Terra: Our 100-Million-Year-Old Ecosystem and the Threats That Now Put It at Risk*. New York: Farrar, Straus and Giroux.

Park, Robert L. 2008. *Superstition: Belief in the Age of Science*. Princeton, NJ: Princeton University Press.

Pinker, Steven. 2011. *The Better Angels of Our Nature: Why Violence Has Declined*. New York: Penguin Group.

Pinker, Steven. 2007. *The Stuff of Thought: Language as a Window into Human Nature*. New York: Penguin Books.

Pinker, Steven. 2002. *The Blank Slate: The Modern Denial of Human Nature*. New York: Viking.

Pinker, Stephen. 1997. *How the Mind Works*. New York: W. W. Norton & Company.

Roberts, Alice, ed., 2011. *Evolution: The Human Story*. New York: Dorling Kindersley Limited.

Saad, Gad. 2011. *The Consuming Instinct: What Juicy Burgers, Ferraris, Pornography, and Gift Giving Reveal About Human Nature*. Amherst, NY: Prometheus Books.

Sagan, Carl. 1995. *The Demon-Haunted World: Science as a Candle in the Dark*. New York: Random House.

Sagan, Carl and Ann Druyan. 1992. *Shadows of Forgotten Ancestors: A Search for Who We Are*. New York: Random House.

Shubin, Neil. 2008. *Your Inner Fish: A Journey Into the 3.5 Billion-Year History of the Human Body*. New York: Vintage Books.

Stringer, Chris. 2012. *Lone Survivors: How We Came to be the Only Humans on Earth*. New York: Times Books.

Stringer, Chris and Peter Andrews. 2005. *The Complete World of Human Evolution*. New York: Thames & Hudson.

Thaler, Richard H. and Cass R. Sunstein. 2008. *Nudge: Improving Decisions About Health, Wealth, and Happiness*. New York: Penguin Books.

Trivers, Robert. 2011. *The Folly of Fools: The Logic of Deceit and Self-Deception in Human Life*. New York: Basic Books.

Wade, Nicholas. 2006. *Before the Dawn: Recovering the Lost History of Our Ancestors*. New York: Penguin Group.

Wade, Nicholas. 2014. *A Troublesome Inheritance: Genes, Race and Human History*. New York: The Penguin Press.

Wells, Spencer. 2002. *The Journey of Man: A Genetic Odyssey*. New York: Random House.

Wheelan, Charles. 2013. *Naked Statistics: Stripping the Dread From the Data*. New York: W. W. Norton & Company.

Wilson, Edward O. 2014. *The Meaning of Human Existence*. New York: Liveright Publishing Company.

Wilson, Edward O. 2012. *The Social Conquest of Earth*. New York: Liveright Publishing Company.

Wilson, Edward O. 1998. *Consilience: The Unity of Knowledge*. New York: Alfred A. Knopf.

Weisman, Alan. 2007. *The World Without Us*. New York: Picador.

Wrangham, Richard. 2009. *Catching Fire: How Cooking Made Us Human*. New York: Basic Books.

Lecture Series

Anding, Roberta H. 2009. *Nutrition Made Clear*. Chantilly, VA: The Great Courses.

Barnhart, Edwin. 2012. *The Lost Worlds of South America*. Chantilly, VA: The Great Courses.

Brier, Bob. 1999. *The History of Ancient Egypt*. Chantilly, VA: The Teaching Company.

Christian, David. 2008. *Big History: The Big Bang, Life on Earth and the Rise of Humanity*. Chantilly, VA: The Great Courses.

Garland, Robert. 2012. *The Other Side of History: Daily Life in the Ancient World*. Chantilly, VA: The Great Courses.

Goldman, Steven L. 2007. *Great Scientific Ideas That Changed the World*. Chantilly, VA: The Teaching Company.

Goldman, Steven L. 2006. *Science Wars: What Scientists Know and How They Know It*. Chantilly, VA: The Teaching Company.

Goldman, Steven L. 2004. *Science in the 20th Century: A Social-Intellectual Survey*. Chantilly, VA: The Great Courses.

Haier, Richard J. 2013. *The Intelligent Brain*. Chantilly, VA: The Great Courses.

Harl, Kenneth W. 2005. *Origins of Great Ancient Civilizations*. Chantilly, VA: The Teaching Company.

Hazen, Robert M. 2013. *The Origin and Evolution of Earth: From the Big Bang to the Future of human Existence*. Chantilly, VA: The Great Courses.

Hazen, Robert M. 2005. *Origins of Life*. Chantilly, VA: The Teaching Company.

Hinshaw, Stephen P. 2010. *Origins of the Human Mind*. Chantilly, VA: The Teaching Company.

Huettel, Scott. 2014. *Behavioral Economics: When Psychology and Economics Collide*. Chantilly, VA: The Great Courses.

Joordens, Steve. 2011. *Memory and the Human Life Span*. Chantilly, VA: The Great Courses.

King, Barbara J. 2002. *Biological Anthropology: An Evolutionary Perspective*. Chantilly, VA: The Teaching Company.

Leary, Mark. 2012. *Understanding the Mysteries of Human Behavior.* Chantilly, VA: The Great Courses.

Novella, Steven. 2012. *Your Deceptive Mind: A Guide to Critical Thinking Skills.* Chantilly, VA: The Great Courses.

Nowicki, Stephen. *Biology: The Science of Life. Chantilly.* VA: The Great Courses.

Patel, Aniruddh D. 2015. *Music and the Brain.* Chantilly, VA: The Great Courses.

Sapolsky, Robert. 2012. *Being Human: Life Lessons from the Frontiers of Science.* Chantilly, VA: The Great Courses.

Sapolsky, Robert. 2010. *Stress and Your Body.* Chantilly, VA: The Great Courses.

Sapolsky, Robert. 2005. *Biology and Human Behavior: The Neurological Origins of Individuality.* Chantilly, VA: The Teaching Company.

Shermer, Michael. 2013. *Skepticism 101: How to Think Like a Scientist.* Chantilly, VA: The Great Courses.

Sojka, Gary. 2009. *Understanding the Human Factor: Life and Its Impact.* Chantilly, VA: The Great Courses.

Vishton, Peter M. 2011. *Understanding the Secrets of Human Perception.* Chantilly, VA: The Great Courses.

Wysession, Michael E. 2016. *The Science of Energy: Resources and Power Explained.* Chantilly, VA: The Great Courses.

Online Courses

Jakoi, Emma and Jennifer Carbrey. 2015. *Introductory Human Physiology.* Duke University. (Coursera)

Mason, Peggy. 2014. *Understanding the Brain: The Neurobiology of Everyday Life.* University of Chicago. (Coursera)

McGue, Matt. 2015. *Introduction to Human Behavioral Genetics.* University of Minnesota. (Coursera)

St. Leger, Raymond J. and Tammatha O'Brien. 2015. *Genes and the Human Condition: From Behavior to Biotechnology.* University of Maryland, College Park. (Coursera)

Index

About the Author

 RONALD M. SMITH has a B.A. in the earth sciences and an M.A. in experimental psychology with an emphasis on human learning. He spent more than thirty years working in the field of education in roles as diverse as classroom teacher, research associate for a federal R&D institution, employee training manager for a large microelectronics firm, and director of curriculum and assessment for a public school system. His most recent academic interests include evolutionary psychology and behavioral genetics. In preparation for writing this book, Mr. Smith read more than thirty thousand pages of source materials and participated in more than thirty university-level science courses ranging from biological anthropology to neuroscience to earth history. He lives in Bend, Oregon. This is his first book.

Learn More

www.humanfieldguide.com

YOU ARE INVITED to visit the book website shown above and sign up for a quarterly newsletter which will include updates and recommended new resources as they become available. In addition, the website provides, free of charge, access to chapter notes and supplemental resources providing the opportunity to study, in more detail, topics introduced in the guide. The website also provides instructions on how to qualify to become a certified field naturalist of the human species. Certification includes a quality certificate suitable for framing and an embroidered patch for attachment to an item of clothing or a favorite backpack. As a certified naturalist, you'll be able to explain, to the delight of your friends, the causes of many of the interesting anecdotes about humans shared on the daily news.

Made in the USA
Lexington, KY
24 July 2017